Scared of the Kids?

Curfews, crime and the regulation of young people

Stuart Waiton

Abertay University Press
University of Abertay Dundee
Dundee DD1 1HG

Cover designed by Alex Cameron
Typeset by Shona Norman, Information Services, University of Abertay Dundee

Printed by Scotprint

©2008 ISBN 189979620 7

ABERTAY
UNIVERSITY
PRESS

Dedicated to John and Lily

Contents

Preface   7

Preface to the Second Edition   11

Foreword   15

1   Zero Tolerance   21

2   Prevention and Fear   37

3   Spotlight on the Curfew   55

4   Curfew on Children: Child's Play   65

5   Curfew on Youth: Nuisance as Crime   83

6   Regulation Regulation Regulation   103

7   Adults   129

8   Summary   149

9   Future Developments and Recommendations   161

Comment   169
    Save the Children curfews on Children and Young People in Communities
    Nancy Ovens Vice Chair – Play Scotland
    Gerison Lansdown Director of the Children's Rights Office
    Joe Parfery Chair of the Hillhouse Community Council
    Tim Gill Children's Play Council
    Roger Smith The Children's Society (written in a personal capacity)
    Scottish Human Rights Centre Legal Issues – Hamilton Child Safety Initiative

Bibliography   179

Index   185

Scared of the Kids?

Preface to the first edition

In December 1996, while talking to a group of young people who used the drop-in centre I ran in Coatbridge, I discovered they had all been stopped and searched by Strathclyde police officers in the previous week. A colleague giving a talk on children's rights at a nearby school found that all the teenagers in the class had been stopped and searched. When discussing this with the teacher of the class, he found that all the young people that went to her Sunday School had also been stopped and searched, as part of the Strathclyde police initiative Operation Spotlight.

Concerned about the impact that this new policing initiative was having on young people who hung about on the streets at night, myself and a number of youth and community workers across Strathclyde formed the research group Generation Youth Issues. The aim of the group was to assess the real impact of crime in the areas we worked, but equally to assess the impact that policing initiatives were having on young people within communities. Following an article in Glasgow's *Evening Times*, about the group's activities, the Generation office received over 50 phone calls from parents whose children had recently come into contact with the police. One of the parents explained that her daughter would no longer go out at night, because she was being searched every time she left the house.

This response from parents provided the incentive to develop a better understanding of the changing role of policing and its impact on young people. It was clear to many youth workers and concerned parents at the time, that the 'zero tolerance' attitude of the police towards young people was a problem that could lead to greater numbers of young people being criminalised

Initial research by Generation aimed to assess the reality of the 'crime epidemic' that was being used to justify the growing level of policing across Strathclyde. The first bulletin published by the group in January 1997 concluded that, 'the popular idea that Britain is overwhelmed by criminality is based on statistical evidence that can at best be described as shaky, at worst as downright deceptive'. A sober appraisal of the crime figures points to a marked tendency to exaggerate both the extent and the growth of crime.

What became clear from this work was that while crime and youth crime itself may not be increasing, and indeed may well be decreasing, the fear of crime is rising. Indeed, much of the reported increase in crime, rather than being a reflection of more crime itself, was due to the growing awareness that people had of crime.

As a community worker I experience this public sensitivity towards crime daily, with elderly people regularly raising the problem of what to do about all the 'lawless kids'. Few of the adults I come across have ever experienced any serious incident with any young person, but it is often commented that you can never be too careful with teenagers today who are 'happy to mug old women'.

The launch of the Hamilton Curfew by Strathclyde Police in October 1997 gave Generation an opportunity to assess the impact of a new form of policing. One that is based on policing the fear of crime and encouraging young people to go home before they get into trouble. This project, officially named the 'Child Safety Initiative', was developed by South Lanarkshire Council, the council's social work department and Strathclyde police and aimed to clear the streets of any under 16 year old 'out after dark without a good reason'.

While focusing on the impact of the Hamilton Curfew, *Scared of the Kids?* incorporates primary research within a wider study of issues ranging from 'the importance of children's play', to questions of 'intergenerational conflict and contact'.

The primary research was developed through detailed interviews with young people who had direct experience of the Hamilton Curfew. Through this research, the book establishes a critique of the numerous crime and safety initiatives that have developed over the last decade across Scotland and the UK.

A key argument within *Scared of the Kids?* is that the exaggerated fear of crime and of young people who hang about the streets at night, has little to do with the mythical growth in antisocial behaviour of young people, but is caused instead by wider sociological and political changes since the 1980s.

In confronting the arguments of criminologist Jock Young, *Scared of the Kids?* challenges the promotion of safety as a way of rebuilding communities. Arguing, 'As the example of the curfew shows, promoting community development via safety has the opposite effect. Now adults are more aware of and frightened of the young people in their area, parents are more risk conscious regarding their children and are subsequently attempting to supervise even more of their free time, and the general level of contact between the generations has decreased even further.'

This book examines in detail the growing 'safety industry' surrounding children and young people – an 'industry' and outlook that is affecting not only how young people are policed, but also how they are perceived and treated by various public sector workers, from teachers to nurses and social workers. The question is put, 'Can we still call ourselves public servants when often our initial instinct when dealing with a young person is to ask "am I safe"?'

The second half of the book looks at the impact that a 'risk conscious society' is having on the lives and relationships of children, young people and adults within the community.

Firstly the trend to overprotect children and thus limit their freedom is examined. With an overview of a growing body of research in this area, I argue that 'ironically in a period when children have never had less free time, the image of them running around wild and the call for more curfews across the country, is greater than ever before'. The impact that this growing regulation of children's time, upon children and the family is explored.

The young people in the curfew-targeted areas were conscious that they were being moved off the street because of adult's fears of them. However *Scared of the Kids?* looks at how the curfew had simply reinforced these fears and reduced further the contact between the generations. This growing distance between the generations is discussed in depth and I attempt to explain why adults no longer feel able to deal with the young people on their estates and in their schools.

Finally and perhaps most significantly, *Scared of the Kids?* explores the impact that growing up within a 'risk conscious environment' is having on young people themselves, concluding that, 'It is not far from the truth to say that "youth" no longer exists – if by youth we mean the freedom-loving rebelliousness so often associated with teenage life'.

Thanks must be given to the students from Glasgow, Strathclyde and Edinburgh University who assisted with the research work in Hamilton. Thanks also go to members of the Generation: Youth Issues group particularly Simon Knight and Stuart Baird, who while not directly involved in this work, have been a constant source of ideas and information. Lastly, I would like to thank South Lanarkshire Council Education Department for allowing me access to children in their schools to discuss what was a highly sensitive issue; the children and young people in the schools; and all the people involved with children's charities and legal reform groups who have questioned the legitimate use of curfews, many of whom have expressed their concerns in this book.

Stuart Walton, January 2001

Preface to the second edition

So are we scared of the kids? And if so why?

According to the IPPR report *Freedom's Orphans* published in 2006 adults are more scared of young people in Britain than in any other European country – or at least they are less prepared to intervene when young people are causing a nuisance: In the UK only a third of adults said they would stop youngsters if they saw them vandalising a bus shelter – in Germany twice as many said they would intervene.

Unfortunately the outcome of research like this, something that is also reflected in the government's approach, is to focus on the problem behaviour of young people rather than the more serious problem of the lack of an active civic sense of responsibility reflected in adults who simply 'walk on by'.

Scared of the Kids has often been interpreted as a book written in defence of 'youth', however it would be more accurate to say that it developed from a concern about 'community' – about both adults and young people, and the relationship between the generations. A relationship that appears to have become, if anything, more problematic.

A lot has happened in 10 years since the Hamilton curfew was introduced and even since *Scared of the Kids* was first published in 2001. Not least of all the unbelievable amount of legislation being passed by the government has grown and grown. New laws have been introduced at an accelerated rate as law replaces politics and becomes the new way to micro-manage society. Nick Clegg, the Liberal Democrat MP recently observed that since Labour came into office they have created over 3000 new criminal offences – one for every day they have been in power.

Despite the intense focus on antisocial behaviour in the last decade, and arguably because of it, the myriad initiatives introduced to help create a 'sense of community' appear to have failed and the concern about our 'yob culture' remains. In this respect the main arguments in *Scared of the Kid*s are perhaps even more important now:– that a sense of community cannot be created by laws, policing or a focus on safety; that the engagement with the public through their fears generally has a negative impact on society as a whole, and that for genuine communities to develop, warts and all, people need space and the freedom to act rather than more curfews, ASBOs and CCTV.

Unfortunately with each passing election of the Labour government the 'politics of behaviour' has become further entrenched and the rate at which offences have been created has accelerated. In 1998, Labour's first full year in power, 160 new offences passed into legislation, rising to 346 in 2000 and 527 in 2005. Liberal

Democrat MP Nick Clegg who uncovered these figures argued that,

> Nothing can justify the step change in the number of criminal offences invented by this Government. This provides a devastating insight into the real legacy of nine years of New Labour government - a frenzied approach to law-making, thousands of new offences, an illiberal belief in heavy-handed regulation, an obsession with controlling the minutiae of everyday life. (*Independent* 16 August 2006)

In the Southside of Glasgow where I live a mini version of what has developed nationally also occurred in the last decade. Here, little had been heard from the local Labour MP Mohammad Sarwar until he called a meeting about crime and antisocial behaviour. Tapping into local concerns and fears about crime and also about the behaviour of some young people in the area, this first public meeting was attended by around 400 local residents. Here, genuine issues of crime were raised by residents but so too were more exaggerated fears of young people – with one street in particular, the street I happen to live in, being described as 'under siege'. The police statistics which indicated that crime was actually down in the area, and that of all the areas covered by Mr Sarwar this was the least problematic in terms of crime appeared to be of no concern, least of all to Mr Sarwar himself: *Fear is rarely if ever questioned by today's politicians.* As is the trend in society, at this meeting the non-criminal disruptive behaviour of some youngsters was mixed with the issue of more serious crime and the eventual solution offered by Mr Sarwar was to introduce CCTV cameras across the estate. Local adults, it appeared were not expected to play any role themselves in attempting to engage the young people in their area who would now be monitored by surveillance cameras and treated as part of the 'problem of crime'.

Unsurprisingly young people continue to hang about the streets in my area and there is little noticeable change to the nuisance behaviour of a minority of these young people. The image of the estate as an area with problems has increased and the sense that young people are out of control fortified. With CCTV on every other street corner replacing the watchful eye of local residents the message to local adults is clear – if young people are misbehaving – walk on by. (As we go to press yet another meeting about this subject has been called – this time with the 'guest' speaker being the Scottish National Party's MSP Nicola Sturgeon).

To promote the idea that local adults should play a role in regulating the behaviour of young people at one level sounds like common sense – but in the last few years this idea has become more problematic. Last year for example, following howls of derision from those on the right who asked, 'How dare you blame us for rising crime', Home Secretary John Reid backed down from introducing an antisocial behaviour initiative with the slogan, 'Don't moan, take action – it's your street too'. The Conservative shadow Home Secretary David Davis similarly said it was, 'brazen beyond belief for the government to turn around and try and shift responsibility on to the shoulders of the public'.

However, this 'outrage' at the idea of ordinary people being more active in their communities to resolve problems has also, indeed more consistently, been ridiculed by those on the 'left', with the idea of a 'have a go hero' being used mockingly to denounce almost any action by adults as 'vigilantism'. As Dennis, Erdos and Robinson have noted,

> What used to be regarded with approval as 'self policing' when practised by a group or neighbourhood, and as 'good citizenship' when practiced by an individual, is condemned as 'vigilantism' – a term that conjures up, and is intended to conjure up, images of innocent men lynched by hate-filled mobs of violent and ignorant bigots under flare of torches in some remote Mississippi town in the 1920s. (Dennis et al 2003: 21).

Perhaps the most important development in the last decade is that informal, spontaneous and unregulated action by people is now seen as a problem. This has developed both in terms of regulating the activities of adults and young people acting in public – but also in the growing regulation of people's private, personal relationships. Often framed in the language of 'safety' previously unregulated activities between adults and young people and indeed between young people themselves are now scrutinised by 'experts' and fettered. Despite the trend in this direction in 1997 it would still have been almost unbelievable to imagine that all adults working with or volunteering to help out with young people in any way would have to be vetted, or that at school nativity plays adults would be asked not to take photographs of their children. Today however, the consequences of the 'Safeguarding Vulnerable Groups Bill' will be that one third of the adult population in the England and Wales will be subject to ongoing criminal checks. And having originally been ridiculed as excessive and unnecessary, the warning to 'not take photographs of the children' has now become commonplace in schools. For young people themselves the regulation of informal areas of their lives that were once seen as not needing adult intervention has also developed - from the bullying campaigns and the concern about 'peer pressure', already well established by 1997 - to now include professional support for would be boyfriends and girlfriends in the form of 'relationship education'.

Today in the area I live CCTV cameras are on every other street corner, I have received an official letter from my 7 year old son's school for his bullying activities, which turned out to be about him teasing a neighbour's son for 'K.I.S.S.I.N.G' my daughter (perhaps they need relationship education before embarking on this 'risky' activity), and I and all the other parents present at a school play were recently asked 'not to take photographs of the children'.

As 'safety' takes over as the basis of 'good practice' trust, informality and ultimately 'community' exits stage left.

Stuart Waiton, January 2008

How to use this edition

This second edition of *Scared of the Kids* has been developed to assist in the education of those studying criminology, community education and youth work, and also for those who work in the community. At the end of each section a number of questions for students to consider are raised, suggestions are made about how to go about researching these questions and also additional reading material is suggested. Wherever possible the reading material chosen has been picked because it is available online. Almost all of the journal articles mentioned are available online and various articles cited are likewise available on the internet. The books that are mentioned are often well known texts that will hopefully be available in university libraries. Where this is not the case, the internet should again be used to locate journal articles by these authors on the relevant themes discussed.

Foreword

Reason can wrestle terror, and overthrow it at last.

Euripides

Youth curfews have a long history elsewhere in the world particularly in the United States. Not so in Britain where, even during war-time, they were only briefly considered as a policy option. Primarily this was because youth curfews were, until recently, viewed as being unnecessary and unwarranted. Unnecessary because the public behaviour of young people although recurrently the focus of concern for some police officers, members of the general public and policy makers, was never judged so bad it demanded such a draconian measure to manage it. Unwarranted because all curfews have historically been perceived as something that could only be justified as a means of dealing with the most extreme and life threatening instances of collective disorder or challenges to national security. By curtailing the liberty of whole communities, innocent and guilty alike, curfews have rightly been viewed as autocratic and unjust. An illiberal stratagem that in a democratic society could only be employed for a brief, time limited period to quell the most extreme problems of social order. Probably only one modern example can be cited, prior to 1997, of a curfew applied selectively to a specific segment of the population. That was the restrictions placed on the free movement of all women, unaccompanied by their husband or close male relative, within the boundaries of a garrison town. Introduced under the auspices of the Contagious Diseases Acts of 1864, 1866 and 1869 it was designed to inhibit the spread of sexually transmitted diseases amongst members of the armed forces by removing prostitutes from the streets. Unfortunately this cruel and inhumane law not only made it illegal for women to be out and about during 'night time', but meant all those apprehended were, until they could provide evidence they were 'clean' and 'respectable', treated as criminals. Eventually repealed in 1886, it had taken almost two decades of campaigning by Josephine Butler and others before this intolerable law was repealed (see Jordan 2001). Of course this curfew was imposed primarily on women from working class background, that is persons who as a consequence of their class and gender were denied the vote. Once the suffrage had been extended to encompass all adults, it seemed reasonable to assume that such overtly discriminatory legislation would be a thing of the past. That a legal device criminalising and harassing the innocent in order to manage the illegal behaviour of a minority would be set aside as a failed experiment from a less fair-minded, perceptive and democratic era. Given democracy is premised on the idea of liberty, exercised responsibly, one might assume blanket curfews have, in normal circumstances, place within their orbit. Sadly that was not to be the case.

Popular at any price

During the 1980s and 1990s many of our politicians and senior civil servants largely stopped thinking for themselves. Instead they took the easy way out and opted to borrow policy from elsewhere to fill the gaps as they arose. As the Thatcher revolution petered out so Conservative and Labour politicians clueless as to what to do that would be both popular and effective began to scuttle backwards and forwards across the Atlantic seeking social policies compatible with the neo-conservative economic agenda they had signed up to. American federal structures ensured that there, unlike Britain, local politicians and policy makers had far greater opportunities to experiment. This enabled our politicians to pick and mix from what they encountered on their travels. With both parties anxious to appear tough on crime, and juvenile crime in particular, they predictably and unashamedly borrowed policies that they were told 'worked' such as - restorative justice; short, sharp, shock disposals; zero tolerance; boot camps; three strikes and out sentencing; and youth curfews. The latter, it should be noted after being abandoned in the 1950s as a failure were 40 years on once again operating, with variable success, in over 100 American cities and towns (Jeffs and Smith 1996). Like cholera in the 1830s arrival was inevitable, the question was therefore always - where and when? For they were too glib and simplistic a 'solution' to the problem of 'troublesome youth' to long escape the attention of a politician or chief constable keen to make a name for themselves.

Fortunately the first place in Britain to introduce a youth curfew, or as it was euphemistically called by advocates a Child Safety Initiative, was Hamilton. I deliberately say fortunately because the author of this book was at that time a youth worker operating in a neighbouring council. If it had been introduced somewhere else it is unlikely that the impact of this policy initiative would have been scrutinised with such energy and assiduousness. Stuart Waiton was uniquely placed to study the implementation, as well as the reactions of the community and the young people living within the designated area to this policy. Thankfully he seized the opportunity to do so and with a team of volunteer interviewers started talking to young people and adults, collecting data, attending meetings and scrutinising policy documents and reportage. Somehow finding the time to embark on a major piece of research whilst working full-time as a youth worker.

Contemporary research into the impact of youth policy and youth work practice is overwhelmingly undertaken by academics and consultants, that is by those who are paid to do so. Individuals whose livelihood and professional status is reliant upon securing grants or contracts to complete research and evaluations. Predictably this arrangement encourages a safety first approach amongst researchers and consultants. They know they must operate with their eyes cast down and their palms up. At worst these research entrepreneurs learn to live with funders scrutinising their questionnaires, monitoring their work and editing their reports and publications. At best they get by becoming skilled at meeting their paymaster's outcomes and dressing-up their findings to avoid offending them. Like an Eighteenth century court portrait painter present-day academics and consultants seem to know instinctively what they can and cannot reveal. Seemingly they do not need to be told or taught the limits of criticism, by a process of osmosis they too often acquire the necessary deference. Waiton as an outsider was exempt from those unframed and unspoken constraints. He was neither answerable to a patron nor inhibited by the pressures of colleagues anxious to make sure he did not produce findings that might embarrass their university department or agency or inhibit their chances of getting further contracts. Waiton may well have been subjected to pressure emanating from his employer, although I have no evidence as to whether this was the case or not. If so that demanded a different sort of courage on his part. Suffice to say what he and his volunteer helpers produced is in a number of crucial respects a radically different research document from anything that would have emerged from a police or local government funded evaluation. As those about to read it for the first time will discover this is a scholarly document, in the best sense of the word. A work of engaged scholarship of the highest order. A meticulous account of a policy initiative but one goes beyond the simplistically descriptive and displays no reluctance to avoid offending those holding the purse strings or of telling them what they do not want to hear. For that reason it is also thoroughly readable because it has no reason to present its findings in a convoluted policy speak designed to carefully veil any hint of criticism.

What helps to make this such a valuable, almost unique, document is that it emerged from the concerns of a practitioner. Waiton possessed the grounded knowledge and understanding that provides an added dimension to what is by any measure an outstanding piece of research.

Uncomfortable results

Scared of the Kids does not make for predictable, or comfortable, reading. From an analysis of one policy intervention, within a restricted locality the author spreads his net to illustrate the extent to which "almost every form of contact between young people and adults is now seen through the prism of danger and safety" (p.33). Recounting also the sort of corrosive fear, rational or otherwise, that results in 40 per cent of young people being unwilling to walk to a friend's house at night and in a quarter frightened to leave their area without an adult. Likewise three-quarters of adults find the presence of young people on the street threatening. It matters not that the roles of potential enemy and victim are inter-changeable for amongst both groups, as Waiton shows, it generates a demand that authoritarian controls be imposed on others. In the case of young people that means those occupying their own age band, and therefore themselves. For those youth workers who have for too long encouraged us to believe that young people were overwhelmingly victims of adult malice, this makes for difficult reading. Many young people may want greater freedom and independence for themselves but clearly, as the itemised support of many for age specific curfews show, they are also willing to purchase that at the cost of imposing arbitrary regulation on others.

Individuals may find elements of the growing imposition of age related restrictions on young people irksome but as Waiton found a high proportion, perhaps a majority accept even support the idea of increasing the controls placed on their peers. As he notes few of those interviewed 'talk of their or others rights'. Perhaps as Beck suggests they, like so many, are 'no longer concerned with attaining something "good" but rather with "preventing the worst"' (1992: 49). If so then youth workers and community educators face a daunting challenge. Bertrand Russell, during the early years of the last century, warned that hope never fear is the 'creative principle in human affairs' (1916: 116), the driving force of social and political reform. Individuals and communities living lives enveloped by fear of, even loathing for, those around them will be easy prey to undemocratic ideas and reactionary policies. Certainly they will be unreceptive to ideas that seek to extend the remit of democracy, and show little sympathy for the liberal pleadings of youth workers and community educators.

Conclusion

One of the great achievements of this book, like the skilful campaigning of Liz Wilkinson Longtown where a similar initiative was introduced shortly afterwards, is that for the time being at least youth curfews are a somewhat discredited policy option. That victory however is likely to be short-lived because within the present political climate 'what works' counts for less than 'what is popular' and as Waiton so adroitly shows curfews, provided the victims are not electors, are unlikely to harm the careers of politicians. For that reason, if for no other this book needs to reach the widest possible audience amongst youth and community workers as well as those who on moral and ethical grounds oppose the introduction of curfews. For they need to know why they must resist the temptation, however strong the pressure from young and old members of the communities in which they live and or operate, 'to give curfews a try'. Thankfully here at hand is a ready aid to help them 'wrestle terror' and defeat it with reason.

Finally one reading of Waiton's book may see it as a confirmation of Raymond Williams view that "The settled pessimism of so much of the culture .... Is in effect an absolute loss of the future; of any significant belief that it can be both different and better. The projection of dates is now more often an anxious calculation of the possibilities of mere survival" (1983: 4). In part that interpretation is correct. However education, unlike training, is rooted in an optimistic belief that it is possible to create a better future. That an open society offers far greater potential for enabling people to secure a life free, informed, creative and chosen than a closed one. And therein lies the positive message that resonates within this superb study. Scared of the Kids contests the naïve belief, widely held, amongst educators that they are working with the grain. If we were once, then those days have long passed. Waiton graphically shows that such a viewpoint will serve them ill, in an age when young people are viewed as a threat not a resource. Within such a context youth policy inevitably tends to acquire a different, more oppressive aspect than was once the norm. Therefore as Waiton argues what must be challenged is the very pessimism that produces dead-end policies such as youth curfews. A pessimism that unless challenged ideologically and politically will ceaselessly churn out variants based on the same model. This book is the record of a small, but significant victory, but it is also pointer to where we might turn in order to create better alternatives to youth curfews, regulation and the micro-management of the social lives of young people. To how we might regain our optimism.

Tony Jeffs (Durham University)

References

Jeffs, T. and Smith, M. (1996) '"Getting the Dirtbags off the Streets": Curfews and other solutions to juvenile crime' *Youth and Policy* (53) Summer 1996.

Jordan, J. (2001) *Josephine Butler*, London: John Murray.

Russell, B. (1916) *Principles of Social Reconstruction*, London: Unwin.

1   Zero tolerance

At a time when being tolerant is promoted as an essential requirement for modern life, and children's rights are universally celebrated, we also find that tolerance levels towards children and young people who utilise public space at night has never been so low. So concerned has society become about the threat posed by young people who hang about on street corners that policing based on the idea of 'zero tolerance' is now widely supported by New Labour politicians and enforced by police forces across the UK.

New Labour has successfully stolen the mantle of the 'Party of Law and Order' from the Conservatives, and under the banner of attacking antisocial behaviour has gone further than previous governments ever dared in criminalising more and more areas of life. Many new police and safety initiatives, like the Hamilton Curfew which is addressed within this research, directly target young people, while other laws targeting antisocial behaviour have a disproportionate effect on young people – who use public space more than any other section of society. Many of these initiatives and laws rather than tackling crime itself, are much more concerned with regulating the basic relationships and conflicts that people have with one another in their neighbourhood.

The growing political preoccupation with fighting crime and enforcing order on the streets has been helped in part by 'radical' criminologists and sociologists who have uncritically accepted the myth of the rising tide of crime and youth crime, which is seen as being largely responsible for undermining community solidarity. This chapter by contrast questions the idea that crime and youth crime in particular has exploded and cites research suggesting that the increasing fear of crime has little to do with crime and antisocial behaviour itself, and more to do with wider social changes that have created a culture of fear.

It is this culture of fear and insecurity that has allowed politicians and the police to introduce measures like the Hamilton Curfew which targets young people who, rather than being picked up for committing a criminal offence, are being moved off the street for not having a 'good reason for being out' at night. Rather than crime being addressed here, it is order and a sense of safety that the police hope to establish, by increasingly regulating the contact that young people have with adults and with one another.

New Glasgow: from City of Culture to Curfew

In 1990, Glasgow took on the title of European City of Culture. In February 1993, Strathclyde P launched Operation Blade, an initiative aimed at ridding the streets of knives by stopping and searching young men. By April 20,000 people had been searched.

21

In March 1993 Phil Gallie, then Conservative MP for Ayr, launched his private members bill – backed by both government and opposition parties – making it easier to charge anyone found with 'an article with a blade or point'.

In the same month of 1993 a night-club curfew was announced in Glasgow's city centre. Implemented in June, the curfew placed a time limit of 2pm on night-club opening hours and banned anyone from moving between clubs and discos after midnight.

In October 1993 a Strathclyde University student led a torch lit demonstration with 200 other protesters, opposing the night club curfew.

In the winter of 1994 Glasgow Development Agency launched City Watch, a CCTV scheme that covered the whole of the city centre, explaining that, 'greater international awareness of Glasgow as a safe city', would benefit Glasgow's tourist industry.

In a System 3 opinion poll, it was found that 95% of Glaswegians were in favour of City Watch, 2% were opposed to it, with 7% believing that it infringed their civil rights.[1]

In the summer of 1996 Glasgow District Council banned street drinking. The ban was not just focused on the city centre, but covered the whole of the district.

In October 1996 Strathclyde Police launched Operation Spotlight, an umbrella operation that aimed to target both crime and the fear of crime. The Child Safety Initiative – or what became known as the Hamilton Curfew, set up in October 1997 – is part of the continuing Operation Spotlight.

Operation Spotlight and Generation

The new policing measures developed in Glasgow have emerged in towns across Scotland, particularly in those areas covered by Strathclyde police.

In October 1996 Strathclyde Police launched their zero tolerance policing initiative Operation Spotlight – Britain's biggest crackdown on crime – in an attempt to tackle crime and more importantly, the growing fear of crime that existed across the region. Chief Constable John Orr promised that 200,000 more police hours would be spent on the beat, by putting every desk bound officer back on the streets.

'We want to remove public fear,' John Orr explained, 'and intimidate criminals.'[2] Within three months over 22,000 young people had been stopped and searched by the police. The process of intimidation had started. But were these the criminals that John Orr was referring to?

In 'Zero Tolerance Policing a Free Society', Strathclyde's Chief of Police, explained that, 'Based on the acceptance that minor crime is not a separate entity from serious crime, and that the two are inextricably linked, the initiative aimed to reduce serious and in particular violent crime through identifying and tackling minor issues'.[3]

By January 1997 the number of people searched by Strathclyde Police had risen to 30,000. In local newspaper interviews John Orr explained that as well as focusing on street robberies and football hooligans, the targets of Operation Spotlight were underage drinkers and any young person causing a public nuisance; this included children dropping litter outside schools and young people being noisy on buses.[4]

This approach to crime prevention follows in the footsteps of New York's policing strategy developed by Mayor Giuliani and Police Commissioner William Bratten, an approach that is equally focused on reducing the signs of crime, as it is on reducing crime itself.[5]

Broken Window

Known as the broken window approach, this form of policing focuses on petty crime, incivility and disturbances. The idea is that antisocial behaviour within a community helps to undermine the community spirit and leads to further disorder and criminality – a broken window in a house and a graffitied wall in a street, if left, will not only demoralise the residents but give others the idea that they too can vandalise the area.[6] If petty crime goes unchallenged, as Strathclyde's chief of police argues, serious crime will soon develop. In the UK the term 'antisocial behaviour' has become a catch all phrase for these types of activities.

New York's Mayor Giuliani explained that to counter the disorder that can develop in society civility must be established across public life by setting up, 'classes in school to teach youngsters civility and respect, introducing dress codes for teachers, by campaigning against rudeness by bureaucrats, and a crackdown on blaring car alarms, litter and reckless driving'.[7]

By ridding society of – what in England Home Secretary Jack Straw labelled 'winos and squeegee men' – Giuliani is being tough on what he sees as the causes of crime. Not the intractable social causes of crime, but the geographical – publicly visible – causes of crime. As such, bad manners have become a focus of policing, with uncivilised taxi drivers in New York – like noisy school children in Scotland – being targeted by the police.

One of the many initiatives carried out by Strathclyde Police, under the banner of Operation Spotlight, targeted after hours revellers, truants and groups of young people. The number of those charged for public drinking during this campaign increased by 240%, with a 320% and 140% increase of those charged with dropping litter and urinating in a public place respectively. It was also claimed that crime in the area fell by 15%.[8]

23

By focusing on antisocial behaviour in public in this way, and inventing new crimes, such as street drinking, it is inevitable that the behaviour of young people who hang about the streets will become a growing focus of police attention. The Hamilton Curfew is an extension of this form of policing.

Antisocial New Labour

Crime was once the issue of the right. The right's demand was for law and order, for a crackdown on crime and a society regulated by and respectful of the powers that be. The right rejected the idea that there were social causes to crime as a liberal excuse. All this has changed: over the last two decades crime has increasingly become an issue defined by the left. From at least the 1990s on, crime has become an issue that politicians of all persuasions have become increasingly keen to talk about. In 1996 Tony Blair explained that,

> When we talk about being tough on crime and tough on the causes of crime, it is a message warmly welcomed on housing estates across the land, where people, often trapped by poverty and unemployment, are tormented by criminal behaviour, antisocial or violent neighbours, and drugs.[9]

During the 1997 election campaign, New Labour made the issue of crime and policing their own. Their focus upon policing low level disorder, which may not necessarily be criminal, has subsequently intensified and with the introduction of the 1998 Crime and Disorder Act they have taken the policing of behaviour to a new level. A level where there is early, pre-emptive intervention and 'many of its provisions are explicitly directed not only at young offenders, but at young people in general'.[10]

One of the measures introduced under this act is the Antisocial Behaviour Orders that can be used to stop any behaviour that is 'likely to cause harassment to the community'. The definition of harassment is likely to be as wide as to include the New Labour belief that everyone has a right to a 'quiet life' – subsequently being noisy could result in action being taken. Violation of such an order carries the maximum sentence of five years imprisonment.

The result of this new law is that 'annoying citizens', whose behaviour does not actually break any law but offends others, can now be imprisoned for five years.

Parenting Orders, Child Safety Orders, Local Child Curfews and the abolition of the assumption that children cannot be automatically assumed to be responsible before the law (known in law as *doli incapax*) have all helped, as Barry Goldson explained, to 'undermine child welfare... deny youth justice and widen the criminalising net by specifically targeting children below the age of criminal responsibility'.[11] With these new powers, the police in England and Wales can make a child the subject of a court order for nothing more than being perceived as being 'at risk of becoming involved in crime'. Similarly a child may be restricted from public areas for being a 'potential' nuisance.[12]

The Crime and Disorder Act has not been entirely incorporated into Scottish law, although aspects of it like the Antisocial Behaviour Orders, have been. In many other ways this form of policing is however already well established, with initiatives like the curfew in Hamilton and the banning of street drinking.

For New Labour, Home Secretary Jack Straw and Strathclyde's Chief Constable, John Orr, policing is no longer simply about law enforcement, but about helping to improve the overall quality of life of a community by regulating and improving people's behaviour. Law enforcement is out, order maintenance is in.

A Scottish Executive publication looking at housing and antisocial behaviour, defined this type of behaviour as ranging from, 'what might seem to be nuisance and lack of consideration on the one hand, to serious criminal activity on the other', and noted that by far the largest category of complaints come within the range of low to medium level. Noise was the problem mentioned most by tenants, with complaints associated with children and teenagers accounting for 24% of complaints to housing managers.[13] This level of regulation by local authorities and ultimately the courts, moves way beyond traditional areas of policing, into areas of civility and politeness.

New Left Realists

New Labour's transformation into the party of law and order was not simply achieved by moving to the right. Instead the issue of crime itself has become 'radicalised'. This redefinition of crime as a problem for radicals – those trying to get at the roots of society's problems, rather than as something linked with the right wing's old calls for stability and a return to some idealised past is an important component in the Labour Party's transformation.

A key influence in radicalising crime, and the leading left realist criminologist, is Jock Young. In the 1980s Young was influential in challenging the right wing view that crime was a result of the decline of conventional values in society. Rather, he argued, 'the values of most working class criminals are overwhelmingly conventional', with, 'individualism, competition, a desire for material goods and often machoism', being the dominant values. Working class criminals, he believed, were not rejecting the values of capitalist society, but carrying them out within their own communities – they were the stockbrokers of the sink estates.[14]

Young helped radicalise crime prevention and turn it into a 'working class issue', demanding that other left criminologists take crime seriously. Unlike past radical criminologists and sociologists that had explained crime as either an issue of labelling or even positive deviance, Young accepted that crime and especially street crime against persons and property, in itself, was a fundamental problem.

New left realists argued that crime had in fact increased and that it was right for the public to be worried about this increase. The victim of the crime, rather than the perpetrators now became the key focus of attention for academics like Jock Young.

Left realism saw crime as a product of a fragmented impoverished community where self regulation and policing had declined. A greedy, self interested society had created working class communities made up of too many individuals acting for themselves alone without regard for their neighbours. The weakening of communal bonds gave people the freedom to act in a selfish antisocial manner – by so doing these people helped further undermine the confidence and solidarity of other people within these communities.[15]

Like the New Labour government today, Young saw the political importance of crime, not simply for its destructive impact on communities but for what he believed was its unifying potential:

> Crime is of importance politically because unchecked it divides the working class community and is materially and morally the basis of disorganisation: the loss of political control. It is also a potential unifier – a realistic issue, amongst others, for recreating community.[16]

With today's increasing concerns about raising the level of public participation in community issues and also empowering the 'socially excluded', involvement by local people in crime and safety issues has been prioritised. Involving the local community in safety initiatives is now the norm, with community safety initiatives in Newcastle and Leeds, for example, aiming to, 'strengthen communities... and build trust', and to 'engage all sections of the community in efforts to reduce crime and fear of crime'.[17]

By focusing on crimes that Young believed undermined working class community confidence, the activities of those people – largely young males – who hang about the street, was elevated in importance. Not only was crime the problem, but like New Labour and the police, left realists saw the civil behaviour – i.e. non criminal behaviour – of these young people as an issue to be addressed. Similarly, ex *Marxism Today* writer Bea Campbell in her book *Goliath*, targeted young working class men as the most destructive force within their communities.[18]

The left realists demanded that crime should be taken seriously and so it has been. The launch of the first British Crime Survey in 1982 reflecting the growing interest and concern about crime as an issue for social analysis and debate. Within politics Conservative and Labour governments have introduced a significant number of new laws that target behaviour or civility as well as crime. Police activity and involvement in community safety initiatives has developed throughout the eighties; inter agency activities that involve social work, housing and health professionals in crime prevention have emerged and the popular perception and support for more safety initiatives and crime prevention is unquestionable.

Newspapers and TV news, over the eighties and nineties, have given more time and space to issues associated with crime. Even the 'entertainment industry', especially television, produces a greater number and variety of 'cop' shows like *The Bill* – with a particular growth taking place in the real life 'America's Most Wanted' type programmes, the most famous British example being BBC's *Crimewatch*.

The popular support for initiatives like the Hamilton Curfew, or for the deployment of CCTV which has taken place across Strathclyde and the UK generally, has been used by the police and politicians to justify many of their crime and safety campaigns. The 'fear of crime', expressed in this public support for more policing, is something that left realists saw the need to address within crime prevention strategies as part of rebuilding communities. Today, it is no longer simply crime that is being policed, but also the fear of crime.

The rise of the fear of crime is popularly seen as a reflection of a rise in crime within society, and is used to justify the need for more policing and surveillance. But is crime on the increase and should we, as Jock Young suggested, take crime more seriously?

Rising crime?

Rising figures of crimes reported by the public and recorded by the police are often used as proof that crime is increasing. However, as former *Times* editor Simon Jenkins has pointed out – recorded crime has increased steadily since figures were collected in the 1830s, not as a reflection of increasing crime, but 'roughly in line with police employment'.

'Today some 60% of recorded crime is by children under 18,' Jenkins explained, 'The Children Acts of 1907 and 1933 brought thousands of children who previously had been at the mercy of local constables within the reach of the courts. Both acts led to 'crime waves' that shocked the nation, but were wholly definitional.'[19]

With the increased policing of more aspects of public behaviour, it is likely that recorded crime will continue to increase as more public acts become redefined as criminal. For example, as a result of the Criminal Justice Act 1994 it is now a crime to dance in a field to a repetitive beat. Likewise in Strathclyde recent reports of an increase in violent crime was recognised by the police as being due to an increase in the stop and search policy by the police and to a change in the law regarding carrying knives, rather than as a result of any increase in violent crime. What in the past would have led to protests about police harassment, is today ignored or seen as evidence of the need for even more policing.

In England and Wales the recording of crimes has changed to the extent that the crime figures for 1998-99 increased by 20%. One reason for this increase is that, under the new recording methods, a burglary will be recorded not as one offence but will depend upon the number of victims living in a house affected by the crime. Also, changes in reporting have increased the number of offences that will be recorded as 'violent' – common assault, carrying an offensive weapon, and harassment – will all now be categorised in this way.

As Jenkins states, 'The first thing to say is that police statistics are totally useless, either as a true record of crime or as a measure of its movement over time. They are simply a record of police station activity'.[20]

Criminologist John Muncie convincingly argues that crime statistics are both partial and also socially constructed.[21] They are partial, in that not all crimes are reported by the public or recorded by the police. And they are socially constructed, in that changes in the law and in the recording and reporting of crime depend on the political and social climate. Some activities are ignored today, which were in the past targeted by police, while on the other hand many activities are now elevated in importance, which were previously ignored or tolerated.

Citing work by Pearson, Muncie notes that, for example, 'welfare inspired legislation governing the treatment of young people in the early twentieth century encouraged law enforcement agencies to proceed with cases they might previously have dealt with informally'.[22] The end result of this process was that more young people were dealt with by the courts, creating an impression of a 'crime wave'.

Scare stories about the 'proof' of rising crime generally come from the public reported or police recorded crime figures. However, the record of court convictions that provides a measure of the outcome of more serious offences, shows an opposite trend. Statistics on burglary convictions show a fall from 65,000 in 1980 to 40,300 in 1993, a decline of more than one third.[23] According to David Rose, 'convictions have tumbled drastically for many types of offences'.

The Barnardo's survey on 'Young People's Social Attitudes' points out that, 'criminal statistics reveal a sharp decline in the number of recorded offences attributable to young people in the decade from 1981-1991'. Concluding that:

> Even taking account of the number of unrecorded offences, demographic changes and the growth of strategies to divert young people from prosecution, there is little evidence that youth crime has actually increased.[24]

Research published in 1999 by the Trust for the Study of Adolescence, similarly concluded that, 'there is little evidence of any great increase in the level of crime committed by young people during the last decade'.[25]

Similarly, in 'Antisocial behaviour by young people', Rutter, Giller and Hagell note that, 'the number of juveniles found guilty or cautioned for indictable offences per 100,000 of the population fell, between 1984 and 1994, by 44% for males aged 10-13 and by 19% for males aged 14-17'. They also note that in the UK, by the mid 1990s, young offenders (aged 10-17) represented 26% of all known offences compared to 36% a decade earlier, and that the proportion accounted for by offenders aged 18-20 remained the same, at 17%.[26]

Despite this, the amount of media and political attention given to the 'problem of young offenders' through the 1990s has led some observers to conclude that these is a new 'moral panic' about youth crime, the 'scare in the community'.[27]

While evidence for increasing crime, and youth crime in particular, is to say the least debatable, there is no question that the fear of crime has risen and risen disproportionately to the incidence of crime itself.

Between 1981 and 1991 the *British Crime Survey* (BCS) found that reporting of crime to the police had increased from 31% to 43%, a trend that has continued throughout the nineties. The suggested reasons for this increase was firstly – that more people had insurance in 1991, which had led to more reporting to allow insurance claims to be made. Secondly, because the average age of the population had increased and older people report more crimes, it was logical to assume that this would lead to growing figures of reported crime. Finally, and relating to the increased fear of crime, the BCS noted that there had been a sharp increase in the reporting of 'less serious' crime due to 'increased public sensitivity'.[28]

More broadly across society, the fear of crime has become an issue in its own right, with politicians now referring to crime and the fear of crime.

Less crime, more policing

In Strathclyde itself, despite falling crime figures, the police discovered that the public's fear of crime was continuing to rise. Frustrated by this, at the end of 1997 Strathclyde Police launched a £95,000 advertising campaign to inform people that crime was in fact falling.[29]

Regardless of whether or not police statistics show a fall in crime. Strathclyde Police, backed by local councils, have continued to develop new initiatives and laws to restrict the behaviour of people, and of young people in particular, in public places. New laws have been developed to allow the police to search people for 'offensive weapons'; Glasgow still has a night-club curfew which restricts access to clubs at night; and street drinking is still banned across the whole of Glasgow and in many other areas covered by Strathclyde Police. At a local level minor safety initiatives are developing on a weekly basis, initiatives that offer new peep holes for doors and safety tapes that warn elderly people to beware of 'scruffy youths' coming to their door.

While Operation Spotlight has helped introduce new laws, its key impact has been in changing the approach the police have to policing young people. A child or young person dropping litter, being rude or impolite, has been redefined as a criminal or at least a potential criminal. Following Chief Constable John Orr's logic – that minor crime, which includes 'nuisance behaviour' i.e. non criminal activities of children and teenagers, leads to more serious crime – activities that would until quite recently have been seen as mischievous or even the norm for many children and teenagers, are now the focus of a major policing initiative. Aspects of growing up like under age drinking in public places are now elevated in importance and targeted as antisocial, with laws developing across Scotland and the UK to clamp down on the petty behaviour of adolescents.

The Child Safety Initiative, or Curfew, which has been developed in Hamilton, has taken this approach one step further. Under this initiative, young people are challenged by the police and sent home or held in a police station, not for committing an offence, but for not having a 'good reason' for being out.

Fear of Crime

According to the International Crime Victimisation Survey, 'The fear of crime in England and Wales is so great that people are more anxious about going out alone on the streets than people in any country'.[30] Included within this report were countries like Columbia, South Africa and Russia.

Subsequently, the public support for more policing and surveillance of society has become significant, with roughly 70% now supporting surveillance cameras, identity cards, censorship and an end to the right of silence.[31]

When introducing policing initiatives like the Hamilton Curfew, the police and politicians invariably explain that these measures are being introduced because of a growing concern about crime by people living in the area. It is assumed that, firstly – the growing fear of crime is directly connected to an increase in crime and 'antisocial' behaviour, and secondly – that by increasing the policing of the area and reducing the risk of crime, this fear will be alleviated. However, as suggested above, the fear of crime is often not related to any direct increase in criminality within a particular area or across society as a whole. It is therefore highly questionable whether increased policing can reduce this fear.

Commenting on a number of community safety initiatives set up in England and Wales, Penny Fraser in the Nacro document *'Community Safety, Community Solutions'* noted that, 'While the risk of victimisation and the extent to which people perceive crime as a serious problem have both fallen these have not been reflected in reductions in fear'.[32]

The authoritative twelfth annual report on *British Social Attitudes*, in looking at public attitudes to crime, indicated that public fear of crime far outstrips the reality. In a chapter on crime by Dowds and Ahrendt, they point out that much research to date on the fear of crime has been preoccupied with looking at crime and how being a victim of crime affects people's fear of it. However, they recognise that to understand the growing fear of crime over the last decade, wider issues must be addressed:

> Although fear of crime clearly is related to personal experience and obviously reflects the conditions in which people live, fear also needs to be considered within the context of society as a whole. How for instance, do broader social attitudes link with our feelings of fear and anxiety about crime? Is fear of crime really a part of wider social attitudes?[33]

Lindsay Brook and Ed Cape, in their chapter *Libertarianism in Retreat*, in the same British Social Attitudes report, point out that Britain has become less libertarian during the 1990s especially in relation to issues of crime and punishment, with no evidence of any section of society or sub group swimming against this authoritarian tide. Brook and Cape had expected the explanation for this increase in authoritarian attitudes to lie with those who had experienced more crime, but they note that this assumption was incorrect, pointing out that, 'We found virtually no association between ever having been threatened or burgled and the tendency to want tougher measures against crime and criminals'.[34]

In attempting to explain this culture of fear, Dowds and Ahrendt describe a growing public concern – something approaching distrust or even fear – about Britain's social and political life. Cynicism towards politicians and insecurity about life generally, they believe, are impacting on the public perception and creating a preoccupation with crime and safety. While supporting the increasing police intervention to alleviate this fear, Dowds and Ahrendt also recognise that, 'whichever measure of fear is used, strong links exist between fear and social attitudes which have little to do with crime and still less to do with the arena of government intervention'.[35]

The Culture of Fear

In attempting to understand the culture of fear that exists in society it is important to refer more broadly to debates within the social sciences.

Sociologists, Ulrich Beck in 'Risk Society' and Anthony Giddens in *Beyond Left and Right*, have attempted to describe and explain what Beck defines as the risk society – and what Giddens describes as a dislocated and uncertain 'runaway world'.[36] Giddens argues that we now live in 'reflexive modernity', a society that has to face the consequences of its own development. Unlike the nineteenth and early twentieth century, which forged ahead with higher productivity, greater scientific understanding and better standards of living, modernity is now reflexive, in that the consequences of these developments react back onto society.

Beck explores this idea using the example of industrial pollution, which he argues creates unforeseen circumstances and can undermine our ability to anticipate the future. The advanced, global, scientific world of the 1990s creates dangers that we can never fully understand. Giddens explains that we can attempt to influence these processes that exist in all areas of life, but can never fully control them. The uncertainty and risks that this creates helps to explain society's insecurity.[37] Society, Beck argues, is out of control, but can be managed by learning to avoid or manage the risks we face in everyday life.

Giddens believes that many of today's panics and insecurities like those surrounding the spread of AIDS have been exaggerated, but he nevertheless argues that creating anxiety can be a positive thing. By creating anxiety in the minds of the powers that be, he believes, the condition for getting things done is established.[38] Rather than challenge the insecurity that people feel today campaigns promoting risks are here seen as a positive source of information to help you reduce the risks within your life.

Frank Furedi in his book *'Culture of Fear'*, challenges this view that promoting risks can be positive. For Furedi, the rising fear of crime 'parallels the panic-like reactions in the sphere of health and the environment', rather than reflecting any real increase in crime this fear he argues is generated by a 'free floating consciousness of risk' across society, that can 'attach itself to one type of crime on Monday, a different one on Wednesday and yet another on Sunday'. Citing the example in the USA of the panic about road rage – where due to the insecurity caused by this scare more people started carrying guns and ultimately more people were killed in car related disputes, Furedi points out that, 'it is unfortunate that high levels of anxiety about crime can only make the world more insecure'.[39]

Furedi situates the culture of fear within the general political malaise in which the Western World finds itself. He argues that this culture of fear has developed due to a society wide pessimism about human possibilities brought on by the failure of past social experiments from both the left and the right – and a scepticism towards change and the chances of finding solutions to social problems. With no direction or dynamic, he believes society – like a man in the dark – feels lost and insecure about where it is going. This general mood filters down to all levels and groups within society.

This social malaise is also coupled with 'the mutually reinforcing combination of economic dislocation and the weakening of social institutions (the family, religion, political parties, trade unions etc.)' which have accentuated the tendency for society to fragment. This fragmentation helps to reinforce the sense of fear and risk that elevates issues like crime and policing in the minds of people throughout society. Ultimately, Furedi argues, a 'risk consciousness' has developed across all groups in society not simply because of the uncertainty of a changing social environment, but also because of a sense that humanity can do little to overcome the problems we face.[40]

In a changing world which has little direction and fewer points of contact between people, a breeding ground for insecurity and suspicion has developed – the fear of crime being one of the outcomes of this process. The fear of crime in this respect has less to do with crime itself, but is, as Downs and Ahrendt suggested, a reflection of a broader sense of uncertainty across society.

Ultimately, Furedi argues that the culture of fear, is an entirely negative development in society and one that the further promotion of risks can only reinforce. Lacking direction or trust in where society is going and in the people in charge of that direction, combined with a lack of social support networks, there has developed a heightened sense of isolation and alienation which has undermined society's confidence in itself and led to a growing distrust of others. With this heightened sense of insecurity, all safety campaigns can achieve is reinforcing the fear that already exists and further alienating people from one another.

One key area where risk and safety are increasingly promoted, and which directly relates to this book's research, is in regard to children. As child researcher Mayer Hillman explains:

> We have created a world for our children in which safety is promoted through fear. The message of campaigns such as "One false move and you're dead" is one of deference to the source of the danger. That such a world can be advertised without apparent embarrassment by those responsible for the safety of children, and without provoking public outrage, is a measure of how far the unacceptable has become accepted.[41]

Left realist criminologist Jock Young believes that growing street crime has been caused by "structural dislocation, marginalisation, relative deprivation and power-lessness". [42] Following Furedi's thesis, it would appear to be more accurate to say that it is the fear of crime, the development of risk consciousness and the promotion of and implementation of crime and safety campaigns, rather than any necessary increase in levels of street crime itself, which is assisting this structural dislocation, marginalisation and sense of powerlessness.

Likewise Jock Young's belief that crime should be taken more seriously must be questioned. Rather than taking many crime statistics at face value and accepting public fear of crime as proof of a growing problem of public disorder, wider social issues need to be examined in attempting to understand this culture of fear. If Furedi, Dowds and Ahrendt are correct, and the fear of crime has little or nothing to do with crime itself, the question is raised – what is the impact of the increasing safety initiatives like the Hamilton Curfew, on both young people and adults within communities?

Scared of the Kids?

Study Guide

A. What are the trends in crime today? Statistically is crime worse than it was ten years ago?

Find the latest British Crime Survey statistics and compare them to the recorded police statistics. What are the strengths and weaknesses of these statistics?

B. Is the idea of a growing problem of youth crime a 'myth'?

The question of crime statistics is a constant source of intrigue and frustration amongst researchers of crime. What factors other than the statistics themselves have influenced researcher's interpretation of these statistics?

C. When people talk about crime and antisocial behaviour today what do they mean?

Ask your friends and family if crime and antisocial behaviour has got worse in the last ten years. What direct experiences of crime have they had and to what extend has the media influenced their views?

D. What is the 'culture of fear' and what impact does it have upon our understanding of people?

Where you live or where you work assess the main fear of and for young people and critically discuss the extent to which these fears can be justified.

Useful Reading

A   1. *Youth and Crime* by John Muncie.
See index for 'statistics'.

2. 'Crime Statistics: The 'data explosion' and its implications' by Mike Maguire in *The Oxford Handbook of Criminology*.

3. *The Failure of Britain's Police* by Norman Dennis, George Erdos and David Robinson. This is available online.

B   1. *'Childhood' in 'Crisis'?* edited by Phil Scraton.
Especially chapters 1, 2 and 6.

2. *Shooting down the myth of the 'gun culture'* by Brendan O'Neill.
This is available online.

3. *The Failure of Britain's Police* by Norman Dennis, George Erdos and David Robinson.This is available online.

4. *American Youth Violence* by Franklin E. Zimring.

D   1. *Culture of Fear* by Frank Furedi.
Also see relevant articles on Frank Furedi's official website.

2. *Who's Antisocial? New Labour and the Politics of Antisocial Behaviour* by Craig O'Malley and Stuart Waiton.

A summary is available online - *Antisocial Behaviour: The construction of a crime.*

Notes

[1]Cummings, D. (1997). Surveillance and the City (Urban Research Group) p7.

[2]The Scotsman, 2 October 1996.

[3]Bratton, W. J., Dennis, N., Mallon, R., Orr, J., and Pollard, C. (1997). Zero Tolerance: Policing a Free Society (IEA Health and Welfare Unit) p115.

[4]The Scotsman, 2 October 1996.

[5]Dennis, N. (1997). Zero Tolerance: Policing a Free Society. London Institute of Economic Affairs.

[6]Wilson, J. and Kelling, G. (1982). Broken Windows, Atlantic Monthly, March p29-38.

[7]Financial Times, 14 March 1998.

[8]The Guardian 13 Jan 1997.

[9]A Blair, 'My vision for Britain', in G. Radice (ed), What Needs to Change: New Visions for Britain, 1996, p8.

[10]Muncie J (1999) Critical Social Policy Vol. 19 (Sage Publications) p147.

[11]AJJUST NOW: The Journal of the National Association for Youth Justice, Issue No 43 Dec 1998, p11-12.

[12]ibid (p12).

[13]Housing and antisocial behaviour: the way ahead (Scottish Office) p3.

[14]Cummings, D. (1999). In Search of Sesame Street: Policing civility for the twenty first century (Sheffield Hallam University Press) p21.

[15]Young, J. (1994). Incessant Chatter: Recent Paradigms in Criminology, in M. Maguire, R. Morgan and R. Reiner, Oxford Handbook of Criminology (Oxford: Clarendon Press).

[16]Young, J. (1986). Confronting Crime (Sage Publications Ltd) p29.

[17]Fraser, P. Community Safety Community Solutions (NACRO) p5.

[18]Campbell, B. (1993). Goliath (London: Methuen)

[19]Jenkins, S. (1994). Against the Grain (John Murray) p83.

[20]Ibid (p81).

[21]Muncie, J. (1999). Youth and Crime: A critical introduction (Sage Publications Ltd) p15.

[22]ibid (p17).

[23]Rose, D. (1995). In the Name of the Law (Vintage) p102-3.

[24]Roberts, H. and Sachdev, D. (1996). Young People's Social Attitudes (Barnardo's and Social Community Planning Research).

[25]Coleman, J. (1999). Key Data on Adolescence (Trust for the Study of Adolescence) p81.

[26]Rutter, M., Giller, H. and Hagell, A. (1998). Antisocial Behaviour by Young People (Cambridge University Press) p70.

[27]Pitts, J. (1995) Scare in the Community: Part 1: Youth Crime (Community Care 4-10 May).

[28]British Crime Survey (1992) HMSO, p18.

[29]Scotland on Sunday, 23 November 1997.

[30]The Guardian, 26 May 1997.

[31]British Social Attitudes: the 12th report (1995) ed Roger Jowells (Dartmouth Publishing Company Limited).

[32]Fraser, P.: Community Safety Community Solutions (NACRO) p10.

[33]British Social Attitudes: the 12th report (1995) ed Roger Jowells (Dartmouth Publishing Company Limited).

[34]British Social Attitudes: the 12th report (1995) ed Roger Jowells (Dartmouth Publishing Company Limited) p204-205.

[35]British Social Attitudes: the 12th report (1995) ed Roger Jowells (Dartmouth Publishing Company Limited) p33.

[36]Giddens, A. (1994). Beyond Left and Right (Polity Press) p3.

[37]ibid (p79).

[38]ibid (p222).

[39]Furedi, F. (1997). Culture of Fear: Risk taking and the morality of low expectations (Cassell) p23-24.

[40]ibid (Chapter 2).

[41]Hillman, M., Adams, J. and Whiteleg, J. (1990). One False Move...A Study of Children's Independent Mobility (London: PSI Publishing) p111.

[42]Hughes, G. (1998). Understanding Crime Prevention (Open University Press) p118.

2.   Prevention and Fear

In Hamilton, the curfew was introduced as a 'multi-agency', 'community led', 'safety initiative' that would help – by intervening in peer groups – reduce the risky behaviour of young people. This initiative aimed to prevent crime happening by monitoring the behaviour of the young people who hung about the streets. It also aimed to protect children and young people from the 'many dangers that they face when out at night'. As such the Hamilton Curfew was concerned with both crime and safety across the whole community and is a good example of the modern approach to the policing of young people. Here the increased regulation of children and young people was achieved by both targeting them as potential criminals and by presenting them as potential victims of crime. The image of young people as both victims and villains has become increasingly influential throughout the 1980s and 1990s among organisations and agencies that deal with children and young people and subsequently leads to increasing regulation of young lives.

The drive to 'take crime seriously' has, over the last decade, incorporated an increasing number of organisations and agencies through multi-agency initiatives, from the health service to schools, youth organisations and social work departments – as well as involving the community in a growing number of safety initiatives. The focus of attention for these organisations is not solely on crime itself, but on the behaviour of young people who are classified as showing risk related behaviour associated with possible future criminality. Today, while arresting 'hard core' criminals, the trend is for social crime prevention to prevent others from becoming criminals in the first place.

Rather than simply relying on the criminal justice system and the threat of punishment through prisons, the responsibility for reducing crime and antisocial behaviour has increasingly been extended into the 'caring professions' who are now held responsible for changing the behaviour of their troublesome clients. However, it appears that this form of crime prevention, which is often perceived as a more radical, social form of crime prevention, has actually resulted in more aspects of behaviour being linked with criminality and an increasingly interventionist approach into child and family life to prevent future criminals forming than was ever seen with the old right-wing law and order panics.

Measures once associated with social welfare pure and simple are now increasingly being promoted, provided and judged useful on the basis of their capacity to reduce crime. Developing a universal nursery system, helping single parents back to work or providing employment, education and training to all 18-24 year olds, are today pushed as 'ways of tackling the roots of juvenile crime'.[1] The new look youth training schemes are similarly incorporating crime and safety initiatives, with neighbourhood warden schemes set up across the UK being studied by the government's Social Exclusion Unit to assess whether or not they can be incorporated into the New Deal programme.

At the same time that preventing crime and antisocial behaviour is becoming more important in the workload of the 'caring professions', these same professionals are becoming increasingly concerned about their own safety when dealing with the public in general and with young people in particular. This fear is leading to an increasing level of 'internal policing' of young people when they are at school, in hospitals or using any public facilities and an increasing number of safety initiatives designed to protect public sector workers from the public.

Another impact of the preoccupation with crime and safety across society, is that children and young people are seen as being constantly at risk themselves. The threat of paedophiles is the most glaring example of this trend in Britain and it and the many other scares that exist have helped to institutionalise safety measures in young people's lives which are as restrictive as the more overtly authoritarian anti crime initiatives.

Potential criminals

Home Secretary Jack Straw sounded little different to his Conservative counterpart when he talked about society being inflicted with a crime breeding 'excuse culture', where, 'today's young offenders can too easily become tomorrow's hardened criminals'.[2] However as Muncie points out, 'what distinguishes the (Labour) legislation from its Conservative predecessors is the centrality afforded to notions of early intervention and prevention as the most efficient and cost effective means of combating crime'.[3] While hard core offenders continue to be locked up, there is now also an expanding range of statutory and voluntary community-based agencies to provide non-custodial sentences. This is something that was recommended by the Audit Commission in 1996 which prioritised multi-agency work by imposing a statutory duty on all local authorities to establish youth offending teams from representatives of social services, health and education authorities, as well as the traditional agencies of law enforcement the probation and police services.

Within schools, crime prevention projects have been set up to reduce the exclusion of pupils and thus, it is assumed, reduce crime. Home school support social workers develop links between teachers and parents in these projects – their success being measured and funding received in terms of crime prevention rather than educational achievement.[4]

The 1998 Crime and Disorder Act builds on these proposals, and aims to prevent youth crime by developing 'early and effective intervention'[5] to stop child misbehaviour developing into further offending. On this basis, the Act allows for child safety orders and child curfews to 'protect' children under the age of ten, who are deemed to be 'at risk' of becoming involved in crime.[6]

By identifying a cycle of violence or criminality among certain people – once named the underclass, now given the softer label of the socially excluded – attempts are increasingly made to intervene in the lives of young people who it is assumed will become 'hardened criminals'. A recent winner of the Scotland-wide competition to find the best community safety project for example, was the East Lothian Council 'Breaking the Cycle' – youth anti-crime plan. The project which received the 'prize' of £192,000, was, like many of these initiatives, an 'integrated co-ordination of community safety strategies and action plans', and was targeted at 'all young people', to make them, 'aware of crime and the consequences should they choose that path'.[7]

The identification of 'risk factors' that can indicate future criminality is now well established in theory and practise when dealing with young people in trouble, and young people generally. The most common indicators include, poverty, poor housing, poor parenting, abuse, association with delinquent peers, truancy and being brought up by criminal parents.[8] However, while little is said about how to intervene to eradicate poverty, intervention to change the behaviour of those in poverty is increasingly widespread.

As John Muncie points out with reference to the Crime and Disorder Act, 'The issue of the causes of offending,' being related to wider social factors, 'was also side-stepped by the identification of "risk conditions" such as inadequate parental supervision, poor discipline, truancy or lack of a stable home'.[9]

Some initiatives may recognise structural constraints and determinants, but their targets invariably become individualised and behavioural. As Muncie points out in reference to Rosenbaum (1998) and Utting (1996), despite the appearance that social crime prevention is challenging Conservative political ideology:

> [T]he way in which social crime prevention has tended to be realised in practise is through a series of programmes which seek either to remove young people from the street by providing supervised leisure activities or to provide special training and opportunities for those considered "at risk" and their parents in order to improve self respect and competency.[10]

Social crime prevention has developed alongside the growing concern with youth crime and antisocial behaviour. The list of the 'risks' that can be used to indicate possible delinquency in later life, are today, so comprehensive that if taken literally would leave few young people untouched. A review of research into young people and offending by the Scottish Office, suggested that as well as those indicators listed above other possible factors that should be taken into account when assessing the future possibility of criminality include:- teenage pregnancy, drug use, drug use during pregnancy, signs of aggression and antisocial behaviour problems, low self-esteem, school failure or not liking school, and impulsive behaviour during childhood.[11] Other factors, like leaving school early, being cruel to animals, having parents who have separated or having a mother who smoked during your childhood, have all been used by different researchers, educational psychologists and social work departments as indicators of potential future criminality.

However, the use of risk indicators as a method of analysing future criminality is highly problematic, especially at a time when more aspects of young people's petty antisocial behaviour are being identified as criminal. None of these risk conditions can be shown to be causal in relation to crime, so for example, many young people who fit some or all of the above indicators will not turn out to be criminals. Also, many factors like teenage motherhood or truancy may simply be indicators of wider social issues that cannot be resolved at the level of individual. The recent Social Exclusion paper Teenage Pregnancy (1999), for example, recognised that low expectations and the lack of the prospect of getting a job was the key reason that teenage girls had children. So addressing the issues of teenage pregnancies or truancy in themselves would miss the point.

Finally, there is a danger that in using these risk conditions that the reactions of young people are seen as being deterministic – almost Pavlovian. John, born to a teenage mother with a criminal past who smokes, having behavioural problems at the age of two, showing cruelty to animals at 8 and drinking alcohol at 13, is a blueprint of tomorrow's criminal. Here rather than John being charged in relation to actual criminal acts, before any crime is committed he has been branded and targeted as a type of person – tomorrow's criminal – with little chance of escaping his social conditioning without the help and support of the caring professionals.

Where crimes have been committed, there is also an attempt to spot 'persistent young offenders', but here too, as Hagell and Newburn point out, there are any number of possible definitions of persistent offender, each of which labels very different young people.[12]

By adopting this approach, behaviour which is common for many young people, like underage drinking and taking recreational drugs, in unison with other risk factors could place many more young people on a social worker's or educational psychologist's at-risk list. A young person caught taking drugs, who lives with their unemployed father who drinks may subsequently get very different treatment and a level of intervention into their lives that would not be seen as necessary if the offender were a middle class teenager from a stable family.

By defining types of people who are at risk of future criminality, the equal treatment of young people who break the law, or act in an antisocial manner, is further reduced.

Get them while they're young

A growing belief has emerged over recent years regarding priorities for intervention to resolve the 'crime problem'. Citing work by Farrington and Rivara (1993) and

Farrington (1986 and 1991) Scottish Office research explains that, 'There is a consensus that the basis for criminal careers begins in childhood'.[13]

For the Scottish Office, early aggression and antisocial behaviour in childhood predicts later delinquency and crime – including violence. Evidence for this includes the Cambridge Study, where 'half of the most antisocial boys at age 8-10 years were still among the most antisocial at age 14 years and 43% were still among the most antisocial at age 18.[14] Another study found that 45% of troublesome boys at age 8-10 years were convicted as juveniles.[15] If early indicators of antisocial behaviour suggest problematic behaviour in later life, then the report argues, early intervention even before school starts is necessary.

The aim of the Scottish Office research into children and crime was to point to how this information could be applied to 'the understanding of, and response to, the offending behaviour of young people in Scotland with the aim of preventing the development of offending lifestyles'.

Focusing on the behaviour of parents towards their young children, Farrington and Rivara believe the answer to resolving violence in society lies with paediatricians who can help in the:

> [P]revention of teenage pregnancy; ensuring adequate prenatal care, especially for high risk mothers...recognition of and intervention in poor parenting; provision of social support to families; recognition and management of behaviour problems through pre-school and early childhood education programmes.[16]

The focus for crime prevention is no longer to merely stop crime, but to stop parents creating criminal children and stopping 'troublesome' children growing up to become criminals. A highly deterministic perception of how criminals are formed has been developed here, where what happens to a small child, sets in stone the pattern of his or her future life.

The Cambridge Study uses the term 'antisocial' to explain the behaviour of these young people, but there is no direct connection between antisocial behaviour which many young people partake in, and crime – especially serious crime. While the results of the two reports above show that half of the 'most antisocial' or 'troublesome' boys proved to continue to be antisocial or were convicted as juveniles later on in life, equally – half did not. There is also a problem in viewing children or adolescents who are troublesome or even delinquent, as the criminals of the future – as Jack Straw does when he says that today's young offenders can too easily become tomorrow's hardened criminals – as longitudinal studies have shown that most young offenders grow out of problem behaviour.[17]

Risk factors are seen as useful for identifying almost all types of criminal behaviour. Dr Sue Bailey, for example, at the Royal College of Psychiatrists' annual conference in Edinburgh, argued that better training for health workers, social workers and teachers could help in the early identification of child killers.[18]

If risk indicators are taken seriously and antisocial behaviour is linked to more serious crimes there is a danger that many children, who will not end up as criminals in later life, will be labelled as potentially dangerous from a very early age, and because of petty antisocial behaviour become criminalised in their youth. By incorporating welfare agencies, schools and youth organisations in crime prevention, there is also the danger that not only do these bodies develop into adjuncts of the criminal justice system, but that the image of these services to young people become framed in a negative, preventative environment. Teachers for example are under increasing pressure to regulate and monitor all aspects of their pupils behaviour, with 'Enforcing Good Behaviour' and 'Teaching Acceptable Interpersonal Skills' competing with education itself. While new exciting technological developments like the Internet are more often than not seen as a potential danger to children who may access pornographic or violent images – leading to warnings from the then Education Secretary David Blunkett that schools should monitor their pupils more closely.[19]

In the process of developing these crime prevention initiatives, 'notions of creative citizenship are de-emphasised through a myopic focus on troublesome behaviour'.[20]

The result, especially in areas targeted for 'social inclusion', is that time, energy and resources are increasingly directed at initiatives that aim to tackle the crime and safety of an area. Funding bids for projects that do not incorporate some aspect of crime prevention and safety are far less likely to be successful. In Easterhouse, a large working class estate outside of Glasgow, the Community Safety Shop is adorned with posters warning customers to 'Stop before you answer the door!'. The shop is part of the Safe Greater Easterhouse Project and has been one of the most successful in attracting Scottish Office money to the area: £680,000 has been awarded to fix mortise locks, door chains, door viewers, hinge bolts and window locks onto every house on the estate.

The image of children generally is changing, with more aspects of their behaviour being seen in the context of crime and safety. The 'truant' – someone who misses lessons at school – for example has been transformed over recent years, and is now seen as a potential criminal. One result of this change is the setting up of pilot swipe card schemes in a number of schools to allow teachers and parents to monitor more closely the time that each child arrives at school. This scheme was announced by Charles Clark, the Home Office Minister, not as part of an education drive, but as part of a £12 million package of anti youth crime measures.[21]

Public Servants?

The Scottish Office research review, entitled Children, Young People and Offending in Scotland, concluded that, 'In terms of policy, therefore, crime prevention strategies should commence not as criminal justice reactions, but via a range of early years health and education initiatives to counter the high-risk precursors of delinquent behaviour'.[22]

While this approach is seen by many as a more social and caring approach to crime prevention, it risks changing the nature of services like the health and education service. Rather than crime prevention becoming more caring, the danger is that caring professions are becoming more preoccupied with crime and the control of young people.

In the area of drug abuse, the health service has already become more preoccupied with crime prevention than with helping their patients' medical difficulties. GP's are becoming increasingly responsible for reducing heroin addiction through methadone maintenance treatment, a programme the BMJ believes has been highly successful.[23] However the mark of success for the BMJ, is no longer a reduction in the number of drug addicts – as the addiction simply shifts from heroin to methadone – but rather the reduction in 'drug related criminal behaviour'.

The National Treatment Outcome Research Study sponsored by the Department of Health, confirmed that prescribing methadone does appear to have reduced crime. However the increase in methadone treatment has also resulted in a dramatic increase in the number of deaths from methadone which now exceeds those from heroin – in Lothian for example deaths from methadone more than doubled between 1995 and 1996.[24]

Despite the evidence of the medical dangers of methadone, for drug users and their families, the multi-agency anti-crime approach towards heroin addicts is now well established. In London, GP's are even being encouraged to join this programme, with financial incentives of £20 per patient, and are coming under moral pressure from the BMJ which has questioned the ethics of GP's who do not join the programme.[25]

So elevated is the role of crime prevention, that the BMJ now believes it is more ethical to take on the role of the police in tackling drug related crime, than in addressing the best interests of their patients.

Public fear of children

As well as the development of crime prevention initiatives within more and more council departments and organisations, there is a move to introduce safety measures to protect workers from their clients. While multi-agency crime prevention initiatives are being promoted within schools, hospitals and social work departments, the 'culture of fear' is affecting the relationship between public sector workers and the young people they work with. Professions once renowned for their caring approach to the public are starting to institutionalise procedures in the workplace to protect their staff from the perceived dangers of violent clients.

Within schools, teachers are increasingly refusing to deal with disruptive children themselves, with educational psychologists, disruptive units and special schools being relied upon. School expulsions are becoming more common, with some children as young as five being expelled. The result of this approach is that, 'pupils are segregated from mainstream schooling, especially those referred to off site units'.[26]

Hospital staff are also showing signs of unease in their dealings with members of the public, and young people in particular, who are perceived to be a threat. Practises, like the introduction of assault books to log the aggressive behaviour of clients, have become common in many hospitals and more widely, the issue of crime and security has become an issue promoted by the British Medical Association itself. The Centre for Action on Staff Safety, for example, has recently been established in England. One staff member in collaboration with the BMA has produced the 80 page pamphlet 'Handling Aggression and Violence in Health Services'. The centre offers staff skills courses, practise procedures and training in legal requirements. While in Scotland, Strathclyde Police have started offering advice on 'surgery layout and security arrangements – panic buttons, CCTV etc. – as well as training in self defence and techniques for preventing and containing aggression'.[27]

A *Guardian* headline recently expressed concern at the rise in attacks on staff that was 'blighting' the NHS. This followed a report into violence in hospitals which found that there had been a 20% increase in attacks on one year. However as one commentator pointed out, while the government had targeted this issue, and in 1998 aimed to reducing attacks by 20%, their own zero tolerance campaign launched in 1999 had encouraged 'staff to report violence and intimidation of all kinds'. In one hospital the introduction of a new incident form for example, led to a 400% increase in the number of violent episodes and the author of the report, 'Getting to grips with work place violence' had to admit that, 'These are shocking findings, although all the figures quoted above should be treated with caution, as employees are now encouraged to report and record incidents, no matter how seemingly trivial'.[27a]

This promotion of safety within the health service has unfortunately had some tragic consequences, as the case of Gordon Niven shows.[28] Hospital staff at Glasgow's Victoria Infirmary, who felt at risk from the aggressive 16 year old Gordon Niven, called the police – who placed him in a cell for three hours. Gordon had fallen off his bike, fracturing his skull and had been taken to hospital where his aggressive behaviour was assumed to be caused by drink or drugs. Despite Gordon's mother's pleas that his behaviour could be due to the head injury, Gordon was taken to a police cell from where he was released after being examined by a police surgeon. He died two days later.

The perceived threat that Gordon posed to the hospital staff of the Victoria Infirmary – despite the possibility that his behaviour may be related to his injury – was enough for staff to call the police to deal with him. Gordon Niven is an extreme example of the dangers of this approach to young people, but the belief that teenagers are more dangerous today and need to be regulated is becoming increasingly common.

Teacher's unions in Scotland have called for more to be done to protect teachers from what they believe is a growing problem. In 1996, the Scottish Secondary Teachers' Association proposed a number of changes in practice within schools to improve the safety situation, these included: visitor's passes, telephones for staff, greater protection for staff working in school outside normal hours, information to be given to staff about pupils with a history of violence or who 'might be violent' and teachers legal right to report violent behaviour to the police to be highlighted. Despite only one local authority at that time having any figures on incidents of violence at school, the Education Institute of Scotland (EIS), which represents 80% of the teaching profession, was convinced that there was a steady increase in the number of assaults on teachers.[29]

The threat that children pose to teachers was recently highlighted by a new Scottish Office report, which had been set up to look in more detail at the level of violence towards teachers, and found that 743 teachers had been attacked in Scotland's schools. Scottish education minister Helen Liddell, who called for a zero tolerance approach to violence in schools explained that, 'It doesn't tell us the whole picture but it certainly tells us enough to let us know that this is something that requires action'.[30]

To deal with the 'growing threat' that children pose to teachers, teachers unions across the UK are campaigning to defend their members from violent school pupils. Nigel de Gruchy, General Secretary of the second largest teaching union in England, the National Association of Schoolmasters/Union of Women Teachers believes that, 'some children have been able to bring the jungle law of violent street gangs into our schools'. The second largest teachers' union in Scotland, the Scottish Secondary Teachers' Association has recently recommended head teachers be given the power to report pupils who consistently misbehave to the Children's Panel, while the largest teachers union in Scotland, the EIS has called for the stalking of teachers to be recognised as a crime. In two local authorities, North Lanarkshire and North Ayrshire, teachers have been offered self-defence classes in response to increased concerns about the level of violence in schools.[31]

High profile acts of violence by young people, like the killing of London head teacher Philip Lawrence, have given weight to the belief that today's school children are becoming more violent towards their teachers, and have helped encourage state departments, like the Scottish Office to set up research projects to look into the violent behaviour of school children.

Despite media splashes about attacks on school teachers, it is difficult to establish whether young people are more violent towards teachers, than in the past. One important reason is that research on this issue has only recently been carried out, however where research has been carried out it is open to question. The recent Scottish Office research which highlighted the figure of 743 violent attacks on teachers in Scotland, and made front page news, is more confusing than clarifying, on the issue of child to teacher violence. Firstly, the number of violent incidents recorded in Scottish schools per 100,000 pupils, was 121. In other words violence is extremely rare. When you break down the 'shocking' figure of 743 attacks on teachers, the scale of the problem reduces even further. Just under half of the 'attacks' were verbal not physical; more than half were carried out by primary school children rather than high school pupils; included within the 743 figure are attacks in special schools rather than ordinary schools; and of the 743 figure only 178 of the attacks were made by pupils in high school – many of these being verbal 'attacks'.

The elevation of verbal abuse by teenagers, or tantrums of five year old children, into 'acts of violence' – punishable by expulsion from school, says more about those interpreting these acts than anything about the incidents themselves.

The fear of young people that can often be found among those who work with the public and especially those working with children has no doubt been elevated further by the changing role of the public sector, the public sector unions and the growing focus upon safety .

The public service union Unison for example, like the NASUWT, has been running a campaign for a number of years to highlight the dangers their members face from the public and a 'landmark judgement' has recently been made by the Court of Session that all people working with 'potentially violent children' have the right to be taught self defence.

Maximum security – fear for children

The issue of crime and safety is not simply an issue for adults who feel at risk from young people, there is also a growing concern that adults must take more and more measures to protect children from crime and violence. This is especially clear with the issues of stranger danger and the concern about paedophiles, where 'Spotting Signs of Abuse' has become standard practice in almost any workplace that deals with children.

Head teacher, Philip Lawrence, who was murdered by a teenager outside his school, has come to symbolise the dangers adults face from young people. In contrast, men like Fred West and Thomas Hamilton are held up as examples of the dangers that children face. Increasingly, isolated extreme incidents such as the shootings in Dunblane, have become the basis for developing safety initiatives in schools and youth clubs that are impacting on the lives of children across the UK. These initiatives, like the growth of school security and the vetting of youth workers, despite their intention, appear to making parents more insecure about their children and are undermining the trust between adults.

After the murder of 16 children and their teacher by Thomas Hamilton in Dunblane, politicians of all persuasions initially warned against a knee-jerk over-reaction to this event. However, within a few weeks the feeling was that 'something must be done' to protect children from this ever happening again. The results: the then Conservative government promised extra money for school security and a review of police powers to deal with intruders at school; a working group was set up in Highland schools to look into the issue of security; the Church of Scotland raised the possibility of vetting all its Sunday School teachers', and the Cullen inquiry was set up to look into issue of school security and the possibility of establishing a vetting system, for all those working with children across the voluntary sector.

The then Shadow Scottish Secretary George Robertson who welcomed the Cullen inquiry as a move to improve school security explained that, 'Labour has already said we will co-operate with any legislation required. Schools must not become like armoured camps, but pupils and teachers have to be given maximum protection'.[32]

A report developed by a government working party after the death of Philip Lawrence was given added weight after the events at Dunblane. The recommendations in the report included: the government should publish guidelines for schools on improving physical security; ministers should give 'every possible priority' to bids from schools for money to install closed circuit TV cameras and measures should be taken to improve liaison between schools and the police.[33]

Lord Cullen, in his report, recommended that every school in Britain should be assessed to determine its security needs. He also recommended that teachers be taught how to deal with aggression, possibly being provided with panic buttons, telephones and personal alarms. Doug McAvoy, of the National Union of Teachers, responding to the report said, 'If schools need to turn themselves into fortresses then so be it'.[34]

Eighteen months later, the first primary school to be built since Dunblane, St Michael's, was completed, with £80,000 worth of security measures attached. The school is protected by a six foot perimeter fence and five security cameras, while once pupils are inside the school, all the doors are electronically locked with admission only possible through a video controlled system.

St Michael's security system is in line with recommendations contained in the Cullen report. Quoted in the Scotsman, the school board chairman said it was sad that schools had to be more security conscious, but this school has been hailed as the shape of schools to come in our 'increasingly violent times'.[35]

The Cullen report's effect is not limited to physical security measures, it also impacts on the relationship of trust in organisations that deal with children. Following the report, across the UK, from 2002 information about employees' behaviour that does not lead to a prosecution, or information about individuals who are charged with abuse but are not convicted, will now be available to the Scouts or other organisations working with children.

The Scouts for example who have checked for convictions of abuse against children via newspaper reports since the 1940s, will now have access to 'softer' information about possible volunteers. The dangers are that innocent people may be labelled as 'potential' abusers; volunteers who now have to be vetted may be discouraged from helping out; and unless the government changes its mind organisations will have to foot the bill of vetting their volunteers. For the Scouts, this vetting procedure would cost £750,000. While vetting will remain voluntary for the organisation, once established it is likely that there will be a moral obligation to access the information, and insurance for organisations may become dependent upon staff being vetted.

This dangerous measure reverses the normal assumption of innocent until proven guilty and opens staff up to malicious charges of 'abuse' affecting their employment prospects or ability to volunteer. It seems that mistrust of adults working with children is set to be institutionalised.

Many of these measures in vetting workers and introducing school security, have emerged 'in the light of Dunblane' and the reports set up in the aftermath of the shootings. However, it is unlikely that any of the measures that have been introduced in schools across the UK would have prevented Thomas Hamilton killing the 16 children and their teacher. As Lord Cullen himself explained in his report, it would be 'unrealistic to expect that the risk of a violent intruder gaining access to a school can be eliminated'.[36]

Like the perception that crime is increasing, the assumption that children face growing dangers from our 'increasingly violent times', does not stand up to scrutiny. There are no more children murdered or abducted today than in the past. Indeed figures for child murder, gross indecency, and cruelty towards children have all fallen in the past 20 years,[37] and as Rob Lyons noted in his submission to the Cullen enquiry – regarding the proposal to vet voluntary workers working with children, 'there are almost no cases in the voluntary sector of child abuse leading to conviction'.[38] This may not prove that child abuse or abductions do not take place, but it does raise doubts about the evidence that such a problem is increasing so that vetting workers and locking children inside their own schools is needed.

One of the consequences of growing school security is that, as Stuart Baird a secondary school teacher in Falkirk High explained, 'Community schools which were attempting to break down barriers between themselves and members of the community, are now closing themselves off from that very community'.[39] Children's perception of school and the dangers they face will also change as schools become more security conscious. This was shown when pupils of St Jude's in Barlanark in the east end of Glasgow were asked, as part of Glasgow 1999 year of architecture, for ideas on how to redesign their school. Two recommendations made by the pupils were for a secure entry system and that children be trained to seek adult help if they see someone at the front door. As Deyan Sudjic, director of Glasgow 1999, said, despite St Jude's good academic track record, he'd found that parents felt, 'coming to school was like walking into Fort Knox', he added that, 'the protection measures such as mesh and cages over the windows are a pretty grim start to life'.[40]

The reaction to the Dunblane tragedy by politicians and local authorities, has been to accept without question the idea that young people are in growing danger of being attacked or abused and must be protected at all costs. But, not only is there little evidence to justify the use of resources to increase the 'policing' of young people in this way, there is also a danger that the insecurity and desire to protect children from all unknown adults will actually intensify the distrust that exists of 'others' and so increase the fear felt by parents and teachers within the community. As Lyons notes, one of the key problems with the move towards the vetting of voluntary workers working with children, is that this approach suggests to staff and parents that,

> No adult should be trusted with children unless they have been checked out and have no previous record of indiscretion. This is the reversal of the traditional view which would be that someone putting themselves forward to perform such work voluntarily has an altruistic desire to help children and should be trusted unless proven untrustworthy.[41]

That adults in Britain are becoming more suspicious of others – especially those that work with or enjoy the company of children – was clearly shown in the 'Euromale' study, which charted the lifestyle and attitude of British men. Asked to look at a picture of a man playing with a young girls' football team and to describe what they saw, unlike French, Spanish, German or Italian men who saw 'a family man who likes children and sports', British men saw 'a paedophile'.

Nick Johnson of research company RSDi whose report was based on interviews with 1000 men explained that, 'The response of all the British men was to won-der why a guy would be spending time with children who are clearly not his own'.[42]

The obsession with paedophilia is such that in the UK, advertisers are being warned off using images of men with children and a new group – Cry – the Campaign for the Registration of Adults Working with Young People and Children has been set up by the Institute of Childcare and Social Education, trade unions and a cross party group of MP's, to urge the Department of Health and

Education to set up a single register for all adults in the childcare business. Spokesman Ronan Dickson explained that the register was needed because of the increase in childcare needs and, he hoped, that once established the register would stop the panic about paedophiles.

Unfortunately, the expectation that the fear of paedophiles will decline because of more security measures is misplaced, as with the fear of crime it is not any real threat from paedophiles or another Thomas Hamilton as such that is leading to this insecurity. Indeed, if the last few years are anything to go by – building schools that resemble 'Fort Knox', vetting workers and volunteers, creating paedophile lists, introducing gun controls and the many other safety initiatives throughout communities – have reinforced the idea that children are in danger and that every adult is a potential threat.

The climate that has been created today, is one based on mistrust. Almost every form of contact between young people and adults is now seen through the prism of danger and safety. Either young people are a potential danger to adults or to one another, or adults are a potential danger to these young people. The Hamilton Curfew has developed within this climate and is promoted as an initiative that can both protect adults from young people while securing the safety of the children within the area.

Many aspects of young people's behaviour that would have been seen as merely immature or 'adolescent' in the past are being seen as problematic and potentially leading to criminality. This will not only result in more young people being unnecessarily incorporated into crime prevention and safety initiatives, but it is already impacting upon the outlook and practise of professionals working with young people who must now be constantly aware of the potentially abusive or abused child.

While most young people will not be incorporated into specific crime prevention programmes, all children and young people are growing up in schools and communities where safety is becoming one of the dominant themes in their lives. What impact this is having on the consciousness of these children and young people and what their views are of adults and other young people will be addressed here in relation to the impact of the curfew.

Study Guide

A. To what extent do the issues of crime, safety and antisocial behaviour impact upon the activities of those working with young people and communities?

Examine for example council policy documents and strategic plans and assess the significance and the potential impact of community safety initiatives on local areas and on the approaches adopted by local authority departments.

B. What are the strengths and weaknesses of the 'risk factor' approach to understanding crime?

Consider your own upbringing and experiences and discuss the extent to which you are a product of your immediate environment.

C. Tony Blair has called for early intervention to help prevent social problems like crime and antisocial behaviour. To what extent can this be understood as a form of 'support' or as an Orwellian form of social engineering?

Research the 'early intervention' strategies being promoted in the press today and assess their underlying assumptions and objectives.

D. To what extent has the issue of 'child safety' emerged as a core framework for addressing the needs of children and young people.

Examine the debate around the growing vetting of youth workers and those working with children and consider the potential problems of this development.

Useful Reading

A. 1. Hughes and Edwards work on community safety in Tilley's *Handbook of Crime Prevention and Community Safety*.

2. *Criminology and the 'community safety' paradigm: Safety, power and success and the limits of the local* by Peter Squires.
Available online.

3. *Community Safety: A Critique* by Daniel Gilling.
Available online.

B. 1. *Children, Young People and Offending in Scotland* by Stuart Asquith et al, published by the Scottish Office.
A summary of this can be accessed online and is useful for its discussion of risk factors and the work of Farrington.

2. 'Review: The Limits of Crime Control' by Richard Rosenfeld in *The Journal of Criminal Law and Criminology*, Vol. 93, No. 1, 289-298 (2002).

3. 'Developmental Criminolgy and Risk-Focused Prevention' by David P. Farrington in *The Oxford Handbook of Criminology* edited by Mike Maguire et al.

D.   1. *The Case Against Vetting: How the child protection industry is destroying adult-child relations.*
This is available online.

2. Visit the Scottish Parents Teachers Council website and do a search for 'vetting'.

3. *After Soham: Taking Liberties* by Jennie Bristow.
Available online.

Notes

[1]Home Office (1997). No More Excuses: A New Approach to Tackling Youth Crime in England and Wales, p10 (HMSO).

[2]Muncie, J. (1999). Youth and Crime: A critical introduction (Sage Publications Ltd) p148.

[3]ibid.

[4]Vulliamy, G. (1999). Meeting need and challenging crime in partnership with schools (Home Office Research).

[5]Home Office (1997) Tackling Youth Crime: in Muncie p152.

[6]Barry Goldson: AJJUST NOW: The Journal of the National Association for Youth Justice, Issue No 43 Dec 1998, p12.

[7]Scottish Executive press release: ref no. Justice – SE0598.

[8]Gerison Landsdown: AJJUST NOW: The Journal of the National Association for Youth Justice, Issue No 43 Dec 1998, p7.

[9]Muncie, J. (1999). Critical Social Policy Vol. 19 (Sage Publications) p151.

[10]Muncie, J. (1999). Youth and Crime: A critical introduction (Sage Publications Ltd) p244.

[11]Asquith, S. et al (1998). Children, Young People and Offending in Scotland (The Scottish Office Central Research Unit).

[12]Hagell, A. and Newburn, T. (1994). Persistent Young Offenders (London PSI).

[13]Asquith, S. et al (1998). Children, Young People and Offending in Scotland (The Scottish Office Central Research Unit) .

[14]ibid.

[15]ibid p14.

[16]ibid p5.

[17]ibid p16.

[18]The Herald, 7 July 2000

[19]Times 11 October 1999,

[20]Muncie, J., Coventry, G. and Walters, R. (1995). The politics of youth crime prevention(p356) in Noaks L et al Contemporary Issues in Criminology, (Cardiff University of Wales Press).

[21]Times 11 October 1999.

[22]Asquith, S. et al (1998). Children, Young People and Offending in Scotland (The Scottish Office Central Research Unit) p52.

[23]British Medical Journal, 5 June 1999.

[24]British Medical Journal, 3 August 1996.

[25]LM Magazine No122.

[26]Asquith, S. et al (1998). Children, Young People and Offending in Scotland (The Scottish Office Central Research Unit).

[27]LM Magazine No 120.

[27]Geldman, A. (2000/01). Getting to grips with work place violence. A Health Service Report, Issue 29.

[28]The Herald Magazine 29 May 1999.

[29]Herald, 8 January 1996.

[30]The Herald Magazine, 29 May 1999.

[31]The Herald, 25 November 1997.

[32]The Herald, 15 May 1996.

[33]ibid.

[34]The Scotsman, 28 October 1999.

[35]The Scotsman, 19 February 1998.

[36]The Scotsman, 28 October 1996.

[37]The Sunday Times, 11 June 2000.

[38]Lyons, R. (http://www.generationyouthissues.com). Vetting of Voluntary Workers.

[39]The Scotsman, 28/10/96.

[40]The Scotsman, 11 December 1998.

[41]Lyons, R. (http://www.generationyouthissues.com). Vetting of Voluntary Workers.

[42]Observer, 27 July 1999.

3   Spotlight on the Curfew

The Hamilton Curfew

The Child Safety Initiative (CSI), commonly known as the Hamilton Curfew, was launched in October 1997 and was to run for a trial six month period, ending in April 1998.[1] Three working class areas within Hamilton in South Lanarkshire were chosen for this pilot project – Whitehill, Fairhill and Hillhouse. The aim of the CSI or curfew (both terms will be used in this book) was to move any under 16 year old off the streets if they were out 'after dark' and could not give 'a reasonable excuse' as to why they were out. While not specifying a strict curfew time, the CSI was clearly aimed at encourage young people to stop hanging around the streets at night and put the onus on them to justify their public presence. Although 'after dark' was the time at which the police stated they would start to act in Hillhouse, most of the young people spoken to in the area believed the police started picking people up around 9pm.

The announcement of the Child Safety Initiative on 23rd October came with speeches from both Chief Constable John Orr and council leader Tom McCabe. From the outset the CSI was promoted as a joint initiative, not simply a police initiative, involving South Lanarkshire Council and in particular the Social Work Department. In numerous radio and television debates about the curfew, it was not the chief of police who explained the purpose of the new policing initiative, but Sandy Cameron, Director of Social Work. Through the Social Work Department the Child Safety Initiative – as its name suggests – was presented as a safety initiative, to prevent young people becoming criminals, and also as a mechanism for ensuring the safety of young children who are allowed to wander the streets late at night. Sandy Cameron explained that, 'This is not a curfew, but an issue of safety and in particular the safety of young people'.[2]

John Orr elaborated on this safety point in his opening speech.

> We come across young people out of doors way after nightfall...yet – and what a paradox – paedophile court cases hit the headlines regularly and there is controversy about the issue of the rights of communities to know where convicted offenders are living. What then can the parents of the children we come into contact with possibly be thinking about.[3]

As well as protecting young people from themselves by stopping their bad behaviour, the initiative is presented as something to protect children from paedophiles by making their 'irresponsible parents' keep them in at night or at least ensure their night time activities are supervised. An aim of the CSI was clearly to ensure that children, young people and particularly parents, were made well aware of all the potential dangers within their communities – even when dangers, for example, from paedophiles – were unheard of within these communities.[4]

The curfew, while being popularly seen as an anti-crime device to protect adults from young people, was promoted as an initiative to improve the safety of young people themselves. As John Orr explained, 'The 6 month long pilot programme seeks to highlight the dangers faced by youngsters allowed out after dark without adult supervision'.[5]

Tom McCabe, Labour Leader of South Lanarkshire Council and Sandy Cameron, Executive Director of Social Work, explained what dangers they were concerned about. In an interview with Sky Scottish, McCabe explained that, 'We are trying to give people their liberty back – especially teenagers who through peer pressure may be led into acts that they will regret for a long time afterwards'.[6]

Young people who commit criminal offences are here seen, not only as criminals, but also as victims – victims of peer pressure who need to be protected by the police. Sandy Cameron makes a similar point, when he notes that,

> It is important to take young people back home into dialogue with their parents – to help them avoid getting into criminal activities... We must also recognise that the misuse of alcohol by young people is a serious problem in our communities, and is something that sets patterns that affect us all.[7]

Here, both McCabe and Cameron portray young people, especially those young people committing offences, as potential victims, victims of their peers or victims of alcohol, and in need of protection from their peers and even from themselves and their 'set patterns'. How this form of policing could work in practise is unclear, but there are many assumptions made here that raise questions about how we treat young people. For example, do we want to start protecting young people from their peers, should we treat all street drinkers as criminals, and should we worry that underage drinkers are merely budding alcoholics?

Scotland's First Citizens' Jury

The development of the curfew involved the council and the Social Work Department, it also involved the wider community through forum discussions and most importantly, through Scotland's First Citizen's Jury set up in Hillhouse, one of the targeted areas. This Jury, made up of a cross section of local people was established to address the issue of community safety and produced a report in May/June 1997 outlining its recommendations which included:

- All possible steps are taken through local action and professional intervention to encourage the growth of community spirit in Hillhouse.
- Adults in the community make a commitment to pass on their skills and encourage the development of skills in young people.
- Children's play areas should be provided.
- Stricter enforcement of the law, against shops which supply alcohol to under age drinkers.

- An additional Community Police Officer be allocated to Hillhouse.
- The police re-examine their attitudes towards the public and adopt a less aggressive, less confrontational approach.[8]

The council and police in an attempt to avoid taking responsibility for the introduction of the Hamilton Curfew, explained that it was this group of local people who had developed the idea of a Child Safety Initiative. This was not true. Not only did this group not develop the idea for a curfew, one of their final demands, as shown above, was for the police to adopt a less aggressive and confrontational approach.

While prioritising the 'safety' *of* children and young people in the curfew areas, the CSI was also promoted as an initiative that could make adults and elderly adults in particular, safe *from* young people. John Orr explained that another reason for the CSI, was the large number of complaints being made by locals about young people disturbing the peace at night. Judging from the level of support given to this initiative by local people, there does indeed appear to be a lot of concern about the behaviour of those people who are out on the streets at night. A survey published by the *Hamilton Advertiser* showed that 95% or 972 people were in favour of the curfew and only 5% or 55 people against it.[9] ITV's teletext telephone poll for Central Scotland found 96% of the 1,918 callers were also in favour of the initiative.

Presented as both an initiative developed for the benefit of young people who hung about on the streets at night, and one that would appease local adults who were complaining about these young people, a Janus-faced initiative was developed. With the CSI claiming to be pro-children to some and anti-children to others, very different aspirations were being appealed to and somebody was bound to be disappointed.

In discussion with residents from Hamilton, and from the number of letters supporting the initiative sent to the local newspaper, it appears that for local adults, the curfew was seen as something that was needed to control the young people who hung about on the streets at night causing a nuisance. Nevertheless this was an aspect of the curfew that the council used less and less in their promotion of it. By presenting the curfew as a 'child safety' initiative, rather than an anti-crime campaign, the council – through the Social Work Department – attempted to deflect criticism of what some commentators saw as oppressive policing based on 'moral authoritarianism'.[10] Some questioning by civil liberties groups, of this aspect of the curfew continued throughout the campaign, but little comment or criticism was made about the child-safety side of the initiative.

Whose Agenda?

Surveys commissioned by the council have shown that safety is certainly an issue for people in Hamilton and across South Lanarkshire. The survey carried out by pollsters, System Three, between April and May 1996 found that, 'The issue about which respondents most commonly said the community should be consulted was Crime and Community Safety (54%)'.[11]

However, when prompted to rate their areas in relation to a number of potential problems or issues, the prominence of highly visible issues of crime and public order diminished and respondents were more likely to raise issues like the availability of job opportunities (rated poor by 84%), the availability of leisure facilities (53% poor), suitable places for children to play (56% poor) and the condition of roads, pavements and street-lighting (48% poor)'.[12]

While safety is clearly an issue for people in Hamilton, when asked to be more specific about the particular problems in their area, the more practical problems of unemployment and poor facilities are clearly prioritised above safety issues.

Despite this, South Lanarkshire Council prioritised community safety as an issue to be addressed, and the Citizen's Jury set up in Hillhouse was established to look at this issue ahead of any other.

The outcome of the Curfew

It is unclear who initiated the idea of a curfew in Hamilton, but it is clear that Jack Straw and New Labour have had the idea on their agenda nationally for some time. Similarly Strathclyde Police have been developing new methods of regulating public space across Glasgow for a number of years, and it is therefore unsurprising that the Child Safety Initiative has been introduced in the Strathclyde Police area first.

In April 1998 the initiative, which was intended to last for only six months, was extended. In justifying the need for an extension to the curfew, Strathclyde Police announced the most extreme examples they had come across while policing the curfew. These were: a four year old out at 9pm; a 14 year old found drunk at 10.30pm; and a 10 year old boy selling newspapers outside a bingo hall.

Of the 229 young people dealt with by the police in this pilot curfew, between October 1997 and April 1998, 63% of interventions were for loitering.[13]

Two hundred youngsters were taken home for breaking the curfew, 4 were taken to Hamilton police station. Of the 229 interventions made, 14% of the young people were under 8 years old. The majority dealt with were 12-13 years olds out on Friday and Saturday nights, with loitering accounting for 63% of the interventions and disorder making up 9%. Strathclyde Police reported that of the 229 youngsters dealt with 87% actually approved of the curfew.[14] However, the Scottish Human Right Centre noted that the police included within this figure those who had expressed no opinion; only 59% of these 229 young people actually expressed support.[15]

On 15th October the result of the Scottish Office research into the CSI was presented to the press at Hamilton Grammar School. Reiterating the message that this initiative was about the safety of children and young people not simply an anti-crime campaign, Chief Constable John Orr and Scottish Home Affairs Minister Henry McLeish hailed the initiative as a great success. Despite this emphasis upon safety, however, the researcher present at this press launch explained that there was 'not enough evidence to say if Hillhouse is safer or not'.[16] The figures used by John Orr to justify his claim that the CSI had been a success were crime figures. The relative fall in youth related crime was held up as proof that the CSI had been effective and would subsequently be extended across the whole of Hamilton. John Orr explained, possibly as a way of overcoming the curfew label, that this extended child and young person's initiative would no longer simply operate at night time, but would now be in effect day and night.[17] By dropping the 'after dark' aspect of the initiative, it is hoped that the stigma of 'the curfew' will be lost. However, in effect, this will allow the police to challenge young people to give a 'reasonable excuse' as to why they are out, at any time of the day.

At this time Henry McLeish raised the possibility that the Child Safety Initiative could be extended across the whole of Scotland. However, by the 3rd December Mr McLeish had backed down on this proposal after the chief constable of Fife, John Hamilton, criticised the 'inefficient and expensive' police approach to juvenile crime.[18]

Research in Hillhouse

The research for this book was carried out in Hillhouse – the largest of the three curfew target areas. Hillhouse has a total population of 2,395. This is the age breakdown of children:

Age	% of population	% in whole of South Lanarkshire
5-11	10.7	9.2
12-15	6.0	5.3
16-17	2.8	2.8
18-21	7.3	4.7

- There are 347 households with children aged 0-15, 29% of those are lone parent households – compared to 18% in the whole of South Lanarkshire.
- Of the 1,100 homes in Hillhouse, just under 80% are rented from local authority/housing associations – compared to 44% in the whole of South Lanarkshire.
- In Hillhouse, 37% of households own one or more cars – compared to 59% in the whole of South Lanarkshire.
- Slightly over 15% of 16-19 year olds are unemployed – compared to 9.7%.[20]

The research took place in three primary and two high schools in and around Hillhouse.

Area	Establishment	Number interviewed
Hillhouse	St Ninian's Primary	8
Hillhouse	Udston Primary	12
High Earnock	Townhill Primary	12
Hillhouse	Earnock High	15
Hillhouse	John Ogilvie High	11
	Total interviewed	58

Total number interviewed in Primary Schools   **32**

Of which 21 came from Hillhouse and 11 came from surrounding areas.

Of the 32, 15 were boys and 17 girls.

Of the 32, 25 were 10yrs old, 4 were 11yrs old and 3 were 9yrs old.

Total Number Interviewed in High Schools   **26**

Of which 13 came from Hillhouse and 13 came from surrounding areas.

Of the 26, 13 were male and 13 female.

Of the 26, 3 were 12yrs old, 7 were 13yrs old,

7 were 14yrs old and 9 were 15yrs old.

The total number interviewed in all schools   **58**

The questionnaires were developed after interviewing five primary school children and a similar number of high school pupils in and around the Hillhouse area. The seven strong research team was made up of students from Glasgow, Strathclyde and Edinburgh University. The children and young people were informed that the research was being carried out independently of the schools and that their answers were totally confidential. Conscious that the school surroundings, within which the interviews were held, may influence the answers of the children in a conservative or 'adult' direction, the interviewers dressed casually and attempted to establish as informal an atmosphere as was possible. Three interviews at a time were carried out within the same classroom. This reduced the awkwardness and pressure that children and young people can feel when being 'interrogated' by a lone adult and generally worked well. In one school a teacher was present during the interviews, which raised the difficulty of gaining honest answers about certain subjects. However the interviewers were able to carry out the interviews so that the teacher was out of hearing range. Some of the interviewers believed this method actually added to the honesty of the answers of the young people, as they became conscious that the interviewers were talking quietly and trying to keep the proceedings confidential.

When talking to children and young people, especially within a school surrounding, it is important to recognise that the answers given to certain questions about hanging about on the streets will be influenced by the interviewer and by the environment the interview takes place. Given more time it would have been useful to run group discussions in a more informal environment with these young people, so as to compare the answers given in the more structured interviews. Having said that, none of the researchers believed that the children and young people felt intimidated by any of the questions and indeed were often surprised at how open and honest the young people were.

It must be remembered however, that there is always the danger when interviewing young people, that by appearing to be keeping this information secret from the schools, the children and especially the young people may give more 'anti-establishment' or anti-police answers than they would normally do.

The answers of the primary school children as would be expected, were very different to those of the teenagers and many of the replies reflected what the children thought was the right answer to a question. Their opinions were therefore often dominated by what they thought adults would believe was good or bad. Despite this difficulty, these interviews were useful especially in establishing more factual information about their time and contact with people within their community.

Similarly, the level of comprehension of the questions being asked differed with the different age groups within the high school. However the overall understanding of the questions by all those interviewed at high school was good. To assist this, the interviewers were allowed to explain questions that they felt had been misunderstood. This may have affected the overall accuracy of the responses when collated, but was necessary for the purpose of clarification.

The schools chosen were either in Hillhouse, or in the catchment area for children and young people from Hillhouse. The children and young people interviewed were chosen alphabetically from the top of the school register. Each child or young person was interviewed for half an hour. Each researcher had a set of questions, some of these were open to gain qualitative information others were closed and used to provide quantitative data. The questions concerned the interviewees' night time activities; their contact and relationships with young people, the police and other adults in their community; their fears and insecurities; and their view of the curfew and its impact on the above. Before asking the primary school children the set questions they were also asked to fill out a diary of their last weeks night time activities. This allowed the researchers to relate the questions – which some of the children found difficult to comprehend – to actual activities they had participated in themselves thus allowing more accurate and detailed answers.

A key reason for interviewing primary school children – rather than just high school pupils who were clearly the more likely targets of the curfew – was a recognition that Jack Straw's curfew, in the Crime and Disorder Act (Sept 1998), is aimed at under 10 year olds, and that this research could subsequently highlight some key issues relevant to local authorities in England and Wales.

Young people from areas surrounding Hillhouse were interviewed to assess the experiences that these and the young people living in Hillhouse had of the curfew, and also to look at any differences in experience that existed between the groups. Where differences existed between those living outside Hillhouse and those living inside they will be stated in the report. The same applies for male/female differences and age differences. Other main areas within which the young people lived included:- High Earnock, Earnock, Burnbank, Fairhill, and Meikle Earnock. While these areas are not all the same nor all very different to Hillhouse, for the purpose of this study they will often be referred to as simply outside Hillhouse, or other. The term young people or teenagers is used in this report to indicate the high school pupils, while the primary school pupils are labelled – children. The names of the children and young people have been changed.

While the numbers of children and young people interviewed is relatively small, and further quantitative work will be necessary to substantiate a number of the conclusions drawn in this report, where possible, comparable studies of the curfew[21] and of young people who hang about the streets[22] will be referred to as supporting evidence. Adults within Hillhouse and Hamilton were also questioned about the curfew and about their relationships with young people.

Areas addressed within the research

The Hamilton Curfew, as it was labelled, was launched on 23rd October 1997 and by the end of the first six month period, in April 1998, the police backed up by Scottish Home Secretary Donald Dewar, claiming it had been a great success. However the measure for this success is narrow – has crime gone down, and do people feel safer. Broader relations between people in these areas are not addressed, for example, if people feel safer since the introduction of the Child Safety Initiative, is this because there is a greater sense of community or simply because there are no young people on the streets anymore?

One of the areas of interest for this research project, was to look at the issue of children's and young people's free time, and analyse how, if at all, this had changed with the introduction of the CSI. Research in England,[23] has found that the space that children and young people have at night, and the level of contact they have with other sections of their communities, is becoming increasingly restricted. These issues were addressed in relation to the experiences of the children and young people interviewed in Hillhouse.

Study Guide

A. Curfew legislation developed with the election of New Labour in 1997 but to what extent have curfews become used by local authorities and the police across the UK?

Do a media search in the last year to assess the extent of the actually use of curfews on young people. Also search for 'curfew and youth' on the BBC website and explore the arguments for and against the use of curfews.

B. What does the support for curfews tell us about the relationship between the public and young people.

Do a survey of friends, neighbours or colleagues and assess the extent to which youth curfews are seen as a good idea.

C. Critically discuss the ways that research can be carried out effectively with young people. What are some of the difficulties with doing research with young people and what are the strengths and weaknesses of the various approaches to overcoming these difficulties.

Use the internet and a research methods text book to answer these questions and write a research proposal explaining how you would attempt to find out young people's opinions about curfews.

Useful Reading

A.   1. 'Curfews; No more hanging around' by Charlotte Walsh in *Youth Justice*, Vol. 2, No. 2, 70-81 (2002).
Available online.

   2. 'Institutionalized intolerance: youth justice and the 1998 Crime and Disorder Act' by John Muncie in *Critical Social Policy*, Vol. 19, No. 2, 147-175 (1999).
Available online.

   3. *Rougher Justice: Anti-social Behaviour and Young People* by Peter Squires and Dawn E. Stephen.

C.   1. *Research with children and young people* by the Chronic Poverty Research Centre. Available online.

   2. *Qualitative Researching* by Jennifer Mason.

Notes

[1]'Information' South Lanarkshire Council, Child Safety Initiative Launch, 23 October 1997.

[2]Sandy Cameron, Executive Director of Social Work, speaking on Sky Scottish 26 October 1997.

[3]John Orr (1997). Launch speech of the Child Safety Initiative, Hamilton, 23 October.

[4]In conversation with Hillhouse Community Council Chairman Joe Parfery, he explained that he was unaware of any knowledge of any paedophile problem within Hillhouse.

[5]John Orr (1997). Launch speech of the Child Safety Initiative, Hamilton, 23 October.

[6]Tom McCabe, Labour Leader of South Lanarkshire Council, speaking on Sky Scottish 26 October 1997.

[7]Sandy Cameron, Executive Director of Social Work, speaking on Sky Scottish 26 October 1997.

[8]South Lanarkshire Council: Chief Executive's Service(May/June 1997). Focus on Hillhouse: Scotland's First Citizens' Jury.

[9]Hamilton Advertiser, 12 November 1997.

[10]The Herald, 13 October 1997.

[11]System 3 (1996). South Lanarkshire Community Survey: Executive Summary, p4.

[12]ibid.

[13]The Herald, 17 April 1998.

[14]The Herald, 17 April 1998.

[15]Springham, K. (1998). Time to Go Home Says Who?, (Scottish Human Rights Centre) p9.

[16]Kevin Power, co-author of 'Evaluation of the Hamilton Child Safety Initiative', speaking at the press conference – 'Strathclyde Chief Constable announces expansion of pilot Hamilton Child Safety Initiative', 15 October 1998.

[17]Chief Constable John Orr, speaking at the above, 15 October 1998.

[18]The Herald, 4 December 1998.

[19]'Information', South Lanarkshire Council, 23 October 1997 (Census 1991).

[20]'Information', South Lanarkshire Council, 23 October 1997 (Census 1991).

[21]See Springham, K. (1998). Time to Go Home Says Who?, (Scottish Human Rights Centre) p13. Also see McGallagly, J., Power, K., Littlewood, P. and Meikle, J. (1998). Evaluation of the Hamilton Child Safety Initiative, Crime and Criminal Justice Research Findings No.24, The Scottish Office Central Research Unit, p3.

[22]See Stirling Council (1997) Are you getting enough...opportunity? p106. Also see Coalter, F. and Allison, M. (1995). Young people in Wester Hailes (The Wester Hailes Partnership) p6.

[23]See Wheway, R. and Millward, A. (1997). Child's Play: Facilitating play on housing estates (Chartered Institute of Housing) p44.
Also see Shimamura, H. and Snell, C. (1996). They don't play out like they used to, do they?

4   Curfew on Children: Child's Play

Environmental planners have become increasingly aware of the 'impossibility' of urban space for children. Parents are reporting more fears about letting their children play in the streets or walk home alone. There is evidence that, despite a growing global emphasis on children's autonomy and rights of participation, certain groups of children are finding themselves segregated from public urban spaces.[1]

Conscious of the forthcoming plan by Home Secretary Jack Straw to introduce curfews for children under 10 years old in England and Wales, 32 children from primary schools in and around the Hillhouse area were interviewed to assess the impact of the Hamilton Curfew on this age group.

The section of Jack Straw's Crime and Disorder Act which gives local authorities the power to enforce 9pm curfews on children, has largely been introduced because of government concerns about irresponsible parents who allow their young children to run wild late at night, causing distress to other residents and leaving the children themselves at risk.(1a) Within Hamilton, similar concerns about bad parents were raised in the promotion of the Child Safety Initiative (CSI). Hamilton South MP George Robertson, the then Defence Secretary, explained that the CSI was, 'designed to reach the very young children who should not be out late at night and to stamp down on rowdiness that makes life intolerable for decent people'.[2]

Citing examples of young children being found alone at night while their parents were drunk, Chief Constable John Orr's CSI launch speech included a scathing attack on parents, whose irresponsible behaviour 'beggars belief'.[3] In this same speech the chief constable questioned parents who allowed their children to go out after dark 'without adults supervision', highlighting the 'paedophile court cases that hit the headlines', as cause for concern.

South Lanarkshire Council leader, Tom McCabe, explained in his CSI opening speech, that some people were ignoring their responsibilities to their children and were subsequently undermining and eroding the very communities in which they lived.[4]

However, looking at the diaries of activities that the children in and around Hillhouse provided, and from interviews about their and other young people's activities, little was found to justify the extreme concerns that have been expressed by politicians, councillors and Strathclyde Police, about street life in Hillhouse. None of these children aged 9-11 years were out late at night and parental involvement with their children's night time activities was extensive.

This chapter looks at the exaggerated sense of risk surrounding children that has been heightened further by the introduction of the CSI. One of the goals of the initiative, promoted by the police and local authority, was to ensure a safe environment for children, and so give parents confidence that their children would be safe when playing out. However by highlighting the various dangers that children face when out at night, rather than making parents more confident, the curfew has resulted in even more restrictions being placed on these children. The implications of this more regulated environment for children is examined and the argument made to end safety campaigns which are frightening the life out of both parents and children.

Limits

The idea that young children across the UK are running wild around estates is not backed up by a number of research projects which raise the opposite concern, that children are in fact playing out less than ever before. Parental fears are seen as key to this more restrictive upbringing for children that, as one report explained, has created a 'bedroom culture'.[5]

The London School of Economics report *Young People New Media* found that 31% of the parents they interviewed said their children spent very little or no time outside the home. Hillman, who has been studying children's mobility for over two decades has found that more and more children are escorted to school and leisure journeys, with this adult supervision continuing until an ever-later age.[6] The personal freedom and choice given to a typical seven year old in 1971, Hillman found, by 1990 was not granted until a child reached the age of nine and a half.[7] Observational research in the UK by Wheway and Millard[8] has found that the distance that children are allowed to travel around their estates is diminishing – a trend that can also be seen in the US, where research shows that restricting children's free space is an issue, with only 16% of a surveyed 323 seven to ten year olds being allowed to go further than their own block unaccompanied by an adult.[9] Valentine and McKendrick found that only 23% of parents questioned in 1997 described their child as an 'outdoors' child, compared with research in 1976 by Newson and Newson, where 60% of parents used this description to define their child.[10] In this same piece of research by Valentine and McKendrick, entitled, *Children's Outdoor Play: Exploring Parental Concerns About Children's Safety and the Changing Nature of Childhood*, it was also found that compared with research in the late seventies by Moore – which found that 'homesites' were the favoured place for only 20% of children to play – by 1997, this figure had increased to 40%. Valentine and McKendrick explained that,

> In other words, a significant amount of children's outdoor play is taking place in 'private' space, rather than 'public' space, so that although children are spending a considerable proportion of their leisure time 'out-doors' most have very limited opportunities to play in or explore the public environment independently of adult supervision.[11]

A Mori poll for the Nestle Family Monitor, of more than 500 parents, found that almost 80% would not let their children play unsupervised in the park during the holiday and only half would allow school-age children to play unsupervised on the street.[12] In response to this situation the group Fair Play for Children is campaigning for more play opportunities, claiming that the child at play is an 'endangered species'.[13]

Brian Stoker, a playground specialist, believes that the daily routine of children has become too structured and the only time where children can revert to being children is when they are playing. However, even while at play, Stoker sees problems for today's children – 'Children cannot play like we played. They've lost the ability to play and to socialise'.[14]

Most parents recognise that their children have less free unsupervised time than they had. A survey of parents by Barnardo's in 1994 found that 83% of those questioned believed children had less safe places to play today than in the past.[15] Important work by Gill Valentine, found that three out of five parents surveyed claimed to have had more freedom to play outside than their own children do.[16] Similarly, a survey by NOP which coincided with National Playday on 4 August 1999 found that 80% of parents believe their children spend less time playing than they did when they were young.[17]

Even within schools, there is a trend towards reducing the amount of unsupervised breaktime allowed. Blatchford found that, 'the prevalence of a negative view about breaktime is leading to more deliberate management and supervision of breaktimes, and a reduction in their duration'. In the United States, he notes that Pellegrini has identified a specifically anti-recess movement.[18] In the UK, Blatchford points out that a negative view of breaktime by teachers is becoming dominant, with a growing concern about bullying and violent incidents. A more general influence on this perception has been press stories and concern being expressed by the teachers unions throughout the 1980s, culminating in the Elton Committee (DES 1989) which identified lunch breaks as the 'single biggest behaviour-related problem that (staff) face'.[19] The result of this more negative view of breaktime and the growing pressure of the new National Curriculum has resulted in more than half of primary schools and slightly less than half of high schools studied reducing their breaktime in the five years between 1990 and 1995.[20]

Likewise, Kate Moorcock, in a study of playground use, points out that free time has also been reduced by the government policy for more school homework clubs – with an increase of these clubs by 52% from 1995-96.[21]

Wandering the streets at night

Chief of Police John Orr, when launching the CSI expressed concern about young children wandering the streets at night in three areas targeted for the curfew. To assess whether or not this was a general problem, but also to get a picture of the night time activities of the primary school children in and around Hillhouse, they were asked to complete a diary of their activities and asked specific questions about how late they were allowed to stay out at night.

From the diary and answers to these questions, it was clear that the amount of free time and space available to children in this area is limited and regulated by parents and that the introduction of the curfew has increased this regulation. Almost half of the primary school children interviewed from both Hillhouse and those living in surrounding estates had to be home earlier at night since the introduction of the curfew. Ten year old Steven from Hillhouse explained, 'Mum doesn't want me taken home by the police'. Classmate Wendy from Burnbank agreed, 'Cos if you stay out too dark the police will pick you up and take you home'.

Those children who had to come in earlier, on average lost one hours play time. Both children living in Hillhouse and those outside Hillhouse were affected. For Hillhouse children, the average 'in-time' before the curfew was 7.45pm; the average 'in-time' after the curfew was 7.10pm. For children outside Hillhouse, the average 'in-time' before the curfew was 7.20pm; the average 'in-time' after the curfew was 7.00pm. The main reason given by both sets of children for having to go home earlier, was the concern parents had about contact with the police. This may simply be a threat that parents were using to encourage their children to come home earlier now that the winter nights were coming in, but no child suggested this.

Another reason for children being told to be in earlier, may be due to the discussion, during the promotion of the CSI, about parental responsibility. Parents may have felt the need to change the 'in times' of their children that had been established over the years, for fear of being labelled a bad parent and having their children labelled as bad kids. The Scottish Office research found, in discussion with parents groups, that parents were now 'more aware of the dangers faced by children out late at night' and that parents were also 'stricter with their children over the time they were called in at night'.[22]

The 'parenting culture and common sense understanding of local geographies of risk', which are developed over time by parents, have here been redefined by this police initiative. Valentine explained the process of parents negotiating their children's free time in this way,

> Through the processes of setting boundaries, punishments and developing subtle care strategies, most parents walk a tightrope, wavering between being anxious that they are being overprotective and fearing that they are placing their children in danger by granting them independence.[23]

Since the introduction of the curfew, this balancing act appears to have tipped in favour of greater protection.

However, it must be born in mind that while there is a lot of evidence to suggest that parents are restricting their children's play space – both in Hillhouse and across the UK – this may also reflect parents concern to be seen to be doing the right thing when asked about how much freedom they allow their child. My latest provisional findings in a pilot research project in Airdrie, for example, show that many parents say they will not allow their children to play in certain areas of their estate, but their children, when asked, contradict this and say that their parents do allow them this freedom. Observational research and more detailed interviews with parents are needed to assess the level to which they feel under pressure to show that they are safe parents – i.e. that they are 'good parents'.

Running wild?

While the majority of children interviewed in Hillhouse walked to school by themselves, walked to their friends' houses by themselves at night and were allowed out of the sight of their parents, a significant minority were not allowed these freedoms. Further questioning of the children who went out alone at night – about where they went and where their friends lived – found that many of those who did travel to their friends houses at night were allowed to do so, only because they lived very close by or because their parents were able to watch them on their travels.

Jane, 10 years old from Hillhouse, explained that she was allowed to walk to her friends house by herself, but only because, 'I'm not even a minute away, and friends parents watch out for me'. Similarly 9 year old Mark walked to his friends house because 'he only lives next door'. While Joanne from Hillhouse explained that, 'Mum watches me go. My friend's mum watches me come, and mum phones her to let her know I'm on my way. But I've never had any bother'.

In no respect could the children interviewed be described as 'running wild'. Before the introduction of the CSI Strathclyde Police may have come into contact with some young children out very late at night – but this should be dealt with on a case by case basis, rather than through a blanket curfew initiative which has effected many more children and parents in and around the area.

Limits on the area in which these children were allowed to play are similar to those found by Mori, the LSE and Wheway (see above). Almost a third of the primary school children said they were not allowed out of the sight of their parents. Most of the other children were allowed to play in their street, or in their friends street as long as their parents knew where they were, or knew that other parents were close at hand. Only a couple of children said they could walk round their entire estate at night and a similarly small number said they cycled around the place.

Whereas past research in the 1970s and 1980s shows that limits on boys' time is less than that on girls', because of a greater concern about girls ability to deal with social dangers, in Hillhouse there was little difference between the times and areas in which boys and girls were allowed out. This supports Valentine who found that parents were equally concerned about their sons' and daughters' safety partly because they believed their daughters were more sensible than their sons who were 'easily led'.[24] This growing concern about boys' safety may be related to a concern about the traditionally more risky activities that boys 'get up to'. The more carefree, adventurous play often associated with boys in today's cautious climate, may be seen by parents as increasingly problematic, unlike the traditional image of girl's play – where fewer risks are taken.

Some of the children interviewed in Hillhouse may have been giving answers that they believed an adult – and their parents – would want to hear – i.e. that they never go far from home. However, observational research carried out by Wheway and Millard into distances travelled by children from their homes, found that while children were travelling beyond the limits set by their parents, they were not travelling much further.[25] A more accurate assessment of the independent travel and play in Hillhouse could only be established by a similar observational survey.

Parents are too responsible!

The children's diaries obtained during the interviews, allowed a detailed assessment of the night time play activities of all of these primary school children. While the initial purpose of the diaries was to help the interviewers relate questions to concrete examples of night time activities given by the children, they became a valuable detailed source of information regarding types of activities undertaken and the amount of parental or adult supervision received by these children.

It is often commented upon today that 'parents aren't what they used to be', either because they are too busy working or because they don't have the parenting skills that past generations had. However, the parents of the primary school children interviewed in and around Hillhouse were extremely involved in regulating their children's activities. This was the case when the children were playing on the street and equally for other activities.

Almost three quarters of these children were in at least one club, many were in more than one and for most children, simply spending a whole night at home watching TV was a rarity, as was just playing in the street. Not only are these children involved in many and varied activities at night, but their parents are often the ones who are taking them there and back. Play may have changed over the years and some limits definitely do exist on these young people, but the range and access to more experiences, clubs and facilities is probably greater than ever before.

However Valentine, who found that two thirds of the parents she surveyed claimed that their children were involved in some form of organised play activity, also found that research in both Europe and in North America, suggests that the increase in these more structured night time activities may have developed primarily, 'in order to prevent [children] playing in public space without adult supervision'.

Thus, 'children's street activities and culture are being substituted with adult-run football coaching or institutional based music classes'.[26] Valentine also notes that this move to subtly regulate children has also been encouraged by parental peer pressure, where 'the watchful gaze of others' encouraged parents to treat their offspring as more incompetent and vulnerable than they perceive them to be.[27]

Further research with adults in the area would be necessary to fully assess the reasons for these more regulated activities being developed in and around the Hillhouse area.

Safe from what?

By promoting a few extreme examples of very young children found out on the streets late at night, Chief Constable John Orr has helped promote the idea that this is a growing problem in the area. However, as Fran Russell from the legal reform group The Howard League, points out, regarding children across the UK, 'no evidence has been produced to suggest young children wandering the streets at night is a serious or growing problem'.[28]

In Hillhouse there does not appear to be a problem of children wandering the streets at night, nor is there any evidence that they are causing trouble on the estate. Janice Meikle, in discussion with three focus groups in the area, found that young people under 10 were not considered to be a problem.[29] Regarding dangers that faced these children, McGallagly, Power and Littlewood, in the same Scottish Office Report, explained that, 'Due to the small number of children who were the victims of crime or road traffic accidents in the 6 month period prior to and during the period covered by the CSI, it was not possible to assess the impact of the initiative on such incidents'.[30]

The lack of any significant danger facing the children in Hillhouse was also expressed by the children interviewed. The children were asked about the level of bother or trouble they faced in their area. Most felt there was not much trouble in their area. No child mentioned having been abused in any way by any adult, rather it was teenagers being rowdy that was the main issue raised. Three children mentioned windows being smashed, two mentioned fights and two others talked about a fire that had been started by teenagers. When asked about personal conflicts, almost two thirds of the children interviewed said they had personally had no trouble. Those that mentioned having 'some bother' explained that they had either been chased or called names.

'Jamie hit me with his stookie (plaster cast), he's always picking on smaller children,' Tim from Hillhouse explained, and 10 year old Steven told me that, 'Teenagers drink sometimes and shout at me, I've been chased as well, but only once'.

While there appear to be some older teenagers drinking and sometimes being antisocial at night, the children have not been put at risk by this group or by 'strange adults'. No paedophile or abusive adult was mentioned; teenagers sometimes chased or called the younger children names, but overall there was no evidence that these children were facing more difficulties in their area than their parents may have faced when they were children. Interestingly, while alcohol was frequently raised as an issue throughout this survey, these children did not mention drugs.

In discussion with Joe Parfery, chair of the Hillhouse Community Council, about the dangers that children faced on the estate, he explained that he was unaware of any great safety problem, especially from strangers or paedophiles. He was equally unaware of any great number of young children wandering the streets at night. He explained, 'There are a few children who stay out, especially during the summer, till about 10.30pm but not many. But what's wrong with that anyway', he said, 'I used to play out all the time when I was a kid'.[31]

At the press conference announcing the results of the Scottish Office research into the CSI, researcher Kevin Power explained that while there was evidence that the CSI had reduced crime in the targeted areas, there was no evidence that this initiative had made the children or young people safer.[32] In discussion with the children in Hillhouse, it was not only unclear whether these children were safer or not, but as the Scottish Office Report itself indicates – with the small number of crimes committed against children in the area – it was equally unclear what they were supposed to be in danger from.

Stranger Danger

Parental insecurity across the UK, has led to children's free time being increasingly regulated. One of the key reasons given by parents in Scotland for the growing restrictions they place on children's play is fear of strangers.[33] The Mori survey (above) found that 56% of parents were concerned about their children being abducted by a stranger;[34] the NOP survey found that 72% of parents gave 'strangers' as the main reason for their fears;[35] Valentine's research based on semi-structured interviews and a survey of 400 parents of 9-11 year olds also found that child abduction was the main concern for parents.[36]

This growing fear which surrounds children in the UK has also been noted in the United States. S.E. Cahill in *Childhood and Public Life* has pointed out that, 'Since approximately 1979, popular concern about children's safety in public places has mushroomed'. Cahill identifies a number of highly publicised child abductions and murders that sparked concern amongst parents across America and regenerated a number of urban myths about strangers. Now even 'morally benign and vehicle free public places', like department stores and shopping centres were seen as dangerous places for children. Interestingly, Cahill explains how serious questions have been raised about the real level of abductions and murders of children in America, with many journalists debunking the 'attempted abduction; and 'mutilated boy' legends. Yet, 'it does not appear that popular concern about children's safety in public places has subsided appreciably because of the widespread publication of such information.[36a]

In promoting the Hamilton Child Safety Initiative, Chief Constable John Orr raised the issue of paedophile court cases hitting the headlines and questioned parents who allowed their children to play out unsupervised. A year later, at a press conference to announce the success of the curfew, he explained that child safety was a concern for the police who had the unenviable job of informing parents when their children were killed. Yet there is no evidence of a paedophile threat in the Hillhouse area, indeed the chances of a child being killed by a stranger across the UK is little more than one in a million. Nor is there evidence that parents and children are not already well aware of these potential dangers.

Further research with parents in Hillhouse would be necessary to assess their concerns regarding child safety, but it is likely that stranger danger is already an exaggerated concern. Despite this, Strathclyde Police used the CSI to visit every school in the targeted areas to make the children aware of the dangers they face on their estate. Across Scotland the police are already heavily involved in the promotion of stranger danger awareness, with some school children being visited every year of their primary school life to be informed about the dangers they face. A key message promoted is that you should 'never talk to strangers'. In this respect, rather than focusing on specific types of 'strange men' who, for example, 'offer you a lift', any adult you don't know is promoted as a stranger and strangers are seen not only as people you don't know but as potentially dangerous.

Throughout the 1990s, stranger danger awareness has been raised not only by the police, but by the media and child care professionals who have focused on the danger of paedophiles. Children's organisations and charities have also promoted this danger, the latest of these campaigns being launched by the NSPCC with their 'Safe Open Spaces Initiative' in August 1999. This campaign aimed to ensure that children and young people 'use open spaces confidently and without fear'.[37] However there is a growing recognition by other child and family organisations that these 'awareness' campaigns are actually fuelling parents' fears and subsequently reducing children's free time.[38] A survey by Barnardo's in 1994 recognised that parental anxiety was becoming a problem for both parent and child.[39]

The level of 'awareness' surrounding the issue of paedophiles was recently demonstrated with the amount of media attention and the anti-paedophile campaigns set up after the murder of Sarah Payne. Preliminary findings of a pilot research initiative in Airdrie found that concerns generated by the murder of Sarah Payne had resulted in half of the 8-12 year olds questioned having their 'time and distance allowed to play' reduced by worried parents.

For those promoting safety campaigns, it is hoped that by making adults and children 'aware' of the dangers around them, they will be empowered to act with more confidence. As Valerie Howarth, Chief Executive of ChildLine explained, 'By giving children information which may protect them from abuse, we're protecting their innocence'.[40] Similarly, the NSPCC through their 'Safe Open Spaces Initiative', believe that by increasing the safety and regulation of play areas more parents and children will feel safe to use these open spaces. However, it is more likely when people are already highly 'risk conscious' that such campaigns will simply re-raise the dangers that children face when they are out playing and will further reduce the use of these facilities.

Discussing the problem of the falling number of children using play parks and safe play areas – despite the improved safety facilities – Kate Moorcock points out that,

> It is believed that parents and children will be more likely to use play areas if they appear to be safe environments. For example, safety surfaces are laid where there is no risk of a fall from a height. However, in the current fear-ridden climate, concerns over safety are likely to actually increase anxiety about outdoor play safety, as parents and children think the changes have been made because play areas are dangerous.[41]

One of the NSPCC's demands in their 'Open Spaces Initiative', is that safe play areas should be established with 'prominent signs' to identify them, 'in which adults can go only if a child accompanies them'. Here once again the message that adults are a threat to children and should not be trusted unless 'accompanied by a child' is raised and more pressure is placed on parents to beware of strangers. This safety campaign also calls for more play areas to be supervised by adults and park rangers who are vetted by the police – the idea being that young children should not be allowed to play without supervision. Even if children do use these supervised play facilities, rather than creating safe 'open spaces' where children can play freely, this will lead to even more controlled play environments where children's play is again regulated.

Clearly stranger danger is not the only risk parents consider when deciding on their child's free time, traffic is often a key issue as well. However the exaggerated sense of risk from strangers and abductions is a useful example to indicate the extent to which children's play is being increasingly regulated not because of any increase in the dangers that children face, but because of an inflated sense of risk felt by parents and encouraged by voluntary organisations and local authorities who constantly promote the child safety message. But as Moorcock points out, 'Children can be forgiven fears about bogeymen and invisible threats hiding in the shadows. Adults need to show them how "getting a grip" is done'.[42]

Dangerous limits

In Hillhouse, stranger danger was something that all the children interviewed were aware of. Two thirds of those questioned said they would never ask an adult for the time if they didn't know them. While over 60% said that they liked talking to adults and thought it was a 'good thing to do', over a third said it was wrong or 'bad' to talk to adults, and every child reiterated that they would only talk to adults they already knew. Some of the older children recognised that this was a problem as they would not get to know most of the people in their area. There was also a minority of children, generally those who had more freedom to play around the estate, that were proud that they knew 'everyone around here' and could always find out what the time was and talk to an adult where ever they were.

Joe Parfery's concern about the limits that the curfew is putting on children is not something that appears to concern the council or the police who have questioned the very idea of children playing out at night unsupervised. This is a serious oversight at a time when children's freedom is becoming increasingly limited. Research has shown that today's generation has less freedom than past generations; there are growing limits on the distances travelled by children today when out playing; there is a falling number of children travelling to school independently; an increased regulation of breaktime at school and when children do go out at night it is often in regulated play activities or under the watchful eye of their parents. This raises a number of serious concerns about children's development.

Despite this some children's charities appear to use fear to generate support. Over the last few years the NSPCC has been criticised by child educationalists for their safety campaigns, which promote the idea that murder of children by lurking strangers is a risk every parent should be conscious of. A senior official of a rival charity explained that, 'They are seriously in danger of pushing their message to the very outer limits of what might be called economical with the truth'. Colin Pritchard, a professor of psychiatric social work believes the NSPCC are 'playing games' as our child murder rates have never been so low with 46 murders in 1995 (only 7 by strangers) compared with 200 in 1973.[42a]

Professor Mayer Hillman has led the way in looking at the wider developmental problems of overprotecting children and has even questioned whether safety campaigns make children less safe, by limiting their learning experiences and independence so reducing their ability to deal with difficult situations. Kate Moorcock, notes that this reduction in play, play which can help children, 'learn to make choices' and 'explore their own personality and creativity', has been overlooked by the New Labour government.[43] Similarly, Blatchford points out that breaktime – which is being reduced in many schools – can help children 'in the acquisition of many subtle social skills essential to later life'.[44] These points are supported by a key text in child psychology by James Youniss, who explains the importance of peer relations for child and adolescent development.[45]

Youniss argues that unlike the adult-child relationship which is dominated by the adult, the very 'structure' of the child-peer and especially child-friend relationship is one that necessarily encourages children to learn to become 'interpersonally sensitive', to 'handle intimacy' and to achieve 'mutual understanding'.[46] Not knowing what the rules of order are when dealing with peers and friends, children must learn to create their own rules through interacting with others.

Children actively develop their relationship with others, as Youniss explains, 'The child's perception of the self as creator of reality,' when dealing with adults, 'will be restricted and his or her opportunities for mutual understanding in relation with others will be limited.' But in relation to other children, 'When self and other are equal agents and recipients, meaning and order depend on co-operation which, in turn, leads to a different understanding of interpersonal relationship, one marked by the potential for mutuality'.[47]

The child, in taking a more active role in relation to peers comes to see itself as being able to construct order *with* peers rather than *through* adults. Adults may have laid down the 'rights and wrongs', but children must learn to recreate these rules between themselves often through play. Children can learn to discover themselves as individuals, but only fully by relating to their friends and peers. Self interest must be co-operatively negotiated and situated within these relationships with others, not because peers know better than adults, but because of the very structure of the relationships developed by peers that encourages mutual understanding and intimacy.

The distinctive nature and structure of child-peer and child-friend relationships, Youniss argues, makes these relationships a major and positive force in a child's development. Peer relations are equally important to adult relations while also having a distinct function. Without free unsupervised peer relations being developed by children, many social and developmental processes would therefore be lost.

Hillman and Wheway also believe that limits on play and the freedom to develop peer relationships, will result in a more limited and less developed young person. Freedom for children is about more than just having a good time, but about acquiring a progressively greater amount of personal autonomy, gaining self confidence and thus growing up. This development often takes place through the creation and negotiation within peer groups.[48]

In and around Hillhouse, a significant minority of children interviewed – around a third – were escorted to school or to their friends houses at night and although the majority of children still played out at night there were definite limits to where these children could play, with many spending time within a supervised environment. Interestingly, there was little difference in the restrictions being placed on boys as well as girls suggesting that the level of concern once exclusively felt towards girls who went out at night has been extended to boys. Further research would be necessary to clarify whether this change in attitude to boys is more widespread.

Despite there being no evidence of any significant risk to these children – within this research, or the Scottish Office sponsored research – the curfew has helped to heighten the awareness of 'potential' dangers faced by children and encourages the idea that children are a 'potential' danger to others. While parents have said that they are more conscious of the risks their children face, the children have explained that their parents are also worried about them coming into contact with the police at night. As Children's Rights Officer Gerison Landsdown explained, the Hamilton Curfew and the curfew for under 10 year olds in England and Wales, gives the message that public space is not a place for children to be – either because children will be at risk, or are a risk to others.[49]

The curfew has increased the limits that are placed on the free time of children in and around Hillhouse, children whose time is already heavily supervised by parents; and while it is impossible to quantify the broader impact this will have on the development of these children, the warning by Nancy Ovens, co-ordinator of the National Centre for Play, must be borne in mind for all those concerned about the development of communities like Hillhouse. Ovens argues that, 'If we are too afraid to let our children play then a generation will grow up finding it difficult to mix with others and to make decisions for themselves'.[50] Unfortunately, within the present risk conscious climate, the government and local authorities appear happy to encourage this fear by promoting safety ahead of any other wider concern.

One likely result of the more regulated environment that children are growing up in, is that they become more used to having their time and space controlled or monitored by others. How this affects young people's expectation for greater independence as they get older is examined in Chapter 6.

As well as affecting children in Hillhouse, the safety concerns supported by the curfew have influenced parents in and around the area. As well as having concerns about their children's safety, parents now have the added burden of worrying about their child coming into contact with the police and the danger of being labelled by the police and possibly by other parents, as irresponsible. In this climate, those parents that continue to allow their children to play out at night will be seen as not only irresponsible but possibly antisocial. Allowing freedom to children that would have been unexceptional 15 years ago is today leading to police intervention to stop these 'irresponsible parents'. Also, where time constraints encourage parents to allow their children to just 'go and play', it is likely that these parents will feel guilty that they are not looking after their children properly.

Part of the reason given by the council and Strathclyde Police, for the implementation of the CSI, was a need to make parents more responsible. However, many parents are now, rather than making their own decisions about what time their child plays out, responding to police decisions about this basic issue of parenting. An example of how this responsibility has now become something decided by police rather than parents was demonstrated on Halloween night. For this night parents and children were informed by officers going to all the schools in the area, that it was OK for children and young people to go out for Halloween. But this relaxation of the curfew came with a warning from a Strathclyde police spokesman, 'We would like all parents to make sure that their kids are supervised and go out that bit earlier in the evening'.[51]

Study Guide

A. Are today's concerns about 'child safety' justified or are parents simply paranoid? Carry out a media search, or discuss with family and friends what 'child safety' issues are of concern today. Consider the extent to which 'child safety' has become not something specific to certain activities but an all encompassing approach to children.

B. A recent child safety issue is paedophile grooming on the internet. Critically assess the extent to which this issue can be viewed as a panic.

Children and young people's use of the internet has become a concern for parents and for the government. Discuss this issue with parents you know and assess the extent of these concerns. Using a media search on 'grooming' explain what evidence there is that proves that this is/or is not a serious problem for children today.

C. Has the nature of play changed today? Critically assess the extent to which today's children and young people can be defined as 'cotton wool kids'

Discuss with older relatives what they did when they where children and what has changed.

Where you live, carry out an observational study of the night time activities of children and young people.

D. The idea of 'unsupervised play' appears to be more problematic today. Why is this and what are the benefits of unsupervised play, for children and for the community?

Youniss argues that peer relations are important because they are 'equal' relationships. Consider what this means and what role do peers, parents and 'strange adults' play in the socialisation of young people. With this in mind discuss the positive or indeed negative role that youth and community work can have on this socialising process.

Useful Reading

A.   1. *Paranoid Parenting* by Frank Furedi.
        See chapter 2. Also see relevant articles on Frank Furedi's official website.

2. 'Paranoid parenting? Rematerializing risk and fear for children' by Rachel Pain in *Social & Cultural Geography*, Vol. 7, No. 2 (2006).

3. 'Geographies of Parents' Fears for Children's Safety in Cyberspace' by Gill Valentine and Sarah Holloway in *The Professional Geographer*, Vol. 53, No. 1, 71-83 (2000).

4. *Are children being held responsible by parental fears?* by Helene Guldberg.

Available online.

5. *Every Child Matters – but so does our privacy* by David Clements. Available online.

6. *Don't touch those kids!* by Josie Appleton. Available online.

C. 1. 'Children's Outdoor Play: Exploring Parental Concerns About Children's Safety and the Nature of Childhood' by Gill Valentine and John McKendrick in *Geoforum*, Vol. 28, No.2, 219-235 (1997).

2. *Cotton Wool Kids? Making Sense of Child Safety* edited by Stuart Waiton. Available at www.GenerationYouthIssues.org

D. 1. *Parents and Peers in Social Development* by James Youniss. See chapters 1 and 14.

2. *Cotton Wool Kids? Making Sense of Child Safety* edited by Stuart Waiton. Available at www.GenerationYouthIssues.org

Notes

[1]Greenfield, J., Jones, D., O'Brien, M., Rustin, M., Sloan, D. *–Childhood, Urban Space and Citizenship: Child Sensitive Urban Regeneration.* Economic and Social Research Council: (Background Information).

[1a]The Guardian, 30 September 1998.

[2]Scottish Daily Mail, 24 October 1997.

[3]John Orr (1997). Launch speech of the Child Safety Initiative, Hamilton, 23 October.

[4]Councillor Tom McCabe (1997). Launch speech of the Child Safety Initiative, Hamilton, 23 October.

[5]The Herald, 19 March 1999.

[6]The Times Education Supplement, 20 June 1997.

[7]Hillman, M., Adams, J. and Whiteleg. J. (1990). One False Move...A Study of Children's Independent Mobility (PSI Publishing) p106.

[8]Wheway, R,. and Millward, A. (1997). Child's Play: Facilitating play on housing estates (Chartered Institute of Housing).

[9]Valentine, G. (1997). 'Oh yes I can.' 'Oh no you can't': Children and Parents' understanding of kids' competence to negotiate public space safely (Antipode 29:1 pp65-89).

[10]Valentine, G. and McKendrick, J. (1997). Children's Outdoor Play: Exploring Parental Concerns About Children's Safety and the Nature of Childhood (Geoforum, Vol 28 No.2, pp219-235).

[11]Valentine, G. and McKendrick, J. (1997). Children's Outdoor Play: Exploring Parental Concerns About Children's Safety and the Nature of Childhood (Geoforum, Vol 28 No.2, pp219-235).

[12]Sunday Telegraph, 9 August 1998.

[13]ibid.

[14]Times Education Supplement: The School Manager, 2 June 2000.

[15]Barnardo's (1994). The Facts of Life: The Changing Face of Childhood (Barnardo's).

[16]Valentine ,G. (1997). 'Oh yes I can.' 'Oh no you can't': Children and Parents' understanding of kids' competence to negotiate public space safely, in Antipode 29:1 (p65-89).

[17]Observer, 8 August 1999.

[18]Blatchford, P.: The state of play in schools, in Woodhead, M. et al (ed) Making sense of social development (1999) (London, Routledge) (p101-2).

[19]ibid p103.

[20]ibid p104.

[21]Moorcock, K. (1998). Swings and Roundabouts (Sheffield Hallam University).

[22]McGallagly, J., Power, K., Littlewood, P. and Meikle, J. (1998). Evaluation of the Hamilton Child Safety Initiative, Crime and Criminal Justice Research Findings No.24, (The Scottish Office Central Research Unit) p6.

[23]Valentine, G. (1997). 'Oh yes I can.' 'Oh no you can't': Children and Parents' understanding of kids' competence to negotiate public space safely, in Antipode 29:1 (p65-89).

[24]ibid.

[25]ibid.

[26]Wheway, R. and Millward, A. (1997). Child's Play: Facilitating play on housing estates (Chartered Institute of Housing) p44

[27]Valentine, G. (1997). 'Oh yes I can.' 'Oh no you can't': Children and Parents' understanding of kids' competence to negotiate public space safely, in Antipode 29:1 (p65-89).

[28]Fran Russell, The Howard League, in conversation August 1998.

[29]McGallagly, J., Power, K., Littlewood, P. and Meikle, J. (1998). Evaluation of the Hamilton Child Safety Initiative, Crime and Criminal Justice Research Findings No.24, (The Scottish Office Central Research Unit), p6.

[30]ibid p3.

[31]Joe Parfery, Chair of Hillhouse Community Council, in conversation 18 August 1998.

[32]Kevin Power, University of Stirling, Press conference to extend the newly named Initiative for Children and Young People across the whole of Hamilton, 15 October 1998.

[33]Scotland on Sunday, November 3 1996.

[34]Sunday Telegraph, 9 August 1998.

[35]Observer, 8 August 1999.

[36]Valentine, G. (1997). 'Oh yes I can.' 'Oh no you can't': Children and Parents' understaning of kids' competence to negotiate public space safely, in Antipode 29:1 (p65-89).

[36a]Cahill, S. E. (1990). 'Childhood and Public Life' in Social Problems, Vol. 37, No. 3.

[37]NSPCC Briefing Note, August 1999.

The Guardian, 2 August 1999.

[39]Barnardo's (1995) Playing It Safe (Barnardo's) p3 and p22.

[40]The Guardian, 7 August 1999.

[41]Moorcock, K. (1998). Swings and Roundabouts (Sheffield Hallam University).42. Moorcock, K., LM magazine No 122, p15.

[42a]Observer, 8 August 1999.

[43]Moorcock, K. (1998). Swings and Roundabouts (Sheffield Hallam University) p32.

[44]Blatchford, P.: The state of play in schools, in Woodhead, M. et al (ed) Making sense of social development (1999) (London, Routledge) p113.

[45]Youniss, J. (1980). Parents and Peers in Social Development (The University of Chicago Press).

[46]ibid p1.

[47]ibid p8.

[48]Hillman, M., Adams, J. and Whiteleg, J. (1990). One False Move...A Study of Children's Independent Mobility (PSI Publishing).

[49]Gerison Landsdown, Children's Right's Officer, in conversation September 1998.

[50]Nancy Ovens (1996). quoted in Panic deepens on child safety, Scotland on Sunday, Nov 3.

[51]The Scotsman, 31 October 1997.

5   Curfew on Youth: Nuisance as Crime

Throughout the twentieth century there has been an 'anti-youth' voice within Western societies – a voice that has generally became more pronounced in times of social change. Wegs, for example, notes the image of 'dangerous' youths in Austria at the end of the 19th century was constructed by an elite at a time of heightened fears about the changing economic, social and political environment.[1] Similarly in *Hooligan: A History of Retrospective Fears*, Pearson notes the dread felt by the British establishment, about the decline of an 'Imperial Race', with 'thousands of boys and young men, pale, narrow chested, hunched up miserable specimens, smoking endless cigarettes, numbers of them betting...'. Others fearing the crowd of young men in the town who, 'in a moment flashes into a delirious mob'.[2]

This negative perception of youth and young men has largely been the preserve of conservative thinkers who have felt threatened by new developments in society. But as we begin the 21st Century, the negative view of young people has become more widespread than ever, with politicians from all sides queuing up to attack the 'teenage louts' blamed for spreading fear across communities.

Whether depicted as villains or victims, the perception of young people is one that demands more regulation of their time and space. In 1994 the former Conservative Prime Minister John Major, attacked what he called a 'yob culture' – white trash that had been identified by right wing thinker Charles Murray and branded the 'underclass;'[3] New Labour are developing curfews and antisocial behaviour orders – largely aimed at young people who they label the 'socially excluded', and at the same time radicals like ex-Communist Party feminist Bea Campbell have also attacked yobs – blaming the rise of violence on working class macho culture.[4]

Campaigning to be first major of London, New Labour's struggling candidate Frank Dobson attempted to play the crime card, denouncing the teenagers who made 'elderly people who fought against Hitler', frightened to walk down their own streets. Rather than stick up for young people, left winger Ken Livingston responded by pointing out that he had supported every law and order policy that Labour had ever developed, and indeed thought more should be done to ensure violent criminals were kept in prison.

The 'youth drugs problem', the concern around teenage pregnancies, and most recently Tony Blair's own attack on the laddish violence of the yob culture all add up to an image of immoral young people running wild with few controls on their nihilistic behaviour. The controls proposed and implemented by government and police are far reaching and yet the public as a whole are increasingly supportive of ever more controls, like CCTV and initiatives such as the Hamilton Curfew, that monitor the behaviour of those young people who hang about the streets at night.

Young people hanging about the streets have always caused trouble and been mischievous. Today however this 'mischief' has been redefined as antisocial or criminal, and laws and police practices have developed around the idea of young people as a threat to others. Indeed mischievous is a term that is no longer used when discussing the petty behaviour of young people. Through the prism of risk and fear this type of immature or 'adolescent', 'rowdy' behaviour has become seen as increasingly dangerous. As Cahill explains,

> [W]hile adults treat younger children in public places as innocent, endearing yet sometimes exasperating incompetents, they treat older children as unengaging and frightfully undisciplined rogues. Among other things, the very violation of public etiquette that adults often find amusing when committed by younger children are treated as dangerous moral failings when the transgressor is a few years older.[5]

New laws have developed with stop and search powers, public drinking bans and antisocial behaviour orders, and public space has become monitored, initially in town centres but increasingly on housing estates, with CCTV, security guards and professional witnesses – to regulate more areas of public life than ever before. While not all of these initiatives are targeted solely at young people, many of them are, and those that increase the regulation of public space have a disproportionate effect on young people who use this space more than any other section of society. In the past, many of these initiatives would have been seen as authoritarian by politicians from both sides of the House, and by many members of the public, but with the heightened sense of fear and insecurity that exists today, public support for these measures is greater than ever before.

With the fear *for* young children and the fear *of* teenagers, Valentine believes that public space is fast becoming a place where children have no role. As she notes, 'research suggests that children's street culture is in decline, leaving adults to produce it as an adult space'.

The Hamilton CSI is an extension of this process of regulating public space. Rather than targeting criminal behaviour, this initiative is directed at young people who, by their very presence upon the street at night are deemed to be a threat to others or to themselves. In Hillhouse it was found that the young people were used to being moved on by the police even before the curfew was introduced, largely because adults on the estate were worried about them standing around in groups. The fear and insecurity felt by these adults towards the young people, regardless of whether they were misbehaving or not, has created a level of intolerance which has been encouraged and institutionalised by the introduction of the curfew.

Where once adults would have ignored the rowdiness of teenagers, or regulated the behaviour of these young people themselves, the curfew has formalised and extended the intervention of the police into the 'adolescent' activities of teenagers who continue to hang about the streets at night. At the same time this CSI has promoted the idea that young people are a danger to one another and need to be protected from other young people – even friends – who apply 'peer pressure'.

Sex, drugs and 'knives'!

Any sense of perspective has been lost in today's discussions about young people and crime. The 'quality' press happily print tabloidesque headlines about violent youth and even in the field of youth research there is a growing concentration upon the excesses of youth, like drinking, drug taking and also crime.

Politicians, backed up by this type of sensationalist research and the shock horror media stories surrounding young people are thus encouraged to push on with their crusade against youth crime. While police forces – such as Strathclyde – use these stories to further justify their authoritarian policing of young people. A vicious circle of further regulating, criminalising and developing laws to clamp down on the activities of young people in public is being created.

In April 2000, 'knife carrying youth' once again hit the headlines after the publication of Professor Neil McKeganey and John Norrie's research into the association between illegal drugs and weapons carrying by young people in Scotland. The 'shocking' results of this school based survey led to McKeganey appearing on Newsnight, BBC Scotland and STV News, with the findings being reported on every national radio station and ending up as front page news in Scotland's broadsheets. The headline stories reading, 'young have turned armed and dangerous' and 'more than a third of Scottish schoolboys are carrying weapons'.

McKeganey explained that his research was 'a wake-up call to schools, parents and agencies working with young people', elaborating that, 'organisers of events attended by young people cannot assume that no weapons will be present'.[6]

One of the key findings of the survey, as stated in McKeganey's press release, was that, 'boys who took illegal drugs were three times as likely, and girls five times as likely to carry weapons as their non drug-taking peers'. The report also argues that as the number of different drugs taken by young people increases, the more likely it is that they will be carrying a weapon – the implication being that more drugs equals more knives which equals more stabbing.

In response to this research Ronnie Smith, general secretary of the EIS remarked that everyone, including parents, should 'sit up and take note'.

Having initially questioned the significance of the research, within 3 days of the findings being published in the British Medical Journal, Strathclyde Police re-launched and extended their stop and search – 'Safer Streets' – initiative, which had already resulted in 20,509 weapons searches in the month of March 2000 alone. Chief Constable John Orr explained that the report painted a 'bleak picture of violence in our society' and 'highlighted only too clearly the potentially lethal mix of young people who abuse illegal drugs and alcohol, which gives them a predisposition to carry knives'.[7]

The message from the research, the media reports and the subsequent police action was that there is a lethal, shocking and violent cocktail of teenagers, drugs and knives in Scotland today, which needs to be addressed by not only the police but by everybody who works with young people. McKeganey's report went as far as to state that, 'although the UK home secretary has advised that adults should be more prepared to intervene when young people misbehave, we suggest the need for caution as some young people may be carrying an offensive weapon'.[8]

However, while the action of the police and the warnings by the EIS and particularly by McKeganey may be serious, the schools survey itself is anything but.

Firstly, the report did not show that over a third of schoolboys *are* carrying knives, but rather that a third have once – at some time in their lives carried a weapon. There is, also no indication of how often young people take drugs – once a week, once a month, only once? Following from this, the report is unable to show whether young people have ever carried a weapon while under the influence of drugs, nor does it show whether young people have ever used their weapons while they are on drugs. Subsequently it is unable to show any link at all between drugs and actual acts of violence.

Secondly, as McKeganey and Norrie note themselves, the research is based on self reporting within confidential questionnaires and as such may be prone to under or over reporting by the 3,121 pupils who filled them out. Indeed it is possible that the results of this survey not only reflect the fact that some young people like to exaggerate their activities, but also that the young people who take drugs are more likely to want to claim to have carried a knife than those who don't.

Finally, there is nothing in the report to indicate whether or not the number of young people carrying knives has increased or decreased. Reference is made to the 'west of Scotland' and its 'association with weapon carrying and gang fights...immortalised in the "no mean city" accounts of life in Glasgow' – a culture which McKeganey argues – 'seems to be continuing'. But that "city" has not existed for over thirty years, and gang fighting today is nothing like it was. All of which begs the question – on what basis did McKeganey feel justified in handing out his 'wake-up call' and warning about the dangers we all face from drugged-up knife-carrying youths?

Some young people clearly do carry knives, but nowhere near the 1 in 3 reported by the press. Of the 20,509 people searched by Strathclyde Police the ratio of weapons found to searches made was around one in forty. Assuming the police target their searches at 'likely' candidates and at 'likely' locations, the real percentage of young people carrying knives at any one time is no doubt far smaller again. Also, and probably more problematic within this discussion, is the direct association being made with young people who have ever carried a knife, and those who have ever used one. Are we really to believe that 1 in 3 young people are capable of stabbing somebody – and if so, why are there so few people being stabbed?

Some young people do also take drugs – different drugs in different places and for different reasons – often as an experiment and often for fun. Indeed it could be argued that some drugs like dope – as the name suggests – make you less rather than more likely to use a weapon. Whatever the truth of this, it is clear that lumping all drugs together and equating them with potential violence is little more than a moral panic.

The danger with this approach is that the distinction between those few young people who do use weapons and the vast majority who don't is lost, while young people who simply use drugs are also now dragged into the discussion about the 'culture of violence'.

Hillhouse youth

Like the pro-active police action in Glasgow, where young people – indeed young adults – are regularly stopped and searched by the police on the assumption that they are a threat to others around them, the Hamilton Curfew started from the assumption that young people under 16 years of age no longer had a right to be out on the streets at night, unless they could prove that they had a good reason to be out.

To assess the impact of the curfew on teenagers in and around Hillhouse, 26 young people aged 12-15 years were interviewed at Earnock High and John Ogilvie High. Half of these teenagers came from Hillhouse. This age group was chosen because early indications of police interventions showed this group was being most affected by the CSI.

The aim of this section of the research was to establish the impact the curfew had had on these young people, the nature of the contact these young people were having with the police, and the reasons they felt they were being stopped, moved on or taken home since the introduction of the curfew.

Most of the teenagers in and around Hillhouse still went out at night, but half of those living in Hillhouse itself believed that their parents were now more worried about them going out in case they came into contact with the police. It was found that the curfew had not substantially altered the amount of contact the teenagers in Hillhouse had with the police – with many young people having had more contact the previous summer when there was no curfew in operation. The young people felt harassed and confused about why they were being stopped by the police – which occurred largely when they were in groups. They were equally confused about why adults felt the need to phone the police when they were out, rather than talk to them themselves.

These young people were being moved on or sent home by the police for simply hanging about with friends. This experience is common to many young people across Scotland. In Edinburgh, in 1994, for example, Anderson found that 44% of 1,000 11-15 year olds had been moved on or told off by the police, and 13% had been stopped and searched.[9] The stopping and searching of young people is something that has been encouraged by the 'zero tolerance' policing initiatives in Strathclyde over the last five years with one such initiative resulting in over 100,000 young people being searched.

Still hanging about after hours

To get an idea about the night time activities of the young people in and around Hillhouse, a number of questions were asked about what they did at night and with whom. It was felt that because these young people could answer the questions being asked of them without first giving a detailed dairy of their week's activities, that such a diary would not be needed. In hindsight, due to the usefulness of these diaries when looking at the activities of the children at primary school, this was a mistake, and a less detailed picture of these young people's weekly encounters was gained. Future work would benefit from including a diary of activities.

Firstly, the impact of the curfew on young people hanging out at night was assessed.

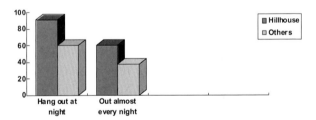

As the chart above shows, hanging out on the streets at night is something most young people – especially those in Hillhouse, do. This had not changed with the introduction of the CSI.[10] Most of the 12-13 year old from in and outside Hillhouse had to be home at night by 9pm. Most of the 14-15 year olds from both areas had to be home before 10.30pm and only two teenage boys – both aged 15 – were allowed to stay out after 10.30pm.

As the curfew time indicated by the police was simply 'after dark' - and in the winter it is often dark in Hillhouse by 4.00pm - all the young people that hung about the streets were clearly out after this time. However, while these young people were unclear about what time the curfew did actually start, most believed the police started picking people up around 9pm.

The number of police interventions during the first six months of the curfew which occurred after 10pm, equally suggests that few young people were out very late at night. Between 8 and 9pm there were 146 interventions; between 9 and 10pm there were 66 interventions; and after 10pm there were one or two interventions.[11]

While only two of the young people from Hillhouse had had their home time changed since the introduction of the curfew, almost half of these young people believed that their parents were now more worried about them going out, in case they came into contact with the police. As 14 year old Laura from Hillhouse explained, 'At weekends I have to be in half an hour earlier now in case I get picked up by the police'.

While some of the young people explained that they hung about at night because there was 'nothing better to do', for most of these young people hanging out gave them a chance to be alone with friends and was something they enjoyed. Fiona liked to, 'go next to the community centre and just drift about or watch the boys play football'. Jane from Hillhouse said, 'I usually walk about and talk with my friends', and fourteen year old Mark explained, 'I just go around on my bike and hang about'. Corrigan through research in Sunderland argues that hanging about doing nothing is something that young people want to do because it provides the best chance that something exciting might happen.[12]

These young people still spent a lot of their spare time with parents, but spent must of their time with their best friend, or with a group of friends.

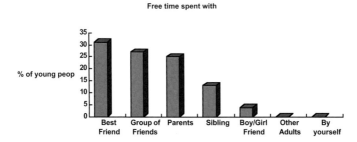

Free time spent with

Clearly being out with friends is an important part of a week's activities for these young people, and while this is often seen by adults as a useless activity or even a nuisance, developing peer relations and relations with adults outside the family is an important part of a young person's development.[13]

As Leo Hendry explains, 'It is in the realm of leisure that young people truly become themselves. Leisure time is the period when different lifestyles can be tried and exchanged. Leisure activities provide the vehicle for socialisation with peers and adults outside the family. Self-identity and group identity are explored and defined'.[14]

The importance of children and young people developing peer relations, is not simply the issues or agendas that are set in these relationships – 'should we take drugs or should we not' – but also the process of creating these relationships independent of direct adult controls. Taking responsibility for yourself and your friends; learning to argue your case within a group; negotiating and relating to others' views and feelings; and ultimately establishing independent relationships without the support of adults, are all important social skills.[15] For these skills to develop young people need time free from adult supervision, time and space during teenage years that is often found while out on the streets at night.

Harassed and Confused

The young people interviewed who lived in Hillhouse felt harassed and confused about why the police moved them on or told them to go home at night. Over two thirds of these young people had had contact with the police since the introduction of the curfew, compared to less than half of those who lived in other areas. A third of the Hillhouse teenagers had been told to go home by the police, another third had been told to move on. None of the young people interviewed had been taken home by the police since the curfew was launched .

Thirteen year old Diane from Hillhouse told me, 'I was sent home on the first day of the curfew, but that's all'. Richard, 15, said, 'I've been moved on, told to be getting in for the curfew, but not much'. The young people who had been spoken to by the police during the CSI were concerned that simply standing around with friends often led to either complaints from adults or action by the police to move them or split up their group. This had increased for the first few weeks of the initiative but had then died down, with a number of young people experiencing more police contact the previous summer when no curfew existed.[16] Laura, 14 years old explained, 'They move us on a lot in the summer. The police tell us there's been complaints, but no one complains to us which they should do 'cos we're never up to much. I guess they're scared of us 'cos we're a big group. There's about 15 of us. They think we'll hit their windows or something if they speak to us – but if they spoke to me I'd tell my pals we'd better move'. Laura's classmate Angela, from Burnbank said, 'The police have stopped us a few times and said there's been complaints. We'd not had anyone complain to us – if they had we'd be quiet. It usually happens when we're in a big group'. Fifteen year old William felt the police use the excuse of adults complaining to do what ever they wanted to, 'They shift us all the time', he said, 'They say there's been complaints, but that's not true'.

The Scottish Office report evaluating the impact of the CSI after six months, found that all of the boys in their survey had had contact with the police compared to only half of the girls. The level of policing was seen by these young people as being more than ever before. One respondent explained that, 'Before the 'curfew' I had been searched once but now it's about every weekend'.[17] This report found that girls appeared to avoid contact with the police, one girl explaining that, 'If we see them coming we run and hide up the closes'.

Over a third of the young people interviewed who had been in contact with the police said that this contact was often because of complaints made by adults when they were standing in the street. This usually happened when the young people were with a group of friends.

Research for Save the Children looking at the experiences of young people aged 12 to 20 found that 62% of the 98 young people they interviewed said they were sometimes 'moved on' because of adults' complaints.[18]

While the initial few weeks of the curfew led to more contact between the young people in Hillhouse and the police, after this the level of contact declined and was little different to that which young people had already experienced when out on the street at night. It was clear from talking to these young people, and from police statistics about why they had told young people to go home at night – i.e. 63% of the curfew interventions were for loitering – that the very act of hanging out with friends was not seen as an acceptable activity by the police.

Despite the activities of the police, the number of young people going out at night does not appear to have changed substantially, although a number of newspaper reports have indicated that adults in the area feel that there are fewer young people on the streets now. This could be because, as Mark told me, the young people are simply more aware of places they get moved from and are now going to other areas in the estate.

Complaints by many of the young people interviewed about being moved on, indicates that as far as they are concerned they are being moved by the police for simply hanging around or messing about with friends. Clearly this is a one sided view and does not take into consideration the feelings of the other residents on the estate, some of whom feel the need to complain to the police about young people in their street. However, the number of young people moved off the street for 'loitering', and the small number of charges brought against the young people picked up by the police during the initiative, suggests that these teenagers are indeed being moved on for being nothing more than a nuisance, or a perceived threat.

Of the 229 interventions made by the police over this six month period only 4 young people were charged with anything. As the Scottish Human Rights Centre points out in their pamphlet, this means that 0.02% of interventions were crime related.[19]

Whether crime in the area falls or not, it is clear from this figure that the curfew is not about crime. The initiative is about cutting out nuisance behaviour of teenagers – shouting, swearing, messing about or being rowdy. This behaviour may be unacceptable to many adults, but rarely in the past has this been seen as a police matter. Through this initiative and others like it, adults are being encouraged to contact the police about the petty behaviour of young people. This approach to policing means that many non criminal activities that young people are involved in are now seen as illegitimate, and a cause for police concern and intervention. This is not a new development, but an extension of the Zero Tolerance police initiatives introduced by Strathclyde Police over the last five years. This intolerant approach to young people has been pushed by the Labour government and has been codified through the Crime and Disorder Act.

Policing play – safe or sanitised?

Shimamura and Snell, researching changes in children's play between the generations in Hull, discovered a grandparent who could recall a local candidate, who come election time would train local children to sing his campaign song, 'Vote, vote, vote for Mr Muff, you can't vote for a better man.' As Shimamura and Snell noted, 'This is a far cry from the local MP (today) who is leading a campaign against young people hanging around menacingly on street corners...one John Prescott MP'.[20]

The above quote gives a sense of how young people playing out has become a political issue today, an issue that is no longer confined to working class sink estates. Concern and complaints about young people hanging about on street corners have become widespread across the whole of the UK. Nuisance behaviour – defined as shouting, swearing, hanging around and fooling around in groups, sometimes outside other people's homes – now makes up between one in ten and two in ten phone calls to the police.[21] A Greater Manchester Police Officer described his daily shift in this way,

> Your busy shift would be the afternoon shift till late in the evening. And you would on a busy day perhaps get 20 plus incidents. And maybe 7 or more dealing with what we call Youth Causing Annoyance. And it would sometimes be young people gathering together and it might be an old lady disturbed by the noise they're making. And she makes a phone call can you come down and move them on. Or maybe it's running across gardens and setting hedges on fire, general vandalism. I would think if we didn't have that problem our job would be a lot easier. It's incessant. It goes on and on.[22]

Many youth and community workers in Scotland are today frustrated at the level of complaints being made by adults about teenagers hanging around at night. This concern stretches across the UK; a youth worker from Epping Forest in Essex recently told me, 'I'm getting more and more adults complaining about kids hanging around the streets, and it's not like up your bit, there's virtually no unemployment down here, no graffiti, no nothing'.

In Hillhouse itself, there are clearly some issues to be addressed regarding petty crime. However, the idea that adults have something to fear from all the young people who hang about or even drink in the streets at night, is not borne out. The Citizen's Jury in Hillhouse, set up specifically to look at the issue of community safety, concluded that the key issue to be addressed in the Hillhouse estate was not violence, drug dealers or even rowdiness. The key issue was vandalism and in particular graffiti.

Policing fear

The fear of crime is such that police initiatives like the Hamilton Curfew have gained support from local people. A similar fear exists south of the border – as mentioned in Chapter 1 a recent crime survey found that the fear of crime in England and Wales is so great that people are more anxious about going out alone on the streets than in any other country.[23] In Scotland also, this insecurity and fear of crime, has allowed Strathclyde Police to develop an intolerant attitude towards anyone in public space who is seen as undesirable. Chief Constable John Orr, in a book *Zero Tolerance Policing* explained that,

> The reality was that the Glesga hard man of the 1960s and 1970s had made way for the doped up, spitting yob standing on the street corner, underpass or local park, drinking buckie and humiliating passers-by, felt-tip pen at the ready to publicly inscribe the current fashionable obscenity.[24]

But as Dolan Cummings in *'Surveillance and the City'* points out, whereas the 'Glesga hard man' was committing acts of violence, the new 'yob' referred to by John Orr 'is not committing a crime at all; it is the kind of juvenile behaviour that has gone on for decades'.[25] This does not make this behaviour by some young people alright, but nor does it make them criminals.

Strathclyde Police are conscious that the fear of crime far outweighs the reality. As well as attempting to explain this through an advertisement campaign, they have also held a conference in Glasgow to help 'break down some of the barriers between young and old'. At this conference, Linda Martin for Strathclyde Elderly Forum explained that, 'There is a stubborn perception among older people that they are likely to become victims of crime, when the opposite is true'.[26] Chief Superintendent Campbell Thomson, Commander of 'Q' division, discussing the curfew stated that, 'It's modern society. There's a fear of crime amongst the elderly that's very seldom justified. A youngster is more likely to be offended against than one of the elderly folk, but that's not the old folks' perception. They're taken aback by a bunch of boisterous youngsters in high spirits'.

Campbell Thomson believes that while communities have a responsibility to provide facilities for kids, kids have also to be aware of the rights of other people.[27] However if the right referred to here is the right of adults to live without fear, then, when elderly people fear the very presence of young people out on the streets at night, there is a clear contradiction between their right to live without fear and the rights of young people to walk around their own estates.

Tackling crime and the fear of crime is what Strathclyde Police hope to achieve through the introduction of initiatives like the Hamilton Curfew. In their flier launching the CSI they explain that, 'The aim of this initiative is not to force young people off the streets; rather it is to make sure that our communities are safer for everyone'.[28] In Councillor Tom McCabe's CSI opening speech, he explained that the CSI was being introduced to help provide, 'the freedom of everyone in the community to live without fear or intimidation'. However, if adults – as has been suggested by Chief Superintendent Campbell Thomson – fear young people standing with their friends on the streets at night, then to ensure adults feel safe, these young people must be removed.

An intolerant attitude to 'yobs' held by the Chief Constable John Orr, has been codified through initiatives like the Hamilton Curfew, and is being supported by an intolerant attitude, stemming from a fear that many adults have, of young people who are out at night in their communities. By moving these young people, it is hoped that this fear will decline. However, Hillhouse community activist Joe Parfery believes more security measures in Hillhouse may be creating more insecurity – especially amongst the elderly, 'We keep having these initiatives for new locks or peephole on your front door, but you just get people worrying even more about why they need these new locks in the first place and whether they'll be strong enough.'

Similarly, there is a danger that the high profile CSI introduced on the Hillhouse estate will only have confirmed the suspicion that many adults have that young people on their streets are a danger to be avoided. It may also result in even more adults avoiding the teenagers they have until now dealt with themselves. Indeed the Scottish Office research into the impact of the curfew, found that fear of 'groups of young people' had increased among adults, and the number of adults who said they would now avoid certain areas also increased.[29]

Talking to sixty year old George who lives in Hillhouse, I found that he and a number of his neighbours felt safer now that the young people who had been drinking in his street at the weekend were no longer there. George had not had any trouble off these young people, but had been worried about what they may do when he walked past them at night. George has had no contact with these teenagers, and given the changes taking place many more adults will become strangers to the young people they still fear in areas such as Hillhouse.

Peer pressure

While young people continue to hang about the streets at night with friends, there is a growing perception and concern which has been adopted and promoted by the police and politicians about the dangers of peer pressure. Discussions about teenager relationships are today largely focused on the negative potential of these relationships and the impact they have to encourage others to take drugs or commit crimes. It is rare to read the word peer in a newspaper without the word pressure following close behind. The assumption here is that this pressure is a negative force, never positive. That some friends may be a positive influence on others is rarely recognised; similarly the element of choice and decision making by young people is ignored; finally the basic fact that young people need to learn to deal with different pressures and influences in their lives as they grow up is also disregarded.

While parental concern about who their children are hanging about with has always existed, the idea about dangerous peer pressure has been given weight by the elevated concern about 'peer abuse'. Children fighting and calling each other names has over the last decade been categorised as and is seen within the framework of 'bullying'. Within this discussion, many aspects of childhood conflicts are seen as abusive and something that could permanently damage a child. In the journal *Aggressive Behaviour*, the most recent bullying theory suggests that most children are involved in the 'group process' of bullying.[30] As Blatchford points out, the negative view of young people's peer relations is one of the key reasons that school break times are being reduced.[31] Through this debate children and young people are increasingly seen as potential abusers and victims of one another. In his book on *Childhood* for example, Chris Jenks explains that, 'An emerging body of work from the USA indicates that most child abuse, sexual, physical and psychological, is, in fact, peer abuse'.[32]

In a Home Office study on young people and crime, the influence of peers was identified as a key factor in offending. Quoting from a report looking at car crime, it notes that the splintering of peer groups reduces pressure to be involved in crime.[33] Breaking up peer groups which can push young people into criminal activities is one of the aims of the Hamilton Curfew. However, the Home Office research also noted in passing that young people who desisted from criminal activities after leaving their delinquent peers, may have left these friends in a conscious effort to stop offending. In other words, it was not the act of being with peers that led to criminal activities, rather individuals *chose* to be part of a group because they wanted to be involved in such activities.

Interviewed on Sky Scottish, South Lanarkshire Council leader Tom McCabe, explained that the CSI helped young people who were out on the streets at night, as the police could now intervene to protect them from peer pressure. The assumption made by McCabe is that it is peer pressure that is forcing many young people to take drugs, fight or even get involved in criminal activities at night. Peers, or friends, here become something that young people need protection from. Whether this is something the police could ever actually achieve appears unlikely. But in this way the police can justify breaking up groups of young people on the assumption that they may be applying negative pressure upon one another.

In Hamilton, Inspector McKenzie informed me while discussing the dangers faced by teenagers in Hillhouse, that if a 13 year old boy was seen hanging about with a group of 18 year olds, this was a clear sign of potential danger to the youngster, and a situation that would have to be resolved. That the spontaneous assumption from Inspector McKenzie about the older teenagers is that they are a danger to the 13 year old, perhaps tells us more about his attitude to young people than it does about any necessary threat posed by them.

The young people interviewed in Hillhouse had had no 'serious bother' with older teenagers and when there was trouble it was usually with their own age group – but not with the friends they hung about with. Nobody mentioned peer pressure, or trouble caused by friends. Rather, it was 'other' teenagers who they did not know very well that were seen as potential trouble makers.

In Hillhouse, teenagers were not under constant adult supervision, and it appears they do have the freedom to develop relations with their peers. However, to what extent the police were intervening to 'protect' these young people from there peers was unclear, but it is an issue that is becoming more prominent in police and council attitudes towards teenagers. The desire to protect young people from their peers, backed-up by police safety initiatives could in the long term be detrimental to the development of these young people who they aim to protect.

Learning to relate to peers and older teenagers is part of growing, and indeed without it young people would have a less all rounded social framework. Traditionally parents felt more comfortable about allowing their children to play out when there were older children around because it was assumed that they would look after them if anything serious happened. Today through initiatives like the curfew, the opposite image is being projected by councils and police forces – other young people are to be feared.

Public space is becoming less and less public

In summary, while there was concern by parents about their children coming into contact with the police at night, most of the young people who hung about the streets in and around Hillhouse still did so, although where they went at night may have changed because they were now more conscious that the police were more active in the area. Where there was contact with the police, the young people felt that they were being moved for no good reason, often due to complaints by adults especially when they were in a group. While there is nothing new about the police moving groups of young people who hang about the streets, the frequency of this type of intervention and the amount of complaints by adults is arguably greater than ever before. The Labour government has introduced even more laws to help the police regulate the behaviour of young people in public space and an intolerant form of policing, based on a fear of young people has emerged.

The culture of fear that exists across society today, is clearly seen in the support for the extended powers of the police to deal with the 'adolescent' non criminal behaviour of young people who continue to use public space to meet with friends. Activities that in the past would have been ignored or resulted in adults intervening to deal with this behaviour, are now seen as threatening and are being criminalised through laws and through 'safety' initiatives like the Hamilton Curfew. Not only has crime been 'taken seriously' by the politicians and the police, but also by the general public, and similarly, it is not only criminal activities that are being targeted, but any action deemed to be a potential risk to others, or even a risk to yourself. This level of insecurity has allowed the police across the UK to extend their powers to enforce order on the streets. The drive for this level of policing is perhaps unsurprisingly coming from the police themselves, however it is also being supported by the New Labour Government, Labour local authorities and a wide number of council departments that have previously had no role in the policing of young people. Councils that should be focusing on broader social policy developments appear to be falling back on crime and safety issues which only reinforce the fear that exists within communities.

The level of fear and insecurity across society, which has its roots outside of the activities of young people, has allowed the development of policing based on the fear of crime. Once established, this form of policing means that the insecurities held by adults and young people alike, can be acted upon, regardless of whether a crime is being committed or not. The curfew is a logical progression of this approach, whereby young people in public are assumed to be a potential problem until they have given a 'good reason' for being out at night. Ultimately, once policing becomes based on other people's fears, then the presence of 'gangs' of teenagers in public space is no longer acceptable. The 'antisocial' act of phoning the police because young children and teenagers are misbehaving on the street, is today being encouraged through initiatives like the curfew.

Discussions with adults from Hillhouse and Hamilton, as well as newspaper reports, suggest that adults feel the streets are quieter now. This may create a greater sense of security in the short term, but there is no indication that this is based on an improved relationship between different generations within the community, rather it is logical to assume that contact between the two groups has declined. Young people have been made more aware of the need to avoid some adults who fear them, and it is possible that by highlighting the 'need' for a curfew, the prejudices that many adults have of young people on their estate will have been reinforced – resulting in greater fear and a fall in the number of adults who are prepared to make contact with these young people.

This new form of policing means that it is easier to criminalise young people who do little more than hang about the streets, sometimes being a nuisance. However, while this 'heavy handed' approach to young people is a problem, a greater problem is the divisions and distrust that already exist between young and old that appear to be being reinforced by this police and council initiative.

Gill Valentine, quoted at the start of this chapter, feels that by forcing young people off the streets adults are creating a public space where only they are allowed to go. However this does not appear to be what is happening in communities like Hillhouse. Rather than young people being moved, so leaving space for adults to control, frightened or unconfident adults are handing over control of public space to the police. The result is that contact between people within communities is being reduced, and the police rather than policing crime are acting as mediators between individuals within communities who are frightened of one another. This 'community policing' is actually leading to policemen and women replacing the community. The curfew, by encouraging adults to increasingly relate to young people via the police, is actively discouraging those adults who do still relate to young people from continuing to do so. The result of this process is that public space is becoming less and less public.

While young people are seen and portrayed as 'villains' who put others at risk, another key aspect of the curfew was its promotion of young people as 'victims' who faced many dangers while out on the street at night. In the discussion about peer pressure, the villain and victim sides of young people can clearly be seen – vulnerable weak teenager being preyed upon by aggressive friends. Through this discussion and the formalising of this outlook into police practice, so called caring, protective policing can be introduced to regulate relationships with young friends who hang around the streets at night. The dangers for young people of being seen as weak and needing constant protection is examined further in Chapter 6.

Study Guide

A. What is meant by a 'yob nation' and is it true to say that today we live in one? Across the political spectrum it has become common to argue that we are living in a yob nation and in communities full of 'neighbours from hell'. Choose one of the books below (numbers 1-3) and critically discuss their ideas about what is wrong with Britain's youth.

B. Within academic and liberal circles it is often argued that young people are portrayed in a negative light today. To what extent could it be argued that 'young people get a bad press'?

Analyse one tabloid and one broadsheet newspaper over a week to assess the way young people are portrayed. Does this portrayal represent a biased image or an honest reflection of reality?

C. 'Respectable fears' and 'moral panics' are understood to have influenced the way young people have been portrayed for decades.

By studying past and present work on moral panics assess the extent to which the portrayal of a youth 'culture of crime' is a modern day panic.

D. Critically assess the extent to which public space has become a no go area for young people. To what extent have the laws developed by the Labour governments since 1997 resulted young people being excluded from public space?

Make a list of new laws that could affect young people's use of public space and discuss with young people you know or work with, or use your own experience, to indicate the extent to which 'hanging about' has been criminalised.

Useful Reading

A. 1. *Yob Nation: The truth about Britain's Yob Culture* by Francis Gilbert.

2. *Neighbours from Hell: The Politics of Behaviour* by Frank Field.

3. *The Great Abdication: Why Britain's decline is the fault of the middle class* by Alexander Deane.

Additional Reading:

4. *What's behind the rise of Yob lit?* by Graham Barnfield. Available online.

C. 1. *Folk Devils and Moral Panics* by Stanley Cohen.

2. *Hooligan: A History of Respectable Fears* by Geoffrey Pearson.

3. *The Politics of Antisocial Behaviour: Amoral Panics* by Stuart Waiton.

4. *American Youth Violence* by Franklin E. Zimring.

D.   1. 'Children should be seen and not heard' by Gill Valentine in *Urban Geography*, Vol. 17, No. 3, 205-220 (1996).

2. *In Search of Sesame Street: Policing Civility for the Twenty First Century* by Dolan Cummings.

3. *Youth Crime* by John Muncie.
See 'youth crime' in the index.

4. 'Young People, Crime and Youth Justice' by Tim Newburn in *The Oxford Handbook of Criminology* edited by Mike McGuire.

Notes

[1]Wegs, R. (1999). Youth delinquency and 'crime' (Journal of Social History Vol32 No 3) p603.

[2]Pearson, G. (1983). Hooligan: A history of retrospective fears (The Macmillan Press Ltd) p71-72.

[3]Muncie, J. (1999). Youth and Crime: A critical introduction (Sage Publications Ltd) p32.

[4]Campbell, B. (1993). Goliath (Methuen).

[5]Valentine, G. (1996). 'Children should be seen and not heard' Urban Geography (Vol. 17) p205-220.

[6]The Herald, 18 April 2000.

[7]ibid.

[8]ibid.

[9]Anderson, S. et al (1994). Cautionary Tales: Young People, Crime and Policing in Edinburgh, (Avebury).

[10]See Springham, K. (1998) .Time to Go Home Says Who?, (Scottish Human Rights Centre) p13.

[11]McGallagly, J., Power, K., Littlewood, P. and Meikle, J. (1998). Evaluation of the Hamilton Child Safety Initiative, (The Scottish Office Central Research Unit) p.15.

[12]Corrigan, P. (1979). Schooling the Smash Street Kids (MacMillan).

[13]See Coalter, F. and Allison, M. (1995). Young people in Wester Hailes (The Wester Hailes Partnership) p6.

[14]Hendry, L. et al (1993). Young People's Leisure and Lifestyles (Routledge) p2.

[15]Corsaro, W .A. and Eder, D. (1990). Children's Peer Cultures (Annual Review of Sociology) 16:197-220

[16]Springham, K. (1998). p10.

[17]McGallagly, J., Power, K., Littlewood, P. and Meikle, J. (1998). Evaluation of the Hamilton Child Safety Initiative, The Scottish Office Central Research Unit, p.58.

[18]Article 12 in Scotland; curfews and crime (Save the Children Fund).

[19]Springham, K. (1998). p10.

[20]Shimamura, H. and Snell, C. (1996). They don't play out like they used to, do they? p35.

[21]Audit Commission Report (1996) p13.

[22]Valentine, G. (1996). 'Children should be seen and not heard' Urban Geography (Vol. 17 No3) p205-220.

[23]Guardian, 26 May 1996.

[24]Bratton, W., Dennis, N., Mallon, R., Orr, J. and Pollard, C. (1997). Zero Tolerance: Policing a Free Society (Institute of Economic Affairs) p110.

[25]Cummings, D. (1997). Surveillance and the City (Urban Research Group) p8.

[26]Linda Martin (1997). quoted in The List 24 October-6 November.

[27]Chief Superintendent Campbell Thomson (1998) quoted in The Face.

[28]Strathclyde Police 'Q' Division (1997) Children and Young People's Safety Pilot Scheme flier.

[29]McGallagly, J., Power, K., Littlewood, P. and Meikle, J. (1998). Evaluation of the Hamilton Child Safety Initiative, (The Scottish Office Central Research Unit) p.57.

[30]Sutton, J. and Smith, P. K. (1999). Aggressive Behaviour (Vol. 25 No2) p97-111.

[31]Blatchford, P. (1999). The state of play in schools, in Woodhead, M. et al (ed) Making sense of social development, (Routledge).

[32]Jenks, C. (1996). Childhood (Routledge).

[33]Home Office (1995) Young People and Crime (p5).

6   Regulation regulation regulation

'Young people have become a separate class. They have their own culture, their own dress sense, and have less contact with other age groups'.[1]

The above quote in *'Psychosocial disorder in young people'*, expresses well the sentiment that there is a significant generation gap today. Young people, it is suggested, have become a separate class of people that adults and society generally can no longer relate to. Elderly friends, often express a similar sense of distance from the experiences of young people, who they recognise have very different lives to their own. The job situation, the lack of respect for authority, the problem with drugs – are the usual suspects that indicate to many that young people's lives and ultimately young people themselves are somehow very different today. In Hillhouse, the Scottish Office research found that adults felt that 'things had changed', and that there was a general lack of respect for adults and elderly people.[2] However, whatever the differences may be, when it comes to the fear for personal safety and a desire for greater regulation of public space, there is no generation gap.

Throughout the curfew, concerns were raised by youth workers and children's charities about the impact this initiative would have on relations between young people and the police. It was suggested that young people, 'who want their freedom', would react against the heavy handed approach by Strathclyde Police. However, while young people may want freedom to go out at night, this is tempered by a strong desire to have their safety guaranteed while they are out. In Hillhouse, despite a feeling among the young people interviewed of being unfairly targeted by the police, they were keen for more policing of others who hung about the streets at night. These young people appeared to be as intolerant of others as the adults on the estate and possibly even more willing to use the police to move them off the street. This supports other research which suggests that across the UK both young people and adults alike are becoming more authoritarian in their attitudes to one another.

From sociological research looking at the image and self image of young people today it seems that young people increasingly see themselves as victims who need protection from others - the research in Hamilton backs up this notion. This outlook has been reinforced by the Hamilton Curfew.

Auntie authority

While running a drop-in centre for young people in Coatbridge, I was surprised by the acceptance shown by the young people who were regularly stopped and searched by the police. These teenagers did not like the police, nor did they like that they were being targeted and searched, but few were overly concerned or even angered about their rights being infringed. Eighteen, and Nineteen year olds, while drinking outside their own homes or in the park, were often stopped by the police who would pour away the alcohol that these young men had. This caused frustration, but rarely was the right of the police to decide what these young people could or could not do in their own estate questioned. It was largely accepted that some people caused trouble when they were out at night, and subsequently the police had the right to do what was necessary. The police were often hated for being 'unfair' to individuals, but this did not stop these young people from accepting the overall right that the police had to regulate young people and young adults, who were out at night.

When the CSI was launched, a number of youth workers and young people who opposed the curfew appeared on a television debate about the police initiative. The youth workers were concerned about the rights of the teenagers they worked with and were opposed to what they saw as authoritarian policing. The young people themselves however, while being concerned about being targeted for simply hanging around the streets, did not have any overall concerns about an increase in policing of young people. Indeed a week after the TV programme, I contacted the most vocal of these young people to get his views on the curfew and discovered that he was now firmly in favour of the initiative because a policeman had explained to him how it would 'target trouble makers and get them off the street'.

With these experiences in mind, I was concerned to examine, not only whether or not the young people in and around Hillhouse were for or against the curfew, but also whether they were generally in favour of more policing of *other* young people.

Youth X-change

The traditional view from the 50s on, of rebellious or anti-authoritarian youth, breaking free of parental and external authority no longer fits. At least in relation to the desire for freedom versus protection, young people today appear to be more conservative and cautious than their predecessors.

Images of British youth in the last fifty years – The Teddy Boys, the Mods and the skin heads – portray young people as rejecting the restrictions put on them by adults, doing their own thing with two fingers stuck up to authority.[3] While these groups did exist and did represent real changes in lifestyle and attitudes of young people, as John Davis points out, most young people, rather than living a life of rebellion, were actually largely conformist.[4]

Even though young people were generally conformist, however, they expected certain freedoms, especially when they were out at night. Safety and a desire for more police protection was certainly not an issue commonly raised by these young people, more characteristic of their attitudes in fact was a desire for more freedom.

In the early 1960s, one author described young people as 'strikingly autonomous'.[5] In 1981 in *Too Much, Too Young*, a book based on interviews with young people aged 11-16, the authors describe 'the kids' as 'bursting to grow up'.[6] These young people they explain, expected to 'break the law, to drink and get into X-rated films'; they were embarrassed to be seen out with their parents and wanted to get out of the house as soon as possible and travel independently with their friends.

While young people today still aspire for freedoms, and conflicts with parents and authority still exists, from research in Hillhouse and with reference to other research with young people in Scotland, there are clear signs that concerns about safety among teenagers is conflicting and to a degree restricting the drive for greater independence.

Safety guaranteed

During the interviews with the young people in Hillhouse, it was clear that, while resentment at being targeted by the police did exist, these teenagers were even more concerned about the need to control other young people, and actually wanted either more policing or some other form of regulation of young people to be introduced in their area.

Like the desire held by many adults, to have the nuisance behaviour of young people more regulated by the police, many of these young people were also keen to have more policing to deal with young people who were being noisy, or who drank on the streets at night. This desire for more regulation of others, meant that the young people had a contradictory attitude to the police. Personal experience of being moved on made many young people feel frustrated at the attitudes of the police and the adults who made complaints about them, but despite this there was still a desire for more regulation of other teenagers. Similarly, while there was an acceptance or even support for more regulation of young people's time, there was some evidence that these teenagers were accepting more limits on their own freedom at night.

That young people appear to share some of the fears and preoccupations of their grandparents raises many questions about the nature of young people today. Further research is needed to look into the impact that the climate of fear within which young people are growing up, and the impact that safety initiatives like the curfew are having on their perceptions of risk.

Anti-curfew

Over half of the young people interviewed from in and around Hillhouse supported the curfew. However, when broken down into areas it was found that while over three quarters of those living outside Hillhouse agreed with the curfew, only a minority, or 38% of those in Hillhouse supported it, with 54% against. The Scottish Human Rights Centre's research, based on interviews with 66 young people on the streets of Hillhouse, found a quarter of these young people supported the initiative and 55% opposed it.[7]

	For	Against	Undecided
All	58%	35%	7%
Living in Hillhouse	38%	54%	8%
Others	77%	15%	8%

High School Support for the Curfew

The young people living outside Hillhouse were generally supportive of the curfew because it was something they believed would not affect them, but also because they believed there were 'trouble makers' in Hillhouse who drank and were rowdy, that needed to be moved off the streets. Despite having some negative experiences with the police themselves, this group were still supportive of more policing of *other* young people.

The Scottish Office evaluation of the CSI found that over half of the 981 young people from Hamilton who were questioned, felt the police did not understand young people, and thought the police stopped young people for no reason. Research by Save the Children and by the Scottish Human Rights Centre, indicates that resentment towards the police had increased since the introduction of the curfew.[8] However, the *Scared of the Kids?* research found that although the majority of young people in Hillhouse opposed the curfew, a third of these teenagers opposed it, not because of a concern they had about their freedom, but rather because they thought it was ineffective.

Fifteen year old Diane from Hillhouse explained that, 'It doesn't change things.' While classmates Michael and Stuart – also from Hillhouse – said, 'No one's going in at 9 o'clock anyway' and 'It makes no difference, people just run from the police'. For these young people the curfew was simply a waste of time and was having no impact on the 'trouble makers who just ran away'.

Power generation

The young people who opposed the curfew were also asked whether they thought the police should be given some other powers to deal with the young people in their area. Two thirds said yes. Which means that of the young people interviewed only 7%, were against the curfew and against any other increase in police powers to deal with young people in their area. These young people who were opposed to any increased regulation in their time, were also the only ones interviewed who mentioned their or their parents' rights being infringed by the curfew.

Fourteen year old Ann from Hillhouse thought that, 'The age', the curfew targeted, 'is wrong', and that, 'It should be just for younger ones 'cos I want more time'. Richard, aged 15 and from Hillhouse, enjoyed hanging out with his friends, and was annoyed by the police initiative, 'They take away our freedom and boss us around', he explained. While 15 year old Leanne explained that, 'It should be up to your mam and dad'. Other research in the area also found conflicting views regarding freedom, with one young man forcefully stating that, 'William Wallace fought for fuck all, we don't have freedom here'.[9] This reaction by these teenagers from Hillhouse may partly reflect their age i.e. that older teenagers want more freedom. But the majority of the 15 year olds from in and around Hillhouse were in favour of more policing of other young people.

All of the young people were asked if they would like to see more policing in their area.

Support for policing by all the young people interviewed

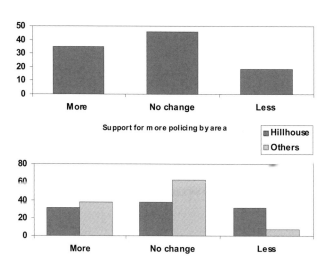

While almost a third of the young people from Hillhouse wanted fewer police in their area, over two thirds wanted more or no change to the amount of policing that their area received. For the majority of even the young people in Hillhouse, the high level of policing undertaken during the curfew was either supported, or thought to be not high enough. Despite the fact that many of these young people were not convinced that the curfew was either fair or effective, there was no overall opposition to more policing itself.

There was no gender difference in the level of support for more police, or more regulation of young people who are out at night. Surprisingly, there was also little difference in the attitudes of the younger and older young people towards the police. It was expected that the younger teenagers who were less independent and would be out on the street at night less, would have a more conservative, pro-regulatory attitude towards other young people. While there was some evidence of this, it was also the case that the majority of the older teenagers had a very similar pro-regulatory approach to other young people, and this despite their own negative experiences of the police in their area. Other research of older teenagers has also found that despite bad personal experiences of policing, young people still wanted more policing. In Stirling, of the 16-25 year olds surveyed, only 1% felt that they were treated well by the police and yet three quarters believed the police should make their area safer.[10]

The first British Crime Survey to look at the experiences and attitudes of 12-15 year olds found that, 'the stereotype of young people as anti-authority – and more specifically anti-police – does not hold'. Indeed the report explained, 'the overwhelming majority of young people recognise the need for the police, and many look to them for protection'. Concluding that young people – many of whom are stopped by the police and sometimes searched – 'may come to expect a degree of monitoring from the police, and not always judge them any worse for it'.[11]

While the majority of young people, even in Hillhouse, felt more police may be a good thing for their area, this was largely because they saw 'others', often older teenagers, as 'more bother' than themselves. For most of these young people, like those recorded in the Scottish Office Report, the curfew was not seen as something that was set up for their safety, with many young people explaining that they 'never felt unsafe before it'.[12]

Contradictory policing

The research in Stirling concluded that, 'Young people seem to have quite contradictory views on policing, or as Anderson and Leitch (Scottish Crime Survey) found 'young people were unsure about how they perceived the police' (1996 p88). Many young people do not feel the police respect young people and are therefore suspicious and distrustful (if not hostile) towards them, however they also argue for increased policing and a more visible police presence to increase their feelings of safety'.[13]

In Hillhouse the young people have a similarly contradictory attitude towards the police. Personal experiences that most of the teenagers have of the police are generally negative. Having been stopped and moved on by the police at night – often for simply hanging around – these young people were frustrated by police attitudes. Most reports by these young people, of being moved off the streets at night, were related to what the police or adults saw as nuisance behaviour. The young people felt that it was unfair to be moved by the police for standing about, or messing about with friends. Despite these experiences, the young people in and around Hillhouse, were not opposed to the general trend towards increasingly regulated public space – and in particular the increased regulation of young people who hung about the streets. Few of these teenagers argued about their *right* to move around their estate without police interference or of the rights of their parents to decide upon the time that they should be allowed out at night. Fewer still were concerned about the rights of all the young people in the area – and like the adults they often criticise for contacting the police – they too were keen to have the police deal with young people.

Rather than seeing the police as a body to deal with crime and criminals, these young people have come to expect the police to regulate the petty nuisance behaviour of young people on their estates.

Downer on drinkers

To assess the level of support that children and young people had for policing of other young people when they were misbehaving or committing petty offences, they were asked:

Do you think the police should be phoned, if a young person is doing the following:

- Sitting on a stranger's wall?
- Running in a garden?
- Knocking on a door and running off?
- Smashing a bottle in the street?
- Fighting in the street?
- Playing football in the street?
- Being noisy in the street?
- Drinking in the street?
- Going out after the curfew time?

% of children and young people in favour of phoning the police

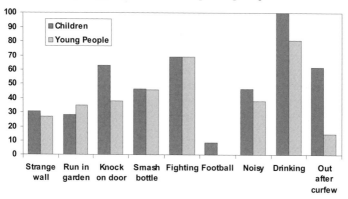

Of note from this table is the large number of primary, but more significantly – high school pupils, who were prepared to phone the police for minor offences. A number of teenagers that were in favour of calling the police elaborated that it depended on why they were 'running in someone's garden' or 'smashing a bottle', and only a small number were in favour of phoning the police if a young person was out after the curfew time. However there was no equivocation about calling the police if a young person was seen drinking under age. This does not necessarily mean that these young people would actually phone the police themselves if they saw a young person drinking at night, but it does reflect a certain attitude and a desire to have other young people – who *may* cause trouble – moved off the street. Likewise it suggests that these young people feel uncomfortable and unconfident about dealing with these other young people themselves.

Even though some of these young people admitted drinking, they still assumed that others who drank on the street would, 'get into a fight', 'cause trouble' or 'go a bit nuts' – and so deserved to be picked up or moved on by the police, just in case.

Over 80% of the young people interviewed said the police should be called if a teenager was seen drinking on the street. Broken down into areas, in Hillhouse the number of those who thought the police should be contacted was still high – 70%. The 80% who favoured phoning the police were asked a follow up question – Do you think it would be better to contact the young person's parents rather than the police? Over 60% answered no to this question. Overall this meant that four fifths of the young people asked, thought the police should be phoned if a young person was seen drinking in the street, and exactly half of all these young people – when given the option of contacting the parents of the young person rather than the police – still said they would contact the police first.

The reason for this attitude towards other young people who drink on the streets at night is partly due to experience, i.e. that street drinkers sometimes cause trouble and can be rowdy, and may reflect the simple fact that drinking is something young people know they should not do. It may also have been influenced by the high profile police campaigns and new laws which have banned street drinking in many areas in Scotland over the last five years – making street drinking and the perception of it, criminal and potentially dangerous. Generally, it reflected a view held by most of these young people that nuisance or antisocial behaviour of other young people was something that should be dealt with by the police. The chance that young people drinking may result in rowdy behaviour, was seen as enough justification for involving the police and moving these young people off the streets.

Intolerant adolescents

While over half of the young people interviewed thought that Hillhouse was an area with 'a lot of bother', only one in eight had personally had any bother. This consisted of fights (by three females), a gang fight and some teenagers being noisy at night. It was mentioned by one 14 year old female that there had been a young man stabbed and killed a few years ago in a fight. However this was clearly the exception rather than the rule to life in Hillhouse and does not explain why these young people had come to accept and even expect the high level of regulation of public space in Hillhouse.

The intolerant attitude that many adults have towards young people is here replicated by many of the young people themselves, who despite their own personal experience of the police are keen to have any *potential* troublemakers cleared off the streets. This desire for a more regulated environment suggests that young people have a changing expectation of freedom within public space, and may also have a more limited expectation of themselves, of what situations, and of what people they are prepared to have contact with and deal with.

The desire by teenagers for greater freedom and independence as they get older, is today conflicting with the desire for more safety and regulation of others. In a survey of young people carried out by the South Lanarkshire Youth Council planning group, when given ten options to chose from as a priority issue, 21% of respondents chose 'crime, violence and personal safety', compared to only 15% who chose 'youth rights'. The right to be safe seems to be winning the battle with the right to be free. As 15 year old Simon from Earnock explained,

'If someone's drinking in my street, it's my right to phone the police if I want to.'

This desire by teenagers for safety and more policing of other young people was also found to be the case in Stirling. Here, a similar youth survey found that half the young people questioned wanted more police on the street; a fifth wanted CCTV to be introduced on their estate; and a quarter said a good way of making the streets safer would be to make sure young people stay off the streets at night[17]. The attitudes of the young people in and around Hillhouse, reflect a broader move away from what could be described as libertarian values, and a move towards a more authoritarian or regulated environment.

The Economic and Social Research Council Children 5-16 Research Briefing Number 16, looking at 10-14 year olds use of public space, notes that 'when asked specifically about "making unsafe areas safe" children particularly London children also wanted enhanced security' (e.g. CCTV, more police and "guards" outside shops and in parks).[14a] (Ironically in the ESRC briefing No. 9 looking at 'young people's use of public space' it is also noted that young people who use shopping centres resent the fact that they are treated with suspicion and as potential criminals, and 'feel that they are being watched at all times').[14b]

The 12th report of the British Social Attitudes Survey contains a chapter entitled 'Libertarianism in Retreat' which assesses the attitudes of the British public towards different forms of policing and surveillance and concludes that, 'Four years ago, we described the British public as "fainthearted libertarians", and our latest data give no grounds for questioning this judgement'.[15] Indeed from the data provided one could also conclude that the support for more policing and surveillance, over a relatively short space of time i.e. 4 years, has increased rapidly. Support for the use of video cameras on housing estates to detect vandals, for example, has increase from 53% in 1990 to 70% in 1994. Like the desire for more policing of street drinking in Hillhouse, the authors of this chapter of the BSA Survey believe that this move to accepting more surveillance cameras on estates, is partly to do with the public becoming used to these new forms of policing. Once established as the norm, it is less likely that people will view new forms of policing as suspect and will therefore come to expect a more regulated environment.

Fundamentally, the changes indicated above suggest that young people today are more likely to resolve conflicts they have with neighbours and other young people via the police rather than attempt to resolve them themselves.

In discussions with elderly men living on working class estates, who have attempted to deal with young people in their area, there is often a level of surprise at the way young people they've 'had a go at' will contact the police to make a complaint about them. Within Hillhouse itself, this was an issue for a local pensioner who had physically confronted some young people who were throwing stones at his window, and found himself under arrest for assault.

Independence?

The regulation of children's lives does not stop once they enter high school and become teenagers. Some of the concerns about stranger danger with this age group does appear to die away, with less of a focus upon this issue by adults, and few teenagers in Hillhouse for example being concerned about any danger they may face from adults on their estate. However new concerns emerge, especially about how young people will cope with their peers and the 'pressures' of growing up. As Valentine notes, parents continue to use the threat of strangers to control their children's free time but that this is often used as a 'catchall threat to keep children off the street and therefore away from drugs, underage sex or mixing with the "wrong crowd"'.[16]

Parental concern about their children's safety continues into their teenage years, with research suggesting that a 'bedroom culture' is developing for many children and young people alike – where parents encourage their children to stay in the house rather than hang about with friends. The L.S.E. report, 'Young People, New Media' indicates a growing concern by parents about young people's free time, and a desire to regulate this time more than in the past. The most extreme example of parental worries leading to a more regulated environment for young people, is the increase in the sales of surveillance equipment being purchased by parents concerned about what their children are getting up to in their bedrooms. Spying on your child with surveillance equipment is clearly not a common practise, and concerns about 'what', 'where' and 'with whom' young people are hanging about with is not new. However the level of concern and intervention by parents into young people's free time does appear to be on the increase.

To assess the level of independence and parental supervision of the young people in and around Hillhouse, they were asked about their freedom to go out at night, to travel outside their area without adult supervision and were also asked about how they travelled to friends' houses at night.

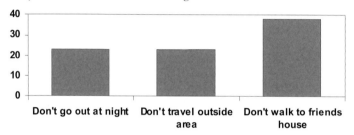

As well as expecting other young people in their area to be regulated by the police at night, a substantial minority had also come to expect other areas of their lives to be restricted and often more regulated by adults. A quarter of young people interviewed said they never went out in their area at night. A similar number never travelled out of their area without an adult, and over a third – more than the primary school children – said they did not travel to their friends' houses at night independently. Despite not having experienced trouble themselves, the reason given for not travelling to their friends' houses independently was a fear that either they or their parents had about potential dangers.

Lucy, 14 years old from Hillhouse explained that, 'It's a 15 minute walk so mum takes me for my own safety', while Lillian from Fairhill said, 'If it's Hillhouse I get a lift. I'm scared to walk by myself – I don't know everyone there'. Fifteen year old Gary from Earnock explained that, 'I get a lift when it's dark, my parents would worry if I didn't', and Christopher said that 'My mother doesn't like me walking in the dark'.

These young people no doubt preferred a lift from their parents partly for convenience, but most mentioned a concern they or their parents had for their safety. It was interesting to note that the young people who had the most regulated 'free time' were usually the young people most concerned or aware of the issue of safety and the ones who generally supported further policing and regulation of other young people. This despite the limited dangers or problems they had ever personally experienced.

Insecurity among young people today is often assumed to be because of their experience of crime, which is disproportionately greater than other sections of the community. The Scottish Crime Survey for example, found that 15% of 16-24 year old males had been victims of personal crime in 1992, compared with 6% of all males, and found that 12% of young women compared to 4% of women generally had experiences of personal crime.[17] However, even if this figure of 'personal crime' for older young people (16-24 years) was also the case for younger teenagers (12-15 years), it would still be a small minority of young people and would not explain the sense of risk that many young people feel. It is also the case that personal 'crime' has always been something that young people have suffered disproportionately to the rest of the population because of the time and type of activities they are involved in, often on the street. And yet young people and young men in particular have not always been so safety conscious and so in favour of more policing of other young people.

The research in Hillhouse supports the notion that young people are less independent today than in the recent past, relying more on their parents for lifts to friend's houses, and being more accepting and supportive of the regulation of young people on the streets by the police. It seems likely that the 'safety conscious' environment within which the young people have been brought up has influenced their perceptions of others and consequently influenced the expectations that these young people have of themselves and their ability to deal with other members of their community.

Risk awareness

Police safety initiatives like the Hamilton Curfew, have added to the safety consciousness of some of the young people living in and around Hillhouse. Thirteen year old Mark explained that he had often thought Hillhouse was a bad area, 'but now I know it is'.

However there are many other areas of life that have been affected by 'risk awareness', leading to a promotion of safety and a drive to regulate the free time of young people. Both schools and youth services have been influenced by this approach to young people, an approach that increasingly puts safety and risk awareness at the top of their agendas. One of the outcomes of this safety consciousness, is that young people become increasingly aware of themselves as potential victims, victims who need to be protected by others.

'Safety' is something that young people are highly conscious of as an issue. The teenagers in and around Hillhouse were extremely aware of what they felt were risky situations they faced on their estate, or when travelling into neighbouring towns. The modern vocabulary of 'risk' and 'safety' was not alien to any of the young people interviewed and none of the teenagers felt the need to ask 'safe from what', when answering questions about their sense of risk when out at night.

This awareness of potential dangers that young people face while out at night is something that has been encouraged by the local authority, who are keen to involve young people in developing safety initiatives in their area.

Consultation with young people is promoted today as good practise. But the topics that are open to discussion are often limited. Overcoming unemployment – a major issue for young people and adults alike – is rarely discussed or promoted.[18] This contrasts with 'safety' initiatives which have been given a high profile by Strathclyde Police and South Lanarkshire Council alike. It therefore comes as no surprise to find that young people are so concerned about the 'nuisance behaviour' of other young people, when the police have highlighted this as a key concern, and adults both locally and nationally are so preoccupied with young people who hang about the streets at night. The fear of crime grew throughout the 1990s and is reflected in the concerns of the young people interviewed, this concern at least in part will have been stimulated by a growing political and media focus upon it. As 14 year old Debbie from Burnbank explained, 'I don't feel safe on my own with all the stories in the papers about rape and murder'.

More widely, the first British Crime Survey to include the attitudes of 12-15 year olds noted that, four in ten young people felt 'fairly' or 'very unsafe' when out alone at night.[19]

Sociologists and child psychologists have noted the development of the promotion of fear through safety campaigns, some have become increasingly concerned with the broader impact this is having on children and young people. Mayer Hillman for example, has compared the lives of young people, with that of prisoners, whose every move is monitored and controlled, with deference increasingly being shown to the source of danger in children's lives,[20] The concern raised here, is not only that fear is being promoted through safety campaigns, but also that by creating fear among children and young people, they are encouraged to avoid all potentially dangerous situations and ultimately grow up ill equipped to cope with life.

The potential dangers that children and young people are said to face today have also grown. As the author of *Culture of Fear* explained, 'In discussions of childhood today, one threat seems to give way to the next. Children are assumed to be at risk not only from abusing adults, but from bullies and abusers among their peers'.[21]

Among professionals working with young people today, there is also a growing sense of responsibility for ensuring that teenagers are made aware of all the dangers they face in their lives. These are often dangers that young people face not only from other young people but from themselves – due to their own 'risky' behaviour.

An example of this approach recently came from a colleague who works with young people, as she described her 'non-judgmental' approach to youth work. 'I always ensure the young people I work with decide what they want to talk about,' she explained, 'so with my first group they wanted to talk about drugs, so we talked about the danger of drugs; the following week they wanted to talk about sex, so we talked about the need for safe sex practices; and the final week they wanted to watch an action movie, so after the film we discussed the dangers of portraying violence through the media.' For this youth worker, like many others, any issue or activity that young people wanted to talk about or do, was turned into an opportunity to explain all the dangers associated with them.

The promotion of safety surrounding children has also developed around teenagers, in particular, with campaigns in schools to stop bullying and with initiatives like the Hamilton Curfew which targets peer pressure as a threat to young people who hang about the streets. With both of these initiatives, the danger of abuse that adults pose to children has been replaced by the dangers that young people face from one another or from themselves. Relationships between young people are today seen in terms of risk and abuse, the logical outcome of this approach is to increase the regulation of these relationships – this is something that is reflected in the huge increase in anti-bullying initiatives which have developed throughout the nineties.

Bullying was a little discussed problem in the 1980s, indeed in 1988 there were no books on bullying in the UK. Yet by 1991 the government stated that all schools should have anti-bullying policies. Today it is the norm for schools to have anti-bullying policies in place and where teachers find little bullying they are often instructed to be more interventionist. The concept 'bullying' now incorporates many aspects of young people's behaviour that would in the past have been seen as unproblematic – name calling and not talking to friends are today described as damaging and abusive. Rather than allowing or expecting young people to resolve many of their problems among themselves, it is increasingly the case that teachers are being encouraged to see peer relations as potentially damaging and to intervene and regulate these relations.

Break time in many schools has been reduced, partly because of a growing concern that teachers have about bullying and violence during this unsupervised period of young people's day. As Blatchford explains, the dominant view of children's behaviour in break time is negative, not only is there a view that children are more violent now, but there is also a perception that children are not as constructive in their play as they used to be.[22]

Like the criminalisation and increased regulation of many aspects of young people's petty behaviour on the street, within schools a similar process appears to be taking place, where petty behaviour like teasing and name calling has been elevated into acts of abuse, and relations between young people themselves have come under increased adult scrutiny.

Discussing the 'victim'-isation of children by society, Gill Valentine notes that children are 'commonly constructed as 'vulnerable' and 'innocent' in public spaces'.[23] This social construction of children as victims is today however, equally the case for teenagers.

The concern for young people as victims is well documented in relation to crime, with most reports on the subject now including a chapter on 'young people and crime' – most making the point that young people are not only the greatest perpetrators of crime, but are also the most likely group to be effected by crime. The first British Crime Survey was published in 1982 and is a good benchmark of how society was becoming increasingly preoccupied with the issue of crime. Similarly, the first British Crime Survey to address the experiences and attitudes of young people was set up in 1992 and published in 1995 reflecting the concern for young people not only as criminals but even more so, as victims of crime. Entitled *Young people, victimisation and the police*, this report not only focused on the old concern of the 'victimisation' of young people by the police, but more importantly looked at young people as potential victims of crime.

The six types of 'crime' addressed in this report were: thefts of unattended property, thefts and attempted thefts from the person, assaults, harassment by adults, harassment by other young people and sexual harassment. Discussed in these terms – of 'crime', 'harassment' and 'assault', the often petty activities of young people become far more serious and threatening. However, the BCS itself concluded that,

> Many of the incidents which young people experienced would unquestionably have been treated as crimes, had the perpetrator or victim been adults. Where the incident is fairly trivial and victim and perpetrator are both school children however, many incidents fall into a "penumbra" of criminality, where they are crimes in little other than a formal sense. This could be regarded as part and parcel of growing up, rather than incidents for the police or court action.[24]

This attitude towards young people who steal or get into fights, as 'part and parcel of growing up', expressed here is refreshing. However the very fact that conflicts between young people are now discussed within the pages of the British Crime Survey reflects a degenerating view of young people who are increasingly seen as both victims and villains.

Most of the incidents initially described as crimes within the survey were not seen as such by the young people interviewed. Overall, a quarter of incidents were said to be criminal, a third 'wrong but not a crime', and a third 'just something that happens'.[25] With the increased focus on crime, bullying and abuse throughout the nineties, it will be interesting to see if these attitudes, which were surveyed in 1992, change over time.

Peer protection programmes

As well as the concern within schools about bullying today, there is also a growing concern about peer groups generally, and the negative impact that peers have upon one another. Discussions in the past about peers or youth cultures, were often targeted at marginal or minority groups like 'teds' or 'delinquents', however in the late 1990s the concern and demand for adult intervention within peer groups more broadly is widespread.

The USA as usual leads the way in this new development, with the negative perception of peers being expressed well by Kathleen McCoy in *Adolescents: Peer pressure and Your Teen*. Here she explains the 'devastatingly corruptive' influence of negative peer pressure that makes 'standing up to peer pressure one of life's greatest challenges'.[26]

McCoy suggests methods to help children avoid negative peer pressure, methods that are necessary because 'you can't rely on the fact that he has friends who'll pressure him to be safe'. Here peers are seen as potentially dangerous because they may involve themselves in 'unsafe' activities. Some of the avoidance techniques include encouraging your child to go to regulated after-school activities where peer influence is minimised, and getting to know the parents of your child's friends so that group rules can be co-ordinated.

This approach, which many would see as over zealous, if carried out would amount to trying to stop peer relations developing at all, and replacing them with adult-led relations. In the UK, few would argue for adults to regulate all areas of young people's lives, and there is a growing recognition among educationalists and psychologists in the benefits of peer relations for children and adolescents. However, despite this, relations between adolescents are increasingly being problematised and regulated.

One of the likely outcomes of this process, is that young people learn to distrust other young people and become increasingly aware of themselves as potential victims needing constant supervision and support from adults.

In the USA, such is the concern among professionals and young people alike, about potential violence in the classroom, that the top youth music channel – MTV, in association with the American Psychological Association, recently launched a Youth Anti-violence web site and a TV show to help young people who are concerned about their 'potentially violent classmates'. The 'Warning Signs' site explains that 71% of youth say they want to learn the warning signs of violent behaviour, the site also explains the need to be able to intervene in the activities of young people before any violence actually occurs. Rare acts of violence like the Oklahoma school shootings have also been held up as proof of the dangers young people face from their peers, and helplines have been set up to encourage young people to tell somebody about the dangerous kid in their class. The result of this approach is that these phone lines have been inundated with calls from frightened teenagers worried about the 'weird kid' in their class. Branded as potentially violent or even killers, growing your hair long and wearing black clothes has once again become a dangerous pastime for young people in the USA. While in the UK through anti-bullying initiatives and safety initiatives like the curfew in Hamilton, young people are becoming increasingly 'aware' of the potential dangers they face from their peers.

Victim – ised Youth

Conflict between young people, and the fear or apprehension that this generates is not new. Most young people at one time or another have to deal with a difficult or even dangerous situation in their lives, with conflicts between young people often taking place within schools or on the street at night where other young people hang about. However, whereas in the past young people would have expected to cope with many of these situations, today teenagers are being educated to rely more heavily upon adults and professionals for protection from their peers. Through 'risk awareness' campaigns and various 'safety' initiatives that involve teenagers, not only has the idea that other young people are a threat become the norm, but the expectation of young people is for adults to resolve this problem for them. As well as being overprotected, the perception of, and therefore the self perception of young people as passive victims has become more influential through the 1990s.

Rather than being encouraged to learn to live and deal with other difficult young people who are out on the street at night, for example, an increasing number of teenagers are learning to rely on their parents to chaperone them from one regulated environment to another. Driven to school, parents now hand over the reigns of protection to teachers who are being encouraged to intervene in almost all peer conflict situations. The anti-bullying slogan, that advises young people to 'tell, tell, tell', reflects this more interventionist approach to young people's lives, an approach that appears, to a degree, to have been adopted by young people more broadly.

Adults, particularly professionals working with young people, are encouraged to be more watchful and protective towards young people. This protection comes not only in the form of anti-bullying initiatives and safety campaigns, but also more broadly there is a move to worry about almost all the pressures faced by teenagers as they grow up. The pressure of exams, for example has recently been described at one teacher's union conference as child abuse. This view of young people as weak often comes from within the 'caring' professions, but the end result is that the lives of teenagers become more controlled and the independence of young people is potentially undermined. Once seen as being at risk and unable to cope with the pressures of growing up, teenagers are increasingly treated as incompetents who cannot be trusted. Within Hillhouse for example, it was the social work department that promoted the idea that the curfew was needed to protect young people from their own excesses of drinking and drug taking which was seen as something almost forced onto them by 'peer pressure'. The image of young people hanging about the street, is here changed, from the aggressive foul-mouthed yob, to the passive bullied victim – the image of victim may appear as more caring and concerned, but the end result in terms of policing teenagers time and space, is the same.

Furedi in *Culture of Fear* explains that the idea of young people as 'victims' is in fact a socially constructed identity, as 'people who have had a bad or traumatic experience do not think of themselves as victims unless society defines them in that way'.[27] Furedi notes that it is increasingly common for the 'status' of victimhood to be pushed onto young people with victimisation being seen by many as the defining quality of childhood. The consequence of this development, he concludes, is that 'children will begin to think of themselves as victims'.

The adult perception of all young people as potential victims of abuse or self abuse, influences almost every area of youthful activity today. Even within the club scene, risk and danger is a pervasive theme where young people are seen as being at risk not only from other young people, but equally from themselves and their drinking and drug taking. This approach to young people clubbing which sees them all as being at risk, as Dave Amis in *Adolescence, Risk and Independence*, explains, is new, and reflects a culture that looks at even the most enjoyable and fun areas of adolescent life in term of 'another risk category'.[28] Amis notes that in the 1950s, 60s and 70s the main perceived danger for young people who went out clubbing came from going to 'dodgy' clubs in 'rough' areas. Young people would make a conscious decision whether or not to go to these areas, aware that there may be trouble. Today in comparison, he explains that clubs that have 'Safe Clubbing' campaigns, treat *all* young people as potential victims not only of violence, and sexual harassment but more significantly, from the 'harm adolescents might do to themselves through abuse of alcohol and/ or drugs'. The implicit assumption, Amis believes, is that the clubbers are not capable of making their own assessment of what, if any, risk is involved in their activity. 'In effect,' he states, 'consumption of drugs and/or drunkenness are seen as manifestations of victimhood where people have lost their self control and have succumbed to temptation'.[29]

Whereas in the past being aware of potential dangers was taken for granted, today it has become a major organising principle and a justification in its own right. Amis explains that risks in the sixties and seventies were often seen in terms of a threat to public order, coming from aggressive rebellious adolescents, especially those from working class backgrounds. These young people were seen as being *conscious* of their actions and were certainly not viewed as helpless victims. This Amis believes, contrast with the view and treatment of 'young people at risk' today who are seen as victims and treated as incompetents.

In the 1990s, the notion of conscious choice has been diminished in a number of ways. People are seen as less in overall control of their lives and more as victims of circumstance or chance. It is in this context that adolescents and young adults who go out clubbing are increasingly seen as being "at risk" from circumstances they are perceived to be no longer capable of controlling without outside intervention.[30]

While many young people would challenge the notion that they are passively accepting a more regulated environment, as Amis notes, they have taken on board the idea that they are 'at risk'.

The broader climate and concern for child safety, is being backed up by local police initiatives like the Hamilton Curfew, where everyone from paedophiles to peers are being held up as a potential threat to the young people of Hillhouse. It is unsurprising then that young people are not only highly conscious of the potential dangers they face, but also that they are less prepared to learn to live and deal with the many and varied situations that face them within their own community. If this increased insecurity results in a reduction in the level of interaction between different sections of the community, then the divisions, fears and intolerance that is developing within communities will increase.

Seen through the eyes of an at-risk victim, the world becomes a more worrying and dangerous place. Like a teacher who has lost his self confidence, fears his pupils and finds himself unable to deal with any unruly behaviour without the support of the head teacher, 'at risk' young people and adults alike who fear those around them, no longer feel able to deal with other young people who hang about the streets at night. The support for the criminalisation of more and more aspects of petty adolescent behaviour makes sense in this context, as adults and young people who feel constantly at risk become less willing and able to cope with unregulated and therefore 'risky' relations with other members of their community.

Criticism of the curfew in Hamilton which came from civil rights groups and children's charities, largely focused on the authoritarian nature of this initiative. There was however, little criticism of the arguments about protecting victimised young people who are in danger from others or from themselves when they are out at night. Indeed an often used argument in opposing the curfew, was that by placing young people back in the home, the police and local authority are simply putting children and teenagers at more risk from abuse in the home. Here, one image of the abused victimised young person is simply replaced with another. Unfortunately, regardless of the often positive aspirations of these groups, by accepting and even promoting the child victim idea, it was impossible for them to consistently challenge this Child Safety Initiative.

More victims less community

Contact and interaction between people within communities is a basis for them to be communities. Shimamura and Snell looking at a working class estate in Hull, recognised that children mixing freely with other sections of the community was a key way that children and adults got to know one another.[31] Similarly for children and young people, the experiences they have with their friends and with other groups of young people – free from adult supervision – are very important for their socialisation. There is a concern today that 'battery-reared'[32] children and young people who are not allowed or encouraged to be independent and take more responsibility for dealing with other people and situations within their communities will grow up unable to cope with life. 'Danger,' as Tim William's explained, 'is part of the human condition and the child protected from everything is protected against nothing'.[33] Moira Gibb, chairperson of the Children and Families Committee of the Association of Directors of Social Services, while criticising the 'decimation' of the youth service and questioning the usefulness of the Hamilton Curfew, explained that, 'I spent my childhood on the streets and there is great working class tradition of hanging out and socialising with your peers. It would be a crime to prevent that'.[34]

However initiatives like the one in Hamilton are actively discouraging young people from learning to deal with different situations and people themselves. By promoting the idea that young people out at night are a risk to others, while being at risk themselves – and by encouraging people to treat 'nuisance' or petty activities as potentially dangerous – young people are being educated to treat other young people as not only dangerous, but too dangerous to approach or cope with by themselves. Whereas in the not too distant past, getting into a fight, dealing with other young people who drank and even drinking yourself, was seen by most young people (and adults) as simply part of life, and something they would expect to cope with. Today, in Hamilton and elsewhere, it is increasingly assumed that where there is a 'risk', young people must call on an external authority to deal with the problem. However, even with the heightened policing involved with the CSI, it is unlikely that Strathclyde police could ever make all the young people, even just in Hillhouse, safe from all possible dangers and unpleasant experiences – many of which often occur among peers (In the Stirling youth survey, 80% of the respondents said they did not believe the police protected them).[35] And yet it is rare to find young people being encouraged to learn to look after themselves – even though in the long term this is the most effective way of becoming safe and being able to live with the rest of your community.

Through these safety initiatives, behaviour of young people, that until recently would have been seen as merely immature or childish, are being criminalised or labelled as dangerous to all those around them. The logical outcome of this process is that communities and the young people within them grow more anxious and hostile towards the 'drinkers', the 'druggies' and the 'trouble makers' – and subsequently become increasingly reliant upon the police to deal with *other* young people. The result is that contact between different sections of the community declines – creating even more isolation within communities.

In conclusion, it is clear that police and council claims before the Hamilton Curfew was introduced, that young people themselves are deeply concerned about their personal safety, are true. It could even be argued that they are more open to crime and safety initiatives than older members of the community who experienced and expected a greater level of freedom on their streets when they were young.

Experience of the curfew and of the police at night, meant that young people felt victimised. Despite this the concern felt by many teenagers, about other young people, meant that they were ultimately in favour of more policing or more regulation of other young people. That this may have an effect upon their own freedom on the streets was of concern, but not of sufficient concern to undermine their desire for public space to become more controlled.

This desire for a more controlled environment was not generated by any extreme experiences that these young people had faced while growing up in and around Hillhouse. Hillhouse itself is certainly not a ghetto, and the young people here are no more 'at risk' than other young people living in working class estates across Scotland and the UK.

However, growing up within an environment where safety issues are increasingly being promoted, appears to have created a generation of young people who perceive the streets as not only a place of freedom and independence – but increasingly as a place of potential dangers. Rather than being eager to 'break free' from adult supervision, a substantial minority of the young people in and around Hillhouse were keen to have their free time more regulated – just in case!

The impact that this will have on communities in the years to come is unclear, but already there is a greater reliance upon the police and the council to deal with others in their community, who's behaviour is often little more than petty or immature.

Study Guide

A. The idea of 'youth' has often embodied a sense of freedom, independence and indeed rebellion, but to what extent can we say that 'youth' still exists today?

Through a study of youth and youth 'subcultures' explore the nature of 'youth' in the 21st century.

B. To what extent has a libertarian outlook been lost amongst the public and amongst young people themselves?

C. Critically discuss the meaning of 'peer pressure'. Are the activities of young people with their peers the result of 'pressure' or preference?

In exploring the idea of peer pressure examine the way the image of young people as 'victims' is embodied within this idea. From personal experience or through discussions with young people assess the role that peers play for young people, and also how young people perceive their own sense of responsibility for their actions.

D. If the nature of 'youth' has arguably changed, what about the 'nature' of the police?

In *Scared of the Kids* an emphasis upon the 'zero tolerance' aspect of policing has been developed. However with the growth of community policing and community police officers have these officers become 'softer' – increasingly dealing with and acting as mediators between people? Discuss with young people and police officers their experiences and understanding of the role of the police within communities.

E. Critically discuss the argument that young people are over regulated today and are not given enough freedom.

Look at the promotion of structured activities for young people, what lies behind the government concern with 'free' young people. Explore the possible benefits and limitations of these types of activities.

A. 1. *Disconnected: Why our kids are turning their backs on everything we thought we knew* by Nick Barnham.

2. *After Subcultures: Critical Studies in Contemporary Youth Culture* edited by Andy Bennett and Keith Kahn-Harris.

3. *Young People and Social Change: Individualization and risk in late modernity* by Andy Furlong and Fred Cartmel.

B. 1. *The British Social Attitudes 23rd Report – Perspectives on a changing society.* A summary of this is available online.

2. *Freedom Should Not Be For Sale* by Dolan Cummings. Available online.

3. *Taking Liberties* by Chris Atkins, Sarah Bee and Fiona Button. See chapter 5.

4. *New Labour flushed liberty down the toilet* by Brendan O'Neill.
Available online.

5. ESRC (2000) Children 5-16 Research Briefing No. 16.

6. ESRC (2000) Children 5-16 Research Briefing No. 9.
Both available online.

C.   1. 'Drugs use among peers: peer pressure or peer preference' by N. Coggins and S.McKellar in *Drugs Education Prevention and Policy*, Vol. 1, 15-26 (1994).

2. *Arrested Development* by Andrew Calcutt.
See chapter 10.

3. 'Peer pressure to smoke: the meaning depends on the method' by L. Michell and P. West in *Health Education Research*, Vol. 11, No. 1. 39-49 (1996).

4. *Random Violence: How we talk about new crimes and new victims* by Joel Best.
See chapters 5 and 6.

E.   1. *Freedom's Orphans Raising youth in a changing world* by Julia Margo et al.
The Executive Summary of this book is available online via the Institute for Public Policy Research

2. 'The roots of 'paedophobia'' by Stuart Waiton and Simon Knight in *Scottish Youth Issues Journal*, Issue 9, 98-94 (2007).
A summary of this is available online.

3. *Tying teenagers down* by Stuart Waiton.
Available online.

Notes

[1]Rutter, M. and Smith, D. (1995). Psychosocial Disorders in Young People (Academica Europa John Wiley & Sons).

[2]McGallagly, J., Power, K., Littlewood, P. and Meikle, J. (1998). Evaluation of the Hamilton Child Safety Initiative, (Scottish Office Central Research Unit) p.61.

[3]Fyvel, T. R. (1961). Insecure Offenders: Rebellious Youth in the Welfare State (Chatto and Windus).

[4]Davis, J. (1990). Youth and the Conditions of Britain (Atlantic Press).

[5]Fyvel, T. R. (1961). Insecure Offenders: Rebellious Youth in the Welfare State (Chatto and Windus) p343.

[6]Fisher, S. and Holder, S. (1981). Too much too young (Pan) p23.

[7]Springham, K. (1998). Time to Go Home Says Who?, (Scottish Human Rights Centre) p13.

[8]ibid. p10. Also see Article 12 in Scotland (1998) Curfew and crime – what young people think.

[9]McGallagly, J., Power, K., Littlewood, P. and Meikle, J. (1998). Evaluation of the Hamilton Child Safety Initiative, (The Scottish Office Central Research Unit).

[10]Stirling Council (1997). Are you getting enough...opportunity? p106.

[11]Home Office Research Study 140 (1995). Young People, victimisation and the police: British Crime Survey findings on experiences and attitudes of 12 to 15 tear olds (p57).

[12]McGallagly, J., Power, K., Littlewood, P. and Meikle, J. (1998). Evaluation of the Hamilton Child Safety Initiative, The Scottish Office Central Research Unit.

[13]ibid. p106.

[14]ibid.

[14a]ESRC (2000). Children 5-16 Research Briefing No. 16.

[14b]ESRC (2000). Children 5-16 Research Briefing No. 9.

[15]British Social Attitudes: the 12th report (1995) ed Roger Jowells (Dartmouth Publishing Company Limited).

[16]Valentine, G. (1996). 'Children should be seen and not heard..' Urban Geography (Vol. 17 No3 p205-220).

[17]Anderson, S. and Leitch, S. (1996). Main Findings from the 1993 Scottish Crime Survey (Scottish Office Central Research Unit).

[18]System 3 (1996). South Lanarkshire Community Survey Final Report, p9.

[19]Home Office Research Study 140 (1995). Young People, victimisation and the police: British Crime Survey findings on experiences and attitudes of 12 to 15 tear olds (p57).

[20]Hillman, M., Adams, J. and Whiteleg, J. (1990). One False Move...A Study of Children's Independent Mobility (London PSI Publishing) p111.

[21]Furedi, F. (1997). Culture of Fear (Cassell: London) p69.

[22]Blatchford, P.: The state of play in schools, in Woodhead, M. et al (ed) Making sense of social development (1999). London, Routledge (p101-2).

[23]Valentine, G. (1997). "Oh yes I can. Oh no you can't': Children and Parents' understanding of kids' competence to negotiate public space safely' (Antipode 29:1) p65-89.

[24]Home Office Research Study 140 (1995). Young People, victimisation and the police: British Crime Survey findings on experiences and attitudes of 12 to 15 tear olds (p25).

[25]Home Office Research Study 140 (1995). Young People, victimisation and the police: British Crime Survey findings on experiences and attitudes of 12 to 15 tear olds (pvi).

[26]Kathleen McCoy: www.parentsplace.com

[27]Furedi, F. (1997). Culture of Fear (Cassell: London) p23-24.

[28]Amis, D. Adolescence (1997). Risk and Independence: Preliminary Findings (Families For Freedom Pamphlet).

[29]ibid.

[30]ibid

[31]Shimamura, H. and Snell, C. (1996). They don't play out like they used to, do they? p35 (available from author).

[32]Mayer Hillman (1996) quoted in 'Stuck on the school run', Scotland on Sunday, November 3.

[33]The Scotsman, 3 December 1998.

[34]Community Care, 23-29 April 1998.

[35]Stirling Council (1997). Are you getting enough...opportunity? p106.

Scared of the Kids?

7   Adults

In Hamilton, the curfew was clearly targeted at young people and children who were out 'too late'. However, the justification for the need of a curfew was often related to adults in the area – either elderly adults who needed protection from teenagers, or irresponsible parents who allowed their children to wander the streets at night. In this way the Child Safety Initiative was never simply about children and consequently the effects of the initiative went much further than simply changing the behaviour of these young people. Adults as well as children had their attitudes challenged by the introduction of the curfew. Indeed it could be argued that the major impact of the child safety initiative was upon adults and the way they relate to the young people on their estates.

This chapter attempts to look in detail at the attitude of adults towards children and young people, both within Hillhouse and across the UK and argues that it is a change in the attitude and confidence of adults, rather than a change in the behaviour of young people themselves, which explains the insecurity felt by these adults. Examples of adults' exaggerated sense of insecurity are re-examined and the level of contact between adults and young people in Hillhouse studied to assess whether or not their is a growing distance between the generations. Neighbourhood wardens, secure accommodation and community policing are often heralded as the progressive alternative to a more hard-nosed criminal justice system. But this approach is questioned on the basis that it runs the risk of simply replacing the community with the police and reducing further the contact between young and old.

The causes of the declining confidence among adults is explored – both with reference to the specific case of Hillhouse and the fear of crime, but also more generally, with reference to research which looks at the wider isolation of adults from young people. The growing isolation of adults from young people, and elderly adults in particular, is both real and something that is sensed by adults who feel that the world has changed and with it the way adults must relate to and discipline children and young people.

Finally, as society places more guidelines down for adults about how they treat young people, an unfortunate side effect appears to be an increasing number of adults opting out of having any contact with these young people.

Not worth the risk

While the promotion and implementation of many safety initiatives like the Hamilton Curfew have come from politicians and the police, it would be a mistake to think that this is not something that has received support from the public. Indeed it is often complaints by adults about the behaviour of those young people around them that kick-start many of these initiatives.

Whether crime rates are rising or falling, there is a constant and growing fear of and concern about crime across society. The British Crime Survey notes that the level of concern by adults about crime is increasing and so is the level and types of crime reported to the police. Britain is fast becoming a surveillance society with more cameras per head than any other. These CCTV schemes have developed and extended beyond private establishments into the public realm and are now moving into estates with the general support of the people living in these areas. At the same time, the number of phone calls to the police about young people's 'nuisance behaviour' is rising and there is a demand for new laws and bodies to deal with antisocial behaviour.

For those people moving into their pensionable years, security appears more of a concern than ever before. A number of police forces across the UK have reported an increasing take-up of security measures in the home among the newer generation of elderly and, according to Age Concern, the generation now in their eighties is the last generation to prefer leaving their back door open and in some cases indiscriminately welcoming the company of youngsters.

Schemes aimed at helping adults to feel safer and so cope with their neighbours – like neighbourhood wardens and secure accommodation – while intended to bridge the gap between old and young, often appear to simply assist the growing distance between these generations and replace community contact with third party mediation. As Hillhouse community council chairman Joe Parfery noted earlier, by giving elderly adults more security locks and peep holes it has simply made them more worried about what lies outside.

Working with tenants groups who live in secured accommodation I have found that once security fences, guards etc. are established, they not only secure the building but become a further barrier between people within communities. One particular group who live in a tower block with a concierge system and security fencing spent a number of months putting pressure on their local councillor to build a safe play park within their compound. Yet by the time the council decided to look at the possibility of building the play park the group had changed their mind. On consideration, they realised that a safe play area would attract other children living outside their security fence compound. This was seen as a potential problem – as with children comes 'noise, graffiti and a lot of hassle'. The park was never built, while a play area half a mile away was dismantled after complaints by adults over looking it about the noise and misbehaviour of local children.

Rather than dealing with the noisy children who came to play in the park, both groups of tenants – despite their concern for the young people in their area – saw this as something that was simply 'not worth the risk'.

While the concierge security system around these flats, which included a number of CCTV cameras, was originally intended to ensure that no undesirable members of the community living outside the compound got access to the new flats. Increasingly, the tenants association has demanded the cameras be turned inwards so that the antisocial tenants and their children can be identified and dealt with by the security guards. Elsewhere in the UK, plans are being drawn up for US-style retirement villages, where the problem of children's nuisance behaviour is resolved by simply not having any children in these villages.

Community or policing

Within Hillhouse and the surrounding area, the level of contact between young people and local adults was assessed and compared to the level of contact these young people had with the police. What impact the introduction of the curfew had on the contact these teenagers had with adults was also looked at.

In a previous chapter it was noted that over two thirds of the young people living in Hillhouse who were interviewed and close to half of those teenagers living in the surrounding areas had had some contact with the police since the introduction of the curfew and that this level of contact was not unusual, with even more police attention during the summer months when young people are out later. A third of all these young people said that they had been moved on by the police because of complaints by adults. It was also noted earlier that the main justification given by the police for moving young people off the streets during the curfew was because they were loitering. In other words these young people were not committing any criminal offence but their presence was perceived as a threat by the police and some adults on the estate

To ascertain the level of contact regarding their behaviour, that young people in there areas had with adults when out at night, they were asked about who tells them off when they are out.

The vast majority of the young people had been spoken to about their behaviour while out at night on their estate. Half of these said that it was adults in their area who normally spoke to them, while almost a quarter said it was normally the police. When broken down into areas, it was found that over a third of the young people interviewed from Hillhouse were spoken to mainly by the police when they were out at night.

The adults who spoke to these young people about their behaviour were usually adults that were known to the young people. However, once these teenagers went out of their own streets into areas where they knew fewer adults, the likelihood of coming into contact with adults decreased and the level of contact with the police rose. While half of the young people explained that adults they didn't know had at some time in the last six months, spoken to them about their behaviour, over half said they had been spoken to by the police – this figure increased to over two thirds for those teenagers living in Hillhouse.

The majority of young people living in and around Hillhouse had more contact with adults than with the police regarding their behaviour when out at night. Much of this contact with adults, may well be 'negative' contact, where groups of teenagers are simply being told to move on. However, this is surely preferable to contacting the police and also suggests that these adults are not too frightened of young people to approach them. But it is still the case that for a third of the young people living in Hillhouse there was more contact with the police than there was with adults and once these teenagers moved to areas they were less well known, this level of contact with the police compared to adults increased dramatically.

Distant relations

The adults who were spoken to in this survey, in Hillhouse and Hamilton, were generally in support of the curfew. Although none of these adults had been attacked or threatened by the teenagers on the estate they were all aware that 'the streets aren't safe' and that it wasn't a place for children'.

The Scottish Office research in Hillhouse found that almost two thirds of adults spoken to had felt unsafe while out on the streets and three quarters said they found the presence of groups of young people threatening.[1] This suggests that the fear of young people is not simply felt by the elderly on the estate but is more common across the age range. Alcohol and drugs, as well as a lack of activities, were blamed for the crime in the area and there had been a daytime mugging recently which was mentioned by a number of those interviewed. Many of these adults complained of the 'bad bits' on the estate and the young men who were unemployed and hung about doing nothing. However, where as the concern about drugs and drink may be relevant for some sections of those living in Hillhouse, regarding the young people picked up by the police during the curfew it was found that 'relatively few children were suspected of having drink, drugs or solvents'.[2] This does not prove that young people under 16 don't drink or take drugs, but does suggest the level of this 'problem' felt by adults may well be exaggerated.

The fear of 'antisocial' young people felt by the adults in Hillhouse is not unusual to this area, indeed the fear of crime is widespread. However this fear is also something adults feel *for* children and young people. A survey by Barnardo's found that three in five adults think childhood today is worse than it was when they were children. The main reasons given for this, from a prompted list, are the 'level of crime' and 'availability of drugs'.[3] More than nine out of ten of these adults agreed that the level of violence in British society is increasing and a similar figure felt that 'children witness more crime these days'.[4]

In Hillhouse the danger that children faced while out at night was not unusual or exceptional. Some of those interviewed had been in fights or been chased but they generally felt safe when out at night, while there was no evidence of there being any crime that had affected the primary aged children's safety before or during the curfew. Similarly for the adults on the estate, while there was a problem with graffiti that was noted by the Citizens' Jury and drinking by unemployed men made them uncomfortable, there was no general threat to these adults and as has been noted earlier – by both Chief Superintendent Campbell Thomson and Linda Martin of Strathclyde Elderly Forum – there is a stubborn perception among older people that they are likely to become victims of crime, when the opposite is true.

Almost half of the adults questioned in Hillhouse said they felt safer in the first six months of the Child Safety Initiative,[5] partly because the streets were quieter.[6] As one young person noted in the Scottish Office survey, 'It makes older people feel safer "cos we're not about"'.[7] Complaints to the police fell during this period,[8] possibly because there were fewer young people out at night or because the police were more active in moving young people before they had a chance of becoming a 'nuisance' or frightening an adult into phoning the police. (Although it is worth noting that the control area in the Scottish Office survey also had a fall in complaints to the police – this, it is suggested could be because of a change in the number of people going out in this area as well, or because less attention to recording youth related incidents was given in the control area compared to the curfewed area).

The perception that many of the adults spoken to had, that there was a problem of people being out of control either because of drink or drugs, appears to influence their perception of young people generally and affects the extent to which they are prepared to deal with young people who are out at night – especially those young people who they do not know. Similarly, perceptions of crime and violence in society – despite limited personal experience of this – is a concern that also influences their image of people on their estate.

In Chapter 1 it was noted that the fear of crime is often a reflection of fear generated by wider social changes, rather than a reflection of an increase in crime itself. In discussion with adults in Hamilton town centre, the issue of how times have changed emerged in relation to the sense of distance many older people have in relating to other people within their community. An often expressed sentiment, within these discussions, was the feeling that local people and young people in particular, could not be trusted anymore. Most of these adults recognise that 'there have always been bad kids from bad families', but as a 67 year old grand-mother explained, 'In the past you knew who the bad ones were, but you also knew that the rest were good kids'. This she contrasts to, 'Today', where, 'you still know who the bad families are but I guess I just don't know if the rest of them are OK or not'.

A lack of knowledge of, contact with and trust of the young people and families living close by, has resulted in the concern about the 'bad families' and 'bad kids' being more generalised and exaggerated. Rather than seeing bad families and bad kids as the exception, there is a concern that it is no longer clear who can be trusted and who cannot. The antisocial activities of some young people and their families now express something more profound to these adults – who rather than seeing acts of individual vandalism and rowdiness, as the petty acts they are, see society, and the young people around them as being generally out of control. These petty antisocial acts therefore take on an importance that in the past they would not have, and which they do not deserve.

This lack of trust, is not simply a matter of contact between individuals, but also a loss of a sense of group norms. Mrs Boyle, who has lived in Hamilton since 1940, explained how in her youth 'everybody' went to the dances and 'you felt like you knew everyone'. This compares with today, where it was felt that, 'everybody does their own thing' and 'people seem to come and go' so that you 'never know who's who'.

Mrs Boyle clearly didn't know everyone in Hamilton in the past, but nevertheless had a sense of commonality which meant that she felt more trusting and secure in her relationships with people she met.

A lack of a sense of commonality today often means that rather than trust between people being the norm, and suspicion something reserved for the 'bad families' or 'outsiders', suspicion has become the norm. Within this climate it is more difficult for people to differentiate between the 'good' and 'bad' families and children on their estate, who are subsequently seen as 'one of them' rather than 'one of us'.

Concern for the kids

Adults in Hillhouse like those interviewed by Barnardo's, are not only concerned about their own safety, but also with the safety of young people themselves. Indeed a key reason given by adults in Hillhouse for there support of the Child Safety Initiative, was that it would protect children and young people from the dangers they faced on the street. However it appears that for many adults, making contact with young people who they no longer feel they can relate to, means they are no longer prepared to do anything themselves to regulate their behaviour or to ensure their safety. One of the groups of adults interviewed in the Scottish Office report, explained that they felt that there was a 'general lack of respect for adults and elderly people',[9] but at some level this respect must be earned – something that is unlikely to happen from behind closed doors.

In discussion with elderly adults in Hamilton, I found that while there was a large degree of support for the curfew – generated by a feeling that some young people were out of control – there was also a genuine concern for young people and a belief that there should be more resources made available for developing youth clubs. However this desire for more centres for young people, in part, reflects a lack of confidence that many adults have today about how to deal with children and teenagers themselves, as well as a belief that the streets are no longer safe places for them to play. In this respect a call for more resources can be seen in part as a way for many adults to avoid the responsibility of dealing with young people.

The insecurity felt by adults often leads to a lack of tolerance of young people and means that unless child and youth facilities are built well away from any residential area, there will be a conflict – with complaints from local people about noise, swearing, fighting, drinking etc. Facilities that are built, to take young people away from complaining adults will clearly do nothing to overcome the divisions that exist between the generations. Indeed by separating young people from the rest of the community, it is likely that they will become even more alien and alienated from many adults.

Unconfident adults

Research with elderly people in England entitled 'Ageing in an Alien World', highlights some of the issues raised above regarding the sense of fear felt by many older adults. This work by Furedi and Brown, which involved in-depth interviews with adults over 60, found that an intense feeling of vulnerability has become a normal feature of ageing. The key factor affecting this sense of vulnerability was isolation from social and family networks. An isolation made worse by a feeling that many elderly people had that they were out of touch with an increasingly unfamiliar world inherited by young people. The result was that for many elderly adults a lack of confidence had developed that made them feel unable to negotiate relationships with children and young people.[10]

How the process of ageing is bound up with disconnection from key family and community networks is addressed in this research and importantly, the issue of fear and insecurity is examined not by narrowly looking at what these adults are afraid of, but rather by looking at the psychological impact which the 'experience of irrelevance' has on their lives.[11] This sense of irrelevance was such that many of those interviewed were no longer prepared to give advice to young people either because they said 'they won't listen', or because 'they know more than me'.

The day to day contact between grandparents and grandchildren in this study was small, while contact was almost nonexistent with any young people outside the family. The authors noted that 'there is no foundation in existence for intergenerational contact for those who do not have grandchildren'.[12] Two significant relationships between the experience of isolation and the intense consciousness of vulnerability were identified. Firstly, the 'Lack of contact and familiarity with the ways of the young tends to inflate the sense of difference between the generations'. One aspect of this process is that many elderly people feel inadequate about the task of rearing or educating children, and in some cases, 'a lack of familiarity with the ways of the younger generation creates a disposition towards accepting negative images of the young'. Secondly, the 'Feeling of irrelevance and lack of familiarity with the ways of the young helps to accelerate the loss of confidence that comes with ageing', which leads to caution and distrust dominating elderly people's perception of youth.[13]

A self-reinforcing trend is identified here which applies to Hamilton, whereby cautious behaviour serves to isolate the elderly from new social networks and this in turn exacerbates feelings of vulnerability.

A surprising finding of this research, was that the older elderly people interviewed – those over 80 – felt less isolated and fearful than their younger 60 something neighbours. A possible explanation for this given by Furedi and Brown is that the octogenarian had grown up during the Second World War, a period of greater communal solidarity and collective experience that made them more trusting of succeeding generations. Whereas the younger elderly were more likely to have experienced the fragmentary impact of the weakening of family networks and possibly have directly experienced wider changes in the workplace and in political and social life generally. All of which could have added to the sense of change that helped undermine their confidence and consequently increase their sense of distance from young people.

These adults like the elderly people interviewed in Hamilton, believe that things have fundamentally changed today. Young people no longer enter similar jobs to ones they had and often face periods of unemployment which they did not; young people have more education, have access to more technology and generally consume much more than past generations. The lives of young people it is felt, are less stable and predictable, having little relevance to older people's experiences. While some of these changes are more significant than others, it is not only the social institutions and life experiences of these adults that are perceived to have changed, but also the intimate aspects of family life such as child rearing.

Many of the elderly people interviewed by Furedi and Brown, believed that their parenting skills had become redundant – especially those aspects of parenting related to discipline. Parents were seen as being much less strict today – partly because they had to work, while teachers were seen to 'want to be on the same level as the kids'. Adults using their authority with children was no longer seen as a matter of common sense as it was when they were young. For example smacking, it was recognised, was no longer looked upon as a straightforward aspect of disciplining children and is seen by some as damaging.

Allowing children to go out and play, was also something that these elderly adults realised was no longer an uncomplicated process. Games that they once played are today seen as risky; the distance from home travelled by children is now far less than previously; and there is an awareness that parents are much more concerned about their children's safety generally – something they did not experience as children or as parents.

The elderly adults in Furedi and Browns survey were keen for children to mix within the community, but this was confused by a recognition that perhaps times had changed and children should no longer do the things they used to. Activities like carol singing around the estate, were seen as 'nice' and elderly people enjoyed them, but they were also seen as problematic because they encouraged young people to go to strangers' houses. Similarly, playing in the fields away from the estate – something many of the adults interviewed did as children – was seen as good in a sense of getting out and having fun – but was now seen as perhaps something that should not happen because of possible abductions.

Many of these adults realised that they were perceived by children in their area as strangers. Most of them wanted to talk to these young people but were unsure whether they should – either because it may scare the child; be something that was unwelcome from parents; be misinterpreted by onlookers; or simply because it was irresponsible of them to talk to children because they were strangers.

These apprehensions about child rearing could help to undermine the role that elderly adults play in childcare within the family, and more certainly are raising doubts in their minds about how to relate to children who they come across on their estate. Establishing boundaries of both discipline and safety are increasingly seen as problematic for these adults.

Strange adults or adults as strangers

One of the outcomes of the growing isolation and the greater sense of alienation that elderly adults have from young people, is that they are more prone to accept the idea that children need greater protection from dangers within their communities. Activities that were the norm when they were children and parents, are seen as being more dangerous today and there is an awareness that talking to children may no longer be the right thing to do. The feeling and often the reality of being a stranger to children felt by many adults, is complicated by the sense of risk and fear surrounding children and the growing image of adults as 'potential abusers' rather than as carers of children.

As a child, the occasional 'stranger danger' campaign I had at school, concentrated on 'strange men', men who did something that was unusual and suspicious. These 'strange men' normally tried to take you away somewhere, 'to see some puppies' or simply offered you a lift, and we were taught – 'Never to go off with someone you don't know'. Today the message taught in schools is more basic – 'Don't talk to strangers'.

Here all unknown adults are depicted as potentially dangerous and are to be avoided. This message is not only something that children are aware of – but especially with the high publicity given to paedophile cases by the media, increasing security in schools, and numerous safety campaigns – is something that adults and men in particular are highly sensitive of. This sensitivity to the 'potentially abusive' relationships that can occur between adults and children, coupled with the broader uncertainty about boundaries and discipline regarding young people, has resulted in men across the UK becoming paranoid about approaching children.

The 'Euromale' study mentioned in Chapter 2 indicates how men who enjoy the company of children are treated with suspicion. Soon after this report came out in the press, a radio debate on the subject was flooded with calls from men worried about whether or not they should approach young children anymore. One caller explained a dilemma of a young girl playing next to a river, unable to approach the young girl – because of what people might think – but unable to leave her, in case she fell in, this man felt he could only watch from a distance for 15 minutes to make sure she was OK. Another caller explained that after strange looks from people when he spoke to some children playing in a park near his home, he had decided not to talk to young people anymore except when he is at church with other adults around him, where his actions would not be misinterpreted. Furedi and Brown found an 82 year old man who after buying some sweets at his corner shop offered one to a young girl who came into the shop with her grandmother. The look of horror on the girls face had upset the old man but he praised her anyway, saying, 'you're right, you shouldn't take sweeties off strangers', but as he explained later, 'it made me feel really dirty'.

It appears that elderly adults and indeed men generally are becoming increasingly sensitive to the potentially negative interpretation of their involvement with young children. While some – especially the younger elderly see these new concerns as a necessary precaution in more dangerous times. Other adults – often the octogenarians, are more bewildered by the lack of trust expressed by adults towards one another. Both these sentiments of bewilderment or acceptance of the need to keep one's distance from children are undermining further the confidence of these adults in dealing with children and young people.

Disturbing discipline

An ex-teacher of 30 years, writing in Glasgow's Evening Times, explained that,

> As a parent and grandparent I endorse the policy which dictates: No talking to strangers...accepting lifts in cars...walking by yourself in parks or isolated places! But we seem near a point where children are programmed to TRUST no one. The result is that many well intentioned adults are terrified of being seen trying to make contact with children. Is it any wonder the generation gap widens by the minute?[14]

The title of this article was, 'My shame over lack of courage', and the author

Catherine McGuinness explained how she had walked past a group of teenagers who were dropping litter in the park, and had said nothing. As well as being aware that approaching children was for many adults more difficult today because children had been 'programmed to trust no one', the ex-teacher explained how she had 'chickened out' of challenging these young people and had to ask herself, 'Had I joined the adults who have opted out of civic responsibility', and 'Have adults become so frightened of the younger generation they're prepared to look the other way rather than tangle with them?'.

For a teacher of 30 years, a parent and grandparent Mrs McGuinness had been surprised that she had opted out of any attempt at disciplining these young people. 'What happened,' she asked herself, 'Surely I could have coped with abuse?' But the question of disciplining children or even talking to young people has become fraught with problems and anxieties for many adults. This has not simply been caused by the sense of risk and danger surrounding children, and the sense of suspicion surrounding adults in their dealings with children, but also by the general problematisation of discipline itself.

Anti-smacking campaigns question whether adults should use any force when dealing with young people, this is often situated within the question of children's rights, as is the debate about discipline in schools and the amount of force that should be used by teachers.

Smacking has become associated by those who argue against its use, as a form of humiliation or abuse with some campaigners stating that, 'all action to cause physical pain to a child, from the little tap to the fatal beating is on one continuum of violence'.[15] Others compare the use of 'violence' against children to that which is carried out by men against women and underlying most discussions about smacking, is a concern that by hitting children, parents are somehow helping to perpetuate the violent society in which we live. A violence that is transferred from generation to generation, as children's rights campaigner Penelope Leach explained, 'Physical punishment is one of many parenting behaviours that is readily passed from one generation to the next'.[16]

The level of concern about smacking was illustrated recently in Scotland when a school teacher smacked his own child in a dentist's waiting room and ended up in court. The end result for this parent was that he avoided a prison sentence, but was struck off the register of teachers and will no longer be able to teach.

Within schools and children's homes, the issue of disciplining children has been complicated by the interpretation of the Children Act 1989. As Head Teacher Bernard Allen explained, 'In the early 1990s the emphasis was on giving power to children, at the expense of the adults who looked after them. A view prevailed that the only way to protect children from abusive adults was to empower children against all adults'.[17]

Allen explains how guidance on permissible force, like that introduced in children's homes, was widely interpreted as preventing staff from taking action to confront difficult behaviour, and giving power to children who misbehave. In this climate he argues, staff would often attempt to avoid a confrontational situation even if it was appropriate to intervene to maintain discipline. But as he points out, 'Unfortunately, giving children power does not prevent them from being vulnerable and the power to reject all adult authority actually places them at an increased risk of harm'.[18]

The consequence that Allen highlights, of the Children Act 1989 – Section 42 which addressed child protection, was that enthusiastic child protection officers began to see issues of assault and unlawful restrictions of liberty everywhere and in some local authorities, inspectors were forced to agonise over issues which 'most reasonable parents would see as common sense'.

The Children Act was also interpreted as significantly reducing the authority of teachers in schools, as Hewett and Arnett argue, the Act meant staff 'can no longer speak to a child in a way that says: "do as I say or I will make you do it"'.[19] The concern about not only disciplining children but also of simply touching them, was raised as an issue by the Scottish Secondary Teachers' Association in 1996. The then acting general secretary, Craig Duncan explained that, 'We have now got to the stage in this country where, if a teacher in an infant class gave a child who fell in the playground a hug, that teacher could technically be prosecuted for assault'.[20]

This may be unlikely, but the union felt it necessary to issue guidelines advising their members not to touch children whenever possible and to avoid being alone with either pupils or parents.

Since this statement, some guidelines regarding disciplining children have changed. In England and Wales, the 1997 Guidance (Laming) relating to children's homes 'reminded' staff that they should not assume they are powerless for example if a young person wants to go out against the advice of staff. Instead they should, 'act as a reasonable parent would in the same situation, and should take account of whether allowing the child to go out could place him or her at risk of harm'. In schools, recent guidance from the Department of Education and Employment has also spelled out that teachers will have a clear legal right to use reasonable force under Section 550A of the Education Act 1996 (DfEE, 1996).

Whatever these guidelines spell out, the very process of developing laws and guidance on how teachers and care workers discipline children, has helped to undermine staff confidence in their own ability to deal with young people. As Simon Knight, a Lanarkshire based youth and social worker explained in relation to the increasing number of regulations within children's homes, 'With detailed procedures for every aspect of a child's life, care workers' spontaneous decision making will be constrained and with it their authority and confidence'.[21]

While there have always been rules and guidelines within schools and care establishments regarding discipline, the point being made by Knight is that the numerous new codes of conduct being developed are increasingly questioning the authority of the adult in charge who must now consult his handbook of disciplinary procedure to ensure he or she is not over-stepping the mark of appropriate behaviour. Many of these new rules and regulations appear to be based on the assumption that adults cannot and should not trust their own judgement and methods of discipline. As Knight remarks, 'If adults don't exhibit trust in themselves and each other, what are the messages we are sending out to tomorrow's adults?'.[22]

Proceduralised parenting

It is unlikely that the many changes regarding the disciplining of children within schools and institutions and the concern about smacking and other aspects of parenting have not had an impact on parents and adults more generally, in the dealings with children and young people. Indeed, today the idea that 'reasonable parents' can simply use their 'common sense' when disciplining and looking after their children is no longer taken for granted. The Laming guidance discussed above, regarding care workers preventing young people from going out at night, advised that staff should 'act as a reasonable parent would in the same situation'. But what is reasonable? Rather than allowing this decision to be made by parents themselves there is a trend to legislate for or at least attempt to educate parents about the 'reasonable' way to discipline their children.

In 1999, Conservative council leader Mike Brundle, prevented his daughter from going out of the house by holding her wrists. Eventually, 15 year old Georgina did go out and reported her father to the police for assault. Mr Brundle was subsequently held in a police cell for a number of hours and his daughter Georgina went into temporary foster care. This act of restraint was clearly not seen as one that should be undertaken by a 'reasonable parent'.

Whether one agrees with the methods used by Brundle or not, what this example indicates is the extent to which parenting and the disciplining of children by parents has started to involve outside agencies. Bad parenting has become the focus of a growing number and variety of government and local government departments. This concern about and focus on parenting and the welfare of the child involves not only agencies like the police and social work, but incorporates the helplines for children and comes at a time when there is a broad move to introduce parenting classes across the country.

In some cases this intervention may have helped parents and children, but the climate of 'support' being offered to both parents and children from professionals, may lead to adults questioning their own right and ability to discipline and look after their children.

In discussion with parents groups in Scotland, it has become the norm to hear of children threatening their parents with a phone call to ChildLine. One group of lone parents explained that their primary school children sing a song, 'If your mammy's getting angry and she's going to skelp your bum, ring 0800 double one double one' – the Childline number.

Carol Baisden who works for Parentline, a helpline set up for parents believes that, 'discipline has become the touchy subject'[23], with on average at least a third of the calls received by Parentline being related to matters about discipline.

One of the issues raised by parents today, is that they never know what other people will think of them if they try to discipline or smack their child in public. The lack of consensus around this subject and the connection made by some between smacking and abuse, helps to make parents feel as if they need official backing before chastising their child.

If the question of disciplining children is more complicated for parents today, then for grandparents and other adults in the community it must be even more problematic – even for ex-teachers like Catherine McGuinness.

For the parents of children living in Hillhouse, the curfew, while being welcomed by many, brought with it new concerns and a new external discipline to ensure they act responsibly.

Many of the children believed that they had to come home earlier during the curfew, because their parents were worried that they would come into contact with the police. Further research is needed with parents to assess this response, but it is not surprising that some parents – even though their children were coming home before 7.30pm – would be concerned about their children being labelled as 'bad kids', or even themselves being labelled as bad parents.

The CSI campaign highlighted the dangers that young children face on the streets at night, as well as raising the issue of 'irresponsible parents' allowing their 'bad children' to wander the streets at night – despite little evidence of these dangers, or evidence that many children were out late at night. This focus on children's night time activities is likely to have increased the pressure on parents – many of whom are already heavily involved with their children's night time activities – to be even more conscious of being seen to be 'good parents'. There is also the danger that those parents who continue to allow their children to simply 'go out and play' – i.e. something that parents have been doing for decades – will increasingly be labelled by other parents as irresponsible. Equally those children allowed to wander around their estate may be seen as bad or even dangerous.

Summary

The initial focus for the research in Hamilton, was the impact of the Child Safety Initiative on children and young people. However, there was always a recognition while undertaking this research, that the role of adults and their insecurities where very important to acquire a more all-round picture of the relationships between people within the targeted estates. More research is needed with adults in Hillhouse and estates like it, to gain a more specific and focused assessment of the sentiment of adults living on working class estates in Scotland. However, there was enough information gained from the adults spoken to on the estate, in Hamilton, via press interviews and the questionnaire answers given by the children in and around Hillhouse to gain some insights into their thoughts and actions. This coupled with wider research on the relationship between young people and adults gives a picture of generations living very much apart.

The insecurities and lack of surety felt by many adults in relating to young people is leading to a growing acceptance that the role of looking after these children is no longer theirs. As Aminatta Forna remarked in the parenting section of the *Guardian*, 'increasingly, few of us can remember the last time we told off a child not our own'.[24] The logical outcome of this approach, is that on estates like Hillhouse the number and level of contacts between adults and young people will decline and the sense of collective responsibility for the safety and well being of children is lost.

The confusion over disciplining children and the elevated sense of risk and safety that surrounds them has helped to undermine the confidence of adults in their dealings with young people and is something that professionals working in this area must be highly sensitive of. As by trying to regulate these relationships and attempting to institutionalise 'correct' ways of dealing with children, adults' spontaneous role in caring for children is being further undermined.

The high level of support by adults across Hamilton for the introduction of the curfew is indicative of the general level of insecurity felt by adults, coupled with the sense of isolation from and confusion over dealings with young people. However, this initiative does nothing to bring the generations closer together, indeed the opposite result is more likely – with the role of talking to and disciplining young people who hang about the streets at night increasingly becoming the job of the police.

New initiatives are already being developed under the New Deal which could supplement the curfew and further institutionalise this regulation of young people within public space. One such initiative is the nation-wide warden scheme, which it is hoped will create up to three times as many wardens as their are police, to patrol council and housing association estates. The result of this kind of scheme will be to create an almost permanent concierge type estate, where adults no longer need relate to any young person directly, but can take all their complaints to their own personal security guard.

The Scottish Office CSI report notes that there has been an increase in the number of people who will avoid certain areas within the Hillhouse estate, since the introduction of the curfew and explains that this may be because of the 'greatly heightened awareness of risk following intense media coverage of the Hamilton Child Safety Initiative'.[25] However, while the media attention no doubt raised the profile of the curfew, the very basis of this initiative was that the streets needed more police because children and young people were not safe on them and adults were not safe from the bad behaviour of these young people. It is perhaps unsurprising then that adults' perception of the dangers on their estate increased. The likely outcome of this is that those adults who were already frightened of young people who hang about in groups will be even more aware of the dangers they represent, while the more active adults who try to deal with young people themselves will be deactivated and come to rely on the police.

Study Guide

A. Critically discuss the various explanations for the apparent 'generation gap' today. It appears to be the case that there is a level of unsureness amongst adults in the UK about how to relate to young people. Where possible discuss with a number of elderly adults their perceptions of young people today and assess the extent to which adults have become 'scared of the kids'.

B. Is the fear of crime a justified concern amongst adults today?

Consider when the fear of crime became an issue, the difficulties with trying to measure 'fear' and the extent to which this fear can be understood as part of a wider culture of fear.

C. What are the potential advantages and disadvantages of 'intergenerational practices' that attempt to bring young and old together?

Consider the positive impact these initiatives can have but also the potential they may have for preventing spontaneous relationships developing between the generations.

D. Consider what intergenerational projects could be of benefit in giving older adults a role with young people today.

Draw up an intergenerational project proposal outlining the aims of the project and the way it will assist the development of the community.

Useful Reading

A.

1. *Freedom's Orphans: Raising youth in a changing world* by Julia Margo et al. The Executive Summary of this book is available online via the Institute for Public Policy Research.

2. 'The roots of 'paedophobia'' by Stuart Waiton and Simon Knight in *Scottish Youth Issues Journal*, Issue 9, 98-94 (2007). A summary of this is available online.

3. 'Do youth have a future?' by Stuart Waiton in *Concept: The Journal of Contemporary Community Education Practice Theory.*

B.

1. 'The Frequency of the Fear of Crime' by S. Farrall and D. Gadd, *British Journal of Criminology*, Vol. 44, 127-132 (2004).

2. *Victims of Crime: A new deal* by M. Maguire and J. Pointing. See Jock Young's chapter on 'Risk of crime and fear of crime: a realist critique of survey-based assumptions'.

3. 'Questioning the Measurement of the "Fear of Crime": Findings from a Major Methodological Study' by S. Farrall, J. Bannister, J. Ditton and E. Gilchrist, *British Journal of Criminology*, Vol. 37, No. 4, pp. 658-6.

4. *Culture of Fear* by Frank Furedi.

5. *The Culture of Fear* by Barry Glassner.

6. *A Review of the Scientifically Evaluated Good Practices for Reducing Feelings of Insecurity or Fear of Crime in the EU Member States.* Published by the European Crime Prevention Network.
Available online.

C. 1. 'Can Intergenerational Practice Offer a Way of Limiting Anti-social Behaviour and Fear of Crime' by Stephen Moore and Elaine Statham in *The Howard Journal of Criminal Justice*, Vol. 5, Issue 5, 468-484 (2006).

2. *Young and Old Meeting Together: Meeting Community Needs through Intergenerational Partnerships* by Tess Scannell and Angela Roberts.
Available online.

3. *Intergenerational Relations and Practice in the Development of Sustainable Communities* by Rachel Pain.

4. Also see the Centre for Intergenerational Practice homepage.

Notes

[1]McGallagly, J., Power, K., Littlewood, .P and Meikle, J. (1998). Evaluation of the Hamilton Child Safety Initiative, (The Scottish Office Central Research Unit) p56/7.

[2]ibid p18.

[3]The facts of Life: Barnardo's, p23.

[4]ibid p24.

[5]McGallagly, J., Power, K., Littlewood, P. and Meikle, J. (1998). Evaluation of the Hamilton Child Safety Initiative, (The Scottish Office Central Research Unit) p59.

[6]ibid.

[7]ibid p63.

[8]ibid p70.

[9]ibid p45.

[10]ibid p61.

[11]Furedi, F. and Brown, T. (1997). Disconnected: Ageing in an Alien World, (Reconnecting).

[12]ibid.

[13]ibid p12.

[14]Catherine McGuinness: Evening Times: Wed 15 Jan 1997).

[15]From 'Children Are People Too, The Case Against Physical Punishment' Peter Newell (EPOCH), (LondonBedford Square Press) 1989.

[16]Leach, P.: Physical punishment of children in the home (National Children's Bureau No. 166).

[17]Allen, B 'New guidance on the use of reasonable force in schools 1998' (British Journal of Special Education Vol 25 No.4 Dec 1998).

[18]ibid.

[19]ibid p187

[20]The Scotsman, 30 October 1996.

[21]The Scotsman 17 December 1997.

[22]The Guardian 27 January 1999.

[23]The Guardian 27 January 1999.

[24]McGallagly, J., Power, K., Littlewood, P. and Meikle, J. (1998). Evaluation of the Hamilton Child Safety Initiative, (The Scottish Office Central Research Unit) p.58.

Scared of the Kids?

8   Summary

The contemporary image of young people as we enter the 21st century has never been worse, with talk of a 'yob culture' coming from all sides of the political spectrum – a yob culture that feeds off a 'culture of violence'. Indeed it often appears that the best young people can hope for in their portrayal by the New Labour government and the media is to be labelled as victims unable to cope with the pressures of life, rather than as villains who are destroying it.

The passion felt by the government and local authorities to stamp out this yobbishness, and the measures they are prepared to go to is reflected well, most recently, by Tony Blair's call for on the spot £100 fines for 'louts' who kick your door or shout obscenities at night: The type of passion once reserved for curtain twitching old ladies being adopted by a prime minister who, through these fines is handing over the power of judge, jury and executioner to the local constabulary.

Despite a recognition by both the police and the government that the fear felt by many adults towards young people is exaggerated, new crime and safety initiatives are being developed almost daily by police forces, local authorities, schools and voluntary organisations, which regulate relations between the two groups.

Talk of rights and responsibilities by New Labour within the context of local communities focuses almost exclusively on responsibilities. Rights of individuals being granted only if they prove they are responsible citizens. Responsibility, something that needs to be actively taken by individuals, is today being forced on people from above. However, what you are expected to take responsibility for is far less than ever before. Any sense that people can take responsibility for and deal with children and young people within their communities has been lost and indeed discouraged. Instead adults are encouraged to passively phone the police to ensure their new 'right to a quiet life' is maintained. Even parents are having the responsibility of deciding the bed time of their children forced upon them by initiatives like the curfew.

The image of local people, held by the government and institutionalised through safety initiatives, is one of weak insecure victims who cannot cope with the daily grind of life without the support of an outside agency. Within this framework, everybody needs protection from everybody else; the elderly need to be protected from teenagers; teenagers need to be protected from one another; and children need to be protected from everybody – even from their own irresponsible parents.

The government's negative image of out of control youth destroying the community, mixed with the belief that we are all fragile individuals, results in a constant attempt to regulate the interactions between people within society – and particularly within public space. By attempting to reconstruct a polite civil society in this way, the most petty aspects of young people's behaviour are castigated and criminalised and the development of communities through developing relationships of individuals within them is undermined.

Ultimately, the level of interference taking place between people in communities – like the Hamilton Curfew – reflects a lack of trust by the government and local authorities in local people. Unfortunately, the culture of fear in which we live has affected all sections of society and the opposition to this increasing diminishment of public space and criminalisation of young people is minimal. While the most passive insecure instincts of people are held up as proof that 'something needs to be done', measures are developed that encourage this passivity and reinforce the fear felt by many adults towards young people.

Part of this focus upon crime and safety by New Labour is an attempt not only to deal with the perceived problem of the yob culture, but also to connect with people and to re-establish public support for state institutions – a problem recognised by sociologist Anthony Giddens, a key intellectual influence on New Labour, who argues that the state in modern society has become, 'inadequate in the provision of public goods, social protection and civic order'. For much of the state sector, the move towards creating civic order through individual protection is already well established.

People are strange – when you're a stranger

Today, within a more atomised and distant society – where few of the post war political and social institutions have any meaning, and 'ways of doing things' in the family or the community have changed – people feel more isolated from those around them. The fear that this creates often takes the form of fear of crime and especially fear of violent crime – muggings of old ladies, or paedophile attacks on children. Safety initiatives, which take this fear at face value and act upon it, can only encourage a greater sense of insecurity and fear within communities. The preventative approach to crime – like the creation of a paedophile register, or the development of schools that resemble prison camps, and streets monitored by CCTV – pushed by government, education authorities and the police give out the clear message: You are not safe in public, the public themselves – cannot be trusted – We are all at risk from one another!

Child safety and the introduction of various child safety initiatives – of which the curfew is but one – is a national preoccupation. A preoccupation which is helping to create an overprotected generation of children and is also helping to further alienate adults, particularly men, from children, who they feel they can no longer even approach.

Through this process, society is encouraging adults and children to remain strangers. The outcome being that people remain strange to one another.

A trip to safety

Travelling to a recent National Association of Headmasters Union of Women Teachers (NASUWT) conference on 'Discipline in Schools', I was handed a Railtrack leaflet about Personal Security. 'Personal Security has always been your number one priority at our stations', it told me, adding, 'We continue to make Waverley Station a safer place to be'. The leaflet noted that, with: security staff on the station day and night; a Duty Station Manager on the station 24 hours a day; British Transport Police patrolling the station at all times; and 16 colour CCTV cameras monitoring station activity around the clock – these measures were proving to be successful and 94% of Waverley Station users, the leaflet explained, now felt safe. Having experienced no 'personal security' problems in my ten years of travelling by train from Glasgow to Edinburgh, I had never considered Waverley Station a dangerous place – but now I had the added security of knowing that all my fellow travellers were being monitored by CCTV and 24 hour wardens.

At the NASUWT conference I was presented with the latest evidence of violence by children against teachers, and wondered whether they would appreciate Railtrack's assistance with their personal security. Zero tolerance of violence by children against teachers was called for, and lawyers speaking at the conference explained how teachers need the law to protect them against assault in the classroom. Nigel de Gruchy, NASUWT General Secretary, explained that the main reason 6th formers were no longer considering teaching as a profession, was because of their concern about a lack of discipline, from what de Gruchy described as the often drugged-up 'unteachable' kids.

Whether it be unions, politicians or even transport organisations, the one sure way these varied organisations feel they can relate to their members, voters or customers – is through a discussion about safety. However while Railtrack may feel they have helped to make people safe, attempting to overcome the insecurity people feel today by increased safety measures can have the opposite effect.

In Glasgow, Scottish Office research looking at the impact of the introduction of CCTV across the city, has found that not only has crime not fallen, but neither has the fear of crime. Jason Ditton, professor of criminology at Sheffield University, who led the research, explained that while most people questioned before the introduction of CCTV in Glasgow said they would feel safer with it in place, after one year of the CCTV surveillance, most said they did not feel safer and more people said they would avoid the city centre.[1] This research backs up similar findings by research in Wales, and questions the idea that people feel safer when CCTV schemes are established.

Despite this research the government plans to extend the surveillance of cities with £170 million more for CCTV across the UK. The Scottish Executive which received the report said it would continue with its own extension of cameras in Scotland.

Part of the extension of CCTV surveillance in the UK is to take place not in city centres but in inner-city housing areas. In Scotland, the Easterhouse estate, the first peripheral housing estate to receive cameras is now to receive a further 15 cameras as part of the Community Safety Strategy. Discussing this development, Superintendent Donald Fraser, explained that not only were these cameras proving useful in the fight against crime, but that, 'it has also contributed very significantly in achieving a reduction in the incidents of group disorder'.[2]

Low level disorder like constant talking and rudeness, rather than extremes of violence, was something MSP Nicola Sturgeon and many of the teachers at the NASUWT conference felt was the main problem with children in their schools. The answer offered by the NASUWT for this bad behaviour, was more support from special educationalists and social workers as well as exclusion from school. However as Alan McLean, principle psychologist in northeast Glasgow, explained at the same conference, 'In terms of resources', to look after difficult young people, 'we've never had it so good'. Elaborating on the point he said that compared to 25 years ago when there were few behaviour units and no support staff, today teachers 'have a huge army of specialists', to help them. One of the effects of this new army of specialists, McLean feels, is that teachers have learned to pass on discipline problems to senior management and to outside agencies. 'Modern structures unwittingly deskill teachers,' he argued, 'and encourage this transfer of ownership and responsibility.'

McLean explained that not only was there no research evidence that discipline was getting worse, but added that in some schools as many as 10% of children had already been removed from mainstream education. Which begs the question - Where do we stop?[3]

The curfew

The behaviour of young people is under more scrutiny today than ever before, and it appears, the intolerance of adults of the 'nuisance' behaviour of young people is also greater than ever. Like the question posed by Alan McLean about the exclusion of young people from schools, the same question must be asked about our attitude towards regulating young people's behaviour in public places – Where do we stop?

In developing and implementing the Hamilton Child Safety Initiative, both the local council and Strathclyde Police were hoping that not only a safer, but a more positive community would emerge. However, by highlighting the potential dangers that exist within Hillhouse, there is evidence to suggest that this initiative has in fact elevated the 'risk consciousness' of local people; reduced the level of contact between different sections of the community; and helped entrench divisions that already existed within Hillhouse.

Further, by increasing the authority of the police – and the level of their activities within this community – there is a danger that rather than creating a 'responsible' community, local people will hand over their ownership and responsibility for the behaviour of local young people, to the police. Within this process, there is clear evidence – especially among young children – that greater limits are being introduced on the activities of young people and their activities at night. The impact of these growing limitations and self limitations are unclear, but raise issues about the independence of these young people – and their reliance upon the police and parents in negotiating their relationships with other members of their community.

Throughout this report, research and trends that address child and youth development nationally have been referred to, and many of the themes looked at in relation to Hillhouse are clearly not specific to this area alone. However, it has been possible, while recognising some of the wider trends identified in other work, to analyse some of the direct impacts and make suggestions about some of the indirect consequences of the curfew itself.

Impact on Hillhouse

As well as leading to greater tension and pressure for parents, the restrictions that the CSI has had on primary school children, is worrying when seen in the context of growing limits that are being placed on the lives of children. Walking to and from school; travelling independently around estates; the limited distances within which children play; and the more regulated 'free' time that children have – are all issues that have been addressed by child researchers over the last ten years. Rather than there being a problem of increasing numbers of children running wild at night, it is recognised that the opposite is the case – i.e. children are leading increasingly limited and restricted lives – often because of fears that parents have for their safety. Talk of paedophiles and dangers on the streets, during the promotion of the CSI, has helped to increase the awareness that parents have about dangers their children face.

Community of strangers

The complexity of children's lives makes it practically impossible to isolate one relationship and clearly see what impact any change in this relationship has upon the child. So, for example, even if children never saw their friends after school it would still be difficult to fully analyse the impact that this would have on their development as they would continue to mix with peers throughout the day. However, there are aspects of peer relations that cannot be replicated by adults, and are unquestionably important for the development of children and young people.[4] Because these relationships are not dominated by one party – like adult child relationships – they allow children and young people to develop their own rules of behaviour. Through this process children develop more equal relationships within which they can develop their independence, in a way they could not do with adults. However, adults are very important within this process especially with young children, as encouragement is often needed before a child 'takes that first step' or 'takes that first bus ride alone'.

If the encouragement given to children to be more independent and take more responsibility for themselves is not forthcoming – and if instead children are increasingly limited in their free time activities and encouraged to be constantly cautious, the development of their independence will be affected.

Also, if adults are constantly depicted as potential paedophiles or 'strangers', not to be spoken to, and if the time and space that young people have in their area is reduced, not only will the experiences they have be reduced, but these children will grow up knowing fewer people within their estate and a community of strangers will develop. As Shimamura and Snell point out, it is not only children who are influenced by the people they meet, indeed many of the relationships that parents develop are generated by the interactions that their children have with other children and also with other adults within estates.[5]

Peer problems?

While it is more common today to hear peer relations discussed in negative terms – regarding the 'peer pressure' that young people come under, it is generally accepted that developing relationships with peers is an important part of growing up. Indeed it is often through the experiences that young people have with their peers that they learn the skills to deal with more difficult encounters and individuals. However, despite this, there is a growing trend – supported by Strathclyde Police and South Lanarkshire Council to increase the regulation of young people who hang about the streets and to be more interventionist in peer relations between them

Through the CSI, the police were encouraged to intervene in the activities of young people – *in case* they became victims of crime, or *in case* they became victims of peer pressure and committed a criminal act themselves.

Here the police are acting *before* a criminal act has been committed. This labelling of some young people as dangerous to others, before a criminal act has been committed is problematic in itself, but is equally a problem, in that it opens up an entirely new area for police intervention i.e. peer relations.

By encouraging the police to be more interventionist regarding relations between young people, the potential exists to further undermine the independent development that takes place within these relationships. This may be unlikely in terms of actual police intervention, but it is possible that young people themselves grow up being more suspicious of their peers – especially other young people who are strangers to them. By problematising the peer relations between young people who hang about the streets at night, all young people who hang about with peers become potential villains who lead others astray or potential victims of these bad boys and girls.

Protection racket

Through the language of protection, the CSI raised the awareness of young people in Hillhouse, not only about their direct peers but also about the irresponsible rowdy teenagers who drink, shout, swear and generally make a nuisance of themselves. The majority of young people interviewed who lived outside of Hillhouse thought the curfew was a good idea. For many the curfew had confirmed that Hillhouse was a bad area with bad young people in it. Within Hillhouse, despite having experienced relatively little 'bother' at night, the issue of underage drinking and nuisance behaviour of other young people was seen as enough of a problem to involve the police in many activities that are not criminal. Whether or not the curfew made these young people more conscious of this as an issue or not is unclear – for many it was more of a confirmation that the streets are unsafe, or that it was best to leave other young people to be dealt with by the police.

The acceptance and indeed support that most young people gave to the idea of increasing the controls on 'other' young people, was the most worrying aspect of this research. Few of these teenagers, even among those who opposed the curfew, talked about their or other young people's rights. Fewer still believed that they should be left alone to deal with the other young people they came across themselves. Clearly there are extreme occasions when the police may need to be called, but for most of these young people – like the adults they complained about – simply being a nuisance and a potential threat was seen as reason to make that call. Rather than learning to deal with other young people in their community and therefore developing greater confidence and independence, young people are developing a reliance on the police that their parents never had. This reliance is being encouraged by the council and the police through initiatives like the curfew.

Young people who have grown up in an environment where public space is being increasingly regulated by surveillance cameras, street drinking bans and safety campaigns – may well have come to expect a growing number of regulations on the activities of other young people within their estates. Whereas young people 10-15 years ago would not have seen street drinking as a criminal act in need of police attention, today they do. Similarly today, noise is something that over a third of the young people interviewed in and around Hillhouse believe is an 'offence' worthy of police action.

Activities like street drinking, that in the past would have been seen as unimportant or simply a nuisance are now elevated into activities that must be dealt with by the police. While many of the young people may not actually phone the police themselves if they see someone drinking in the street, the fact that 80% believed the police should be phoned, says something about the intolerant attitude these young people have towards others. It also reflects a lack of confidence and expectation that these teenagers have that they can live and deal with difficult and annoying situations themselves.

Learning to deal as best as you can with others who live around you – becoming street-wise and getting to know the different characters in your area – is a key way that young people have traditionally developed their independence. It is also a more positive and more practical way for young people to be safe and feel safe in their estates. Indeed if this independence is not developed today, it is likely that an increasing number of young adults will never feel confident about dealing with other members of their community, and will instead look to the police to mediate these relationships for them.

The concept of rights for young people today, is often very different from the concept that prevailed in the past. Rights are less about giving people freedom and the space to do what they want but rather they are about eliminating the freedom and space of others. Brought up on a diet of concerns about safety and security, autonomy and independence are viewed as risky and the mediation of relationships with others from outside agencies becomes the preferred option for young people. In this respect these new rights are antisocial in that they discourage young people from developing social relationships themselves.

Generations apart

The street, and the freedom it provides young people, is an important area for their development. As one of the few places that teenagers have to be free from adult supervision it has long been a place where they hang out. This has always resulted in tension between young people and some adults within communities. Today, however, it is increasingly the case that 'nuisance', i.e. non criminal petty activities of teenagers has become a police matter, rather than something that is tolerated or sorted out within these communities themselves.

A key reason given by the teenagers interviewed, for being moved on by the police, was complaints from adults. Across Britain a growing number of phone calls to the police are about petty behaviour of young people. The young people in and around Hillhouse were confused about why adults made complaints to the police about them when they were simply hanging about with friends. Fear of young people is such that contact between the generations appears to be declining. Rather than talk to young people who hang about the street, today adults often assume that young people would attack them verbally or physically. Rather than taking some responsibility for the behaviour of these young people, by assuming the worst many adults are handing this responsibility to the police. In the minds of these adults, it is likely that the curfew will have confirmed their worst fears about these young people, who will remain strangers to them.

Rather than policing criminals, the role of the police has developed into a baby-sitting service for the entire community, with non-criminal petty activities carried out by children being a focus of attention. Policing based on fear, rather than criminal acts, is prejudiced policing. Stereotype views that some adults have of young people, and indeed stereotypes that some young people have of others on their estate, are being institutionalised in police practice. Rather than being picked up by the police for acts committed, young people now run the risk of being charged with being scary!

Some adults in Hillhouse said the CSI had been a success and they said they felt safer now. But this safety was based on having streets with no children in them. Public space, without the public. Once the police leave these streets or the young people return, the fear will likewise return.

The lack of surety that many adults have in relating to young people has also been made more problematic by the confusion surrounding discipline and the question of rights and responsibilities surrounding children today. The more complicated, regulated and legalised relationships developing between young people and adults had influenced schools – as discussed in the previous chapter – and no doubt has added to the insecurity that some teachers feel when dealing with young people. Like these teachers, as Alan McLean explained, who are no longer expected to deal with difficult children but hand them over to guidance teachers or outside agencies, the 'modern structures' like the curfew being developed by the police and politicians are also 'deskilling' adults in estates like Hillhouse, and encouraging the 'transfer of ownership and responsibility' for young people, from the community to the police, social work departments and other outside agencies.

Taking responsibility

While being critical of the police involvement in the CSI and their approach to community policing, one must also feel some sympathy for the 'bobby on the beat' who is being asked to intervene in a growing number of incidences and relationships that he would not have expected to be involved in the past. Where young people would learn to be street-wise and adults would like wise expect to resolve difficulties with young people who hung about the streets, today the responsibility for these relationships are increasingly being handed over to the police.

While many young people and adults do still take responsibility for these relationships, and more work is needed to assess the contact that these groups have with one another, the growing involvement of the police and the council in these areas is likely to reduce this contact further. For adults in particular, rather than becoming more responsible for the behaviour of the young people in their communities, increasingly this will be seen as something that the police do.

Likewise for young people, what they are expected to deal with in their lives is likely to be reduced, when the local council encourage them to phone the police rather than learn to live with their peers.

Study Guide

A. Critically discuss what the meaning of 'adulthood' is today.

Scared of the kids raises issues not only to do with young people but perhaps more importantly with the changing role of adults in society. Consider what points in life are a clear guide to becoming an adult today and how these have changed in the last few decades.

B. Critically assess the extent to which young people are portrayed not only as villains but also as 'victims'. To what extent is the 'image' of young people one based on the notion of 'vulnerability'? Contrast this to the past image of 'rebellious youth' and consider the implications of this new 'image'.

As a counter to the argument that young people commit most crimes 'radicals' often point out that it is young people themselves who are the greatest victims of 'crime'. Carry out a media search of 'young people' and 'victims'/'vulnerable' and assess the way the idea of 'youth as victim' is constructed today.

C. Since Labour came to power 'freedom' and 'rights' have often been used to mean something very different from how they were classically understood. Discuss the changing meaning of 'freedom' and 'rights' today.

Consider for example the idea of the 'right to a quiet life', or the 'freedom from fear' that were used to promote the curfew and contrast this with the notion of liberty discussed by John Stuart Mill.

D. Should people in their communities 'have a go'.

Being a 'have a go hero', an adult who intervenes to stop crime or misbehaviour is often portrayed negatively and even as right wing. Discuss with adults you know whether adults should intervene when young people are 'rowdy' and consider the implication for communities if instead adults phone the police when they are worried about young people at night.

Useful Reading

A   1. *Arrested Development* by Andrew Calcutt.
See chapter 10.

2. 'Cultivating Suspicion' by Frank Furedi in the *Cotton Wool Kids: Making Sense of Child Safety* bulletin.
This is available online at www.GenerationYouthIssues.org.

3. *Young People and Social Change* by Andy Furlong and Fred Cartmel.
See chapter 9.

4. *The children who won't grow up* by Frank Furedi.
Available online.

B   1. *Random Violence* by Joel Best
See chapters 5and 6.

2. *Antisocial Behaviour: The construction of a crime* by Stuart Waiton

3. *One Nation Under Therapy* by Christina Hoff Sommers.
An online article entitled 'One Nation Under Therapy' is also available in the *Cotton Wool Kids: Making Sense of Child Safety* bulletin, at www.Generation YouthIssues.org

4. *Bully for who?* by Josie Appleton.
Available online.

5. 'The kids are alright' by Stuart Waiton in the *Times Education Supplement Scotland*.
Available online.

6. *Therapy Culture* by Frank Furedi

C   1. *On Liberty* by John Stuart Mill
Available online.

2. *Free speech is more than a slogan* by Dolan Cummings.
Available online.

3. 'Am I guilty of oldthink or is this sensefree?' by Mick Hume in the *Times Online*.

4. 'The left has been infected by the disease of intolerance' by Brendan O'Neill.
Available online.

D   1. *Don't grass take responsibility* by Josie Appleton.
Available online.

2. *The Death and Life of Great American Cities* by Jane Jacobs.
See part one.

3. *The Politics of Antisocial Behaviour: Amoral Panics* by Stuart Waiton.
See the concluding chapter.

Notes

[1]The Guardian, 15 July 1999.
[2]The Glaswegian, 16 December 1999.
[3]The Scotsman, 5 April 2000.
[4]Youniss, J. (1980). Parents and Peers in Social Development (The University of Chicago Press).
[5]Shimamura, H. and Snell, C. (1996). They don't play out like they used to, do they? (p35) Available from author.

9   Future Developments and Recommendations

In April 1998, after the initial six month trial curfew period, the police, council and Scottish Office reaction to developments in Hamilton were all favourable. Six months later, in October, it was announced that the success of the Child Safety Initiative, in the three targeted estates, was such that it was to be extended to all areas of Hamilton. Scottish home affairs minister Henry McLeish was so pleased with the initiative that he speculated that before too long, similar initiatives could develop across the whole of Scotland. However by December, John Hamilton – Chief Constable of Fife – gave a speech denouncing the attitude of many police forces to young people, and explained that he would not be introducing a Child Safety Initiative in his area. Indeed, he elaborated, rather than a curfew, what was needed was more consultation and joint work between the police and young people. In response to this speech Henry McLeish has withdrawn his support for the CSI to be introduced across Scotland.

So why the turnaround? After all, the public in Hamilton remain largely supportive of the initiative, and even young people in Hamilton – as Chief Constable John Orr states – are in favour of safety initiatives being developed in their area. Indeed external public pressure on the police and Scottish Office has been minimal – even within South Lanarkshire Labour Council – opposition to the initiative was almost non-existent.

A major problem for the initiative was that it was immediately labelled as a curfew on young people, and was thus seen – especially by civil liberties groups and children's charities – as a form of authoritarian policing. Targeting young people up to the age of 16 – rather than, as Jack Straw in England has done – targeting only children under 10 years of age, meant that the 'safety' image of the initiative was often lost and the police were seen as being heavy handed towards teenagers. For an initiative that is supposed to be community driven and for the benefit of young people themselves, this is clearly a problem, and is no doubt one of the reasons that the extended initiative in Hamilton has been launched as a safety campaign for day and night – rather than just a night time initiative which was seen as simply a way of pushing young people off the streets.

Despite these concerns as we go to print Strathclyde Police have launched another dusk 'till dawn scheme designed to reduce juvenile crime in the targeted areas of Blantyre and Larkhall and the government has re-raised the spectre of the lout, with Tony Blair's plans for on the spot fines for antisocial young people.

While for those who oppose the CSI, the backing down by the Scottish Office is to be welcomed, the new proposals by John Hamilton, for the development of further safety initiatives through consultation with young people may be equally problematic. Firstly, because the consultation processes that are set up by councils are often weighted to produce a result that favours existing council policies. Secondly, there is a danger – as some children's charities have done – in asking the police to 'listen to what young people have to say', as many young people when pushed, will prioritise safety ahead of the freedoms that many liberal minded adults think they should have. Through consulting with young people, it is therefore possible that even more authoritarian forms of policing could be developed.

More and more and more facilities

In opposition to the curfew, it has been argued that what Hillhouse needs is more facilities for young people and more community police on the ground. However, while more facilities are always welcome, these demands often reinforce the idea that children and young people should either not be on the streets in the first place, or that more police are needed to mediate relations between adults and young people who are out at night.

While interviewing adults in Hamilton, everybody at some point mentioned the need for better facilities for young people. Indeed the demand for more youth workers and youth clubs has been the main alternative offered by those who have challenged the curfew. Rather than simply sweeping these kids off the streets, it is argued, let's give them something better to do with their time.

In Hamilton this was always part of the council's plans, and since the launch of the initiative a new youth internet drop-in centre has been developed in the centre of town. Some people argued that this was not that useful for Hillhouse youngsters who live a few miles out of the centre of Hamilton, but nevertheless it was generally seen as a positive development.

However, since the new centre opened, there have been an increasing number of complaints by adults who live nearby about the noise of the young people who hang about the centre. The problems of nuisance behaviour, appears to have simply moved to a new venue.

How the council will react to this development is unclear, however it is unlikely after spending so much money on the new centre that they will introduce a new initiative that moves these young people away from it. It is more likely that the complaints will simply be ignored. Whatever further developments take place, this example indicates that more facilities cannot resolve the 'problem' of young people hanging about at night, unless they are literally barred from being on any street after dark.

It is often assumed by those arguing for more facilities, that part of the reason for the tension that exists between children, young people and adults on estates, is that there has been a major decline in places for young people to go at night, so that 'kids have got nothing better to do than hang about the streets'. However, while the impact on different areas will no doubt vary, recent research suggests that at least in relation to outdoor facilities, there has been a dramatic improvement – with better play areas for both children and teenagers that are closer to home than ever before. Interestingly though, this report notes that these facilities are underused, largely because either parents are overcautious and won't allow their children to travel to the play areas, or that the equipment in these areas are so safe that older children are bored by them.[1]

In Hillhouse itself as the Scottish Human Rights Centre noted, there were facilities being provided by both churches and also by a local primary school – although the funding for this project was running out. Sports facilities are also good and there is a park and a number of grassy areas and open spaces for recreation.[2] Three quarters of the children interviewed from in and around Hillhouse were involved in at least one club, and many more were in more than one club – often outside the estate itself.

The debate about more facilities, while representing an attempt to deal with young people and also offer them 'something constructive', is often pushed as simply an alternative way of getting young people off the streets. The idea that young people should be allowed to hang about the streets is rarely seen as an alternative. The options being offered to young people are either to be sent home by the police or pushed into centres away from complaining or frightened adults.

Young people want decent facilities and somewhere to go at night. However many young people, like those in Hillhouse, want to 'just hang out' with their friends, or when they do go to youth clubs and sports centres, often enjoy hanging about outside as much as they enjoy the activities themselves.[3] Young people are not going to go away.

The needs of young people are often perceived in terms of more facilities being provided by adults. However, the important developments of children and teenagers that take place within peer groups – free from adult supervision, are largely ignored. Peer groups are in fact often seen today as problematic for young people – something that they need to be protected from.

Agenda setting

While consultation between, the police, the council or any other agency, is to be welcomed as part of a process of developing young people's involvement and understanding of decision making, there are a number of problems with this consultation.

The consultation process being promoted by Chief Constable John Hamilton is itself potentially problematic because of the agenda of the agencies involved in these processes, and the issues that are open – and equally importantly – closed to discussion.

For example, in the major survey carried out by South Lanarkshire council, while safety was a general issue, with regard to what were the major problems for people in their area, unemployment was the main concern. And yet 'Scotland's First Citizens' Jury' – as it was promoted, was not set up to look at the issue of overcoming unemployment, but was set up to specifically look at the issue of community safety.[4]

A similar agenda setting can be observed in the 'third citizens' jury', which was set up by the council to look at the issue of young people's access to leisure and entertainment. The jury was set up because of a recognition that in the major (System 3) survey of South Lanarkshire residents, a key concern highlighted, was the lack of leisure facilities for young people. A representative group of young people was gathered to discuss leisure, from which a report of the recommendations was written.[5]

Eight proposals were reported in this report, the fourth of these was on safety and security. Three proposals were made in this section – more visible policing, better lighting, and more youth workers on the ground. However, it is not clear why this section was written, as the first few lines of the page reads, 'The issues with regard to safety and security are varied. In general, the Jury did not view them as being overly important'. Young people may be concerned about safety – but when asked about leisure facilities in this jury – these young people did not 'view them as overly important'. And yet safety and security remained one of the eight key areas addressed in the report, possibly because it is an issue that is being prioritised by the council itself.

Finally, the outcome of consultation processes – like the citizens' juries – may not be adhered to by the local authorities that set them up. The jury in Hillhouse, for example, made a recommendation that the police improve their attitude to the public, while they did not recommend a curfew. Despite this the council not only set up the CSI, but claimed that it was a community-led initiative. Strathclyde Police often explain while justifying their safety initiatives, that they are only carrying out the people's will, 'The people want more police and we will give them more'. However if the local people in Hamilton decided they wanted fewer police on their streets, would this also be acceptable to Chief Constable John Orr?

More and more safety

However, even if consultation was open and controlled entirely by young people, it would be a mistake to believe that this would result in more 'humanitarian' policing and attitudes towards street life and public space.

In discussion with the volunteers who helped with this research project, the key issue of concern was not the overly heavy handed nature of the curfew, although this was an issue, rather the main concern was that – young people appeared to be already overly conscious of the potential dangers they faced at night; they were highly intolerant of the other young people who hung about the streets; and subsequently had come to expect the police or some other agency to remove any potentially 'dodgy' character off the streets. If this assessment is correct, there is a danger that when the police 'consult with young people', the result may be even more restrictive than the curfew.

There is also a danger that through the process of discussing more and more safety initiatives, young people themselves increasingly relate to issues through the prism of 'safety first' – experimentation, experiences and developing independence being further relegated in the minds of the young people themselves.

Children's agencies who, in opposing the Hamilton Curfew, have demanded that the police listen to young people, may soon find that this 'listening' process results in even more rules, regulations and laws that restrict the behaviour and activities of young people within communities. If the police 'listen' to many of the young people in Hillhouse they will discover that despite their irritation at being harassed themselves, they are largely in favour of 'other' young people being 'swept off the streets'.

Rather than encouraging more consultation on safety issues, the council and also the children's charities and other concerned bodies would be advised to encourage young people's self reliance and independence.

Recommendations

The main problem this book has tried to address, is the fragmenting and increasingly distant relationships developing within and across generations. As such, the following recommendations are seen as a way of countering this trend and encouraging a more trusting and also more active individual within communities.

In effect we must attempt to make public space more public – for young and old; encourage local people to resolve local problems; and ultimately foster an environment within which individuals within communities feel able to relate to one another without recourse to a third party.

Public space

There needs to be a recognition that safety initiatives within communities are helping to create an environment that suggests 'we are under siege'. There must be an end to – CCTV in communities, fenced-in concierge flats and caged-in schools – all of which reinforce the exaggerated sense of risk within areas and foster a sense of us and them.

Similarly, in developing play areas for children – the label 'safe' should be dropped from all future developments – as this again elevates the issue of child safety, and encourages the idea that these are in fact the only places children should be allowed to play.

Children should be encouraged to use public space more freely – rather than simply having set designated areas set aside for them. Children being street-wise should also be encouraged as part of their social development – a by-product of which will be safer children

Areas should be developed for play, away from houses, for balls games and other activities – but should not be somewhere children and young people are corralled into.

Planners should be conscious of issues of noise and cars when developing estates – but should attempt to design estates that build children and young people into public space, rather than push them out of it.

Policing

Police safety initiatives, from safety advice tapes for pensioners to curfews for children, encourage the sense of fear that already exists within communities and should be stopped.

Initiatives like the curfew and the stop and search campaigns carried out by Strathclyde police – the most recent of which, up to August 2000, has resulted in 100,000 people being searched – specifically undermine young people's rights and should be stopped. These initiatives add to the sense of young people being out of control, but also degrade young people's sense of themselves.

The police focus should be on law and catching criminals rather than enforcing order and preventing crime happening. The latter often does not stop crime and also leads to the criminalisation of many non-criminal young people.

Nuisance behaviour of children should be differentiated from more serious criminal activities that threaten life or property and the police should play a less active role in regulating this type of behaviour.

Ultimately, the police need to develop policies that accept that public space is an acceptable place for children and young people to be.

Adult-child relations

Contact and relations between adults and children need to be promoted. Significantly this means creating an atmosphere that accepts and indeed encourages other adults to relate to children and young people within the community.

Within schools, 'stranger danger' campaigns which foster mistrust should be stopped, or replaced by initiatives that inform children about particular 'strange adults' who do 'strange things'. Strangers per se should not be presented as dangerous people to be avoided.

Schools should encourage local adults to 'pass on their skills' (something the Hillhouse Citizens' Jury promoted). This could include actively pursuing a community development approach within primary schools that involves adults helping in class activities – story telling, sports days etc.

More contact between young and old should be encouraged and helped by involving children in community support initiatives helping elderly people with shopping, gardening etc.

Child's play and youth provision

Local authorities should encourage play and youth provision to focus on activities that develop the experiences of young people, rather than focusing on issues of safety and risk.

Play areas and the equipment in them, should be developed to encourage adventurous play. The benefits for child development of unsupervised play should be promoted by local play schemes. And local adults should be encouraged to help out with special play days within these play areas.

These initiatives should be promoted as positive, fun facilities – there for the enjoyment and development of children and young people – rather than as initiatives aimed at making young people safe, keeping them off the street or helping to reduce crime and drug taking.

Freedom and responsibility

The government and local authorities should encourage freedom ahead of regulation within communities – thus encouraging local people to take more responsibility for their actions and those of others within their area. Greater freedom will encourage adults to take a more active role in regulating public space and the activities of children and young people – making adults themselves more streetwise – and communities safer.

Finally, rules governing petty 'anti-social' behaviour should be scrapped thus providing a space within which more genuine communities and community relations can be established between people – issues of concern being resolved face to face rather through state agencies.

Notes

[1]Moorcock, K. (1998). Swings and Roundabouts (Sheffield Hallam University).
[2]Springham, K. (1998) Time to go Home Says Who? (Scottish Human Rights Centre) p5.
[3]Stirling Council (1997) Are you getting enough...opportunity?
[4]System 3 (1996) South Lanarkshire Community Survey: Executive Summary, p4.
[5]South Lanarkshire Council (1998) Access to Leisure and Entertainment: Findings from a Citizen's Jury.

Comment

During the research into the impact of the Hamilton Curfew, a number of agencies and individuals were contacted about their concerns regarding this initiative. Their thoughts are printed below.

Save the Children: Curfews on Children and Young People in Communities

Save the Children (SCF) is an international organisation dedicated to upholding the human rights of children and young people. SCF is concerned at the introduction of curfews in this country because it is a measure which denies children and young people their civil rights under international treaty (UN Convention on the Rights of the Child – Article 15). In addition we understand the main aim of curfews to be the control of children and young people's behaviour within their communities. SCF believes that curfews are a simplistic response to a multi-faceted problem which may create significant negative spin-offs.

The debate was sparked off in Scotland by the introduction of the 'Child Safety Initiative' in South Lanarkshire. The scenario presented was confusing; were the problems identified in the community perceived to be arising purely from the actions of children and young people? Were children and young people seen as victims or perpetrators? Was the concern about children's safety on the streets after dark, or reducing the level of youth crime, or removing young people who were perceived to be a nuisance from the street – or all three? Media reports of the initiative and quotes from the authorities involved appeared to raise different justifications on different occasions. Given government commitment to integrated approaches, the Child Safety Initiative appears to ignore the call for 'joined up' thinking.

The issue splits into two parts: the acceptability in principle and indeed in law (The European Convention on Human Rights – Article 8) of enforcing a curfew on a particular category of people (children and young people), and the pragmatic argument that, principles aside, action needs to be taken in the wider public interest. If a pragmatic justification is advanced we need to be reassured that the local situation does indeed demonstrate extraordinary problems, that the objectives and targets of the initiative are clear, and that proper evaluation is in place. Criticisms have been levelled at the South Lanarkshire initiative in relation to all three of these requirements.

Two key articles within the UN Convention on the Rights of the Child define general principles which should guide the actions of those in authority in relation to children and young people; Article 3, Best Interest of the Child, and Article 12, Participation. In terms of Article 3, SCF questions whether confinement to the family home necessarily serves the best interest of the child. We must consider at least two issues which arise from the restriction of children's freedom to leave their home; the possibility of domestic violence or other forms of harm, and the

169

importance of freedom to play and associate with others out of doors. In relation to Article 12, children have the right to be listened to and have their views taken seriously in order to determine what is in a child's best interest. This is both logical and necessary and should be undertaken as a matter of course in making important decisions affecting children and at the earliest point in the planning process. The strategic decision to impose a curfew in response to perceived problems in South Lanarkshire was we understand, taken without reference to the views of children and young people living in the area.

In contravention of Article 15 of the UN Convention, curfews seek to curtail the movement of young people. No one would deny that bored young people on the street can be noisy, cause damage and be a considerable nuisance, but many young people who are not causing trouble locally will inevitably have their rights infringed by curfews which is clearly unfair. Would it be deemed acceptable to curfew all adults between certain hours because some adults were behaving inappropriately? In responding to problems of antisocial behaviour we must seek to understand the causes and work alongside all of the stakeholders to resolve them.

On grounds of principle and practicality we must listen to what young people have to say and negotiate appropriate resolutions where there is conflict. Without their active involvement as partners in working towards consensual norms of community living, we risk further alienation and mistrust. Importantly we also deny young people the opportunity to become active players in community life. Instead we should be supporting them in the transition to adulthood by including them in debate.

Nancy Ovens: Vice Chair – Play Scotland

CURFEW – Chambers' Dictionary Definition – in feudal times the ringing of a bell at eight o'clock as a signal to put out all fires and lights. From the French couvrir – to cover: feu – fire.

Article 31, UN Charter – States Parties recognise the right of the child to rest and leisure, to engage in play and recreational activities appropriate to the age of the child and to participate freely in cultural life and the arts.

The essence of play is in the right of the individual to choose – the intrinsic process of play identifies the rewards as related to the goals set by the individual. Whether these be also linked to external rewards is irrelevant to the process. Through play, the individual experiences the choices through social interaction with others also engaged in the search for opportunities to play.

At the National Centre for Play, there is considerable evidence of the reduction of the opportunities for children and young people to have freedom of choice in play. To go 'out to play' has been traditionally a feature of Scottish life for generations of children and young people. Adults, likewise, 'go out to play' but their conditioning has led them to reflect the process by defining it in such acceptable terms as going to the pub or playing a round of golf, or awa' tae the fitba', or going round to see Jeannie, etc.

Today's concerns on safety have led to over-protection by anxious adults of their children and young people. In the Stranger Danger campaign, the reality of the facts were ignored. Most children are abducted by people they know – likewise, most children and young people are abused by people well known to them in the family or close friends. So fear, often fostered by media presentation of horror pictures interviews, etc. is increasing rather than allayed by the production and dissemination of helpful information, guidance or advice to the public at large on how to ensure a safe environment for play within which priority can be given to the choices which children and young people can then make.

Safety on the roads is another issue which relates clearly to the work of this topic. While no one today could deny that roads belong to traffic, nevertheless the rights of children need to be considered. The statistics are there to demonstrate conclusively that few children anywhere in rural and urban environments now walk to and from school. Natural social groupings with peers and siblings are therefore no longer at the behest of the children and young people. After school provision, which ensures safety for the children and peace of mind for adults not able to be at their family home, does not meet the need for free choice of peers which is the basis of play. Care provision is a form of social control and until out of school provision is open to all children and young people in the community and until it includes a wide range of activities covering all aspects of human development, the physical, social, intellectual creative and emotional needs – as presently occurs in some other European countries – then such aspirations as social inclusion will not be achieved.

Access to outdoor play environments is an essential part of freedom of choice. Over the years such initiatives as designated streets for play and open playgrounds at schools, have been undertaken but have not survived to any real extent. Adults need to listen to children and young people and they must also reflect on their own memories of their play at that stage in their development. Perhaps we don't want children to fall [into the burn], or climb up the quarry, or play behind the bike sheds, but if we don't provide children with the opportunities to explore their environment, to develop skills in problem solving, to engage with others in planning and negotiating, shall we see adults in the future isolated from their own peers?

Of course we don't want to see young children walking the streets aimlessly – but grounding them only addresses the need for ensuring the streets are empty of pedestrians (albeit the youth in this case). Where might this stop? What of the families where the technology of video, computer and internet may have a far greater future impact on the human race?

171

Is keeping the children off the streets going to lead to reducing the flames of ambition in adults?

Gerison Lansdown: Director of the Children's Rights Office

The Crime and Disorder Act 1998 empowers local authorities to impose curfew on all children under ten years old after 9pm. In other words, it legitimates state intervention to deny freedom of association to all children of a given age during the evening. The protection of our civil rights should be guarded with the utmost rigour – respect for the human rights of individuals is the linchpin of a humane and civilised society. The imposition of a blanket ban of the freedoms of any group within a democratic society should only ever be imposed where there is an overwhelming case that to do so is absolutely necessary to the maintenance of public order and safety, the protection of public health or morals or to protect the rights and freedoms of others. Does the presence of young children out in the evening pose such a threat to society in these ways?

But, you may say, it is only common sense – small children should not be out late unsupervised, they would be at risk, causing trouble, exposed to danger. Such a ban is merely reinforcing good parenting and protecting children whose parents fail to provide adequate supervision. The logic of this argument is that the assumption of a desirable outcome – in this case better supervision of children – justifies the withdrawal of a fundamental freedom. But is this a sufficient defence for such draconian measures? After all, most violent crime is perpetrated by men, much of it late at night after they have been drinking. If we are keen to reduce violence, as I am sure we all are, then the state could also consider banning all men from being out on the street after 9pm. It would undoubtedly make the streets safer. But the cost in terms of loss of civil rights would render such a ban unthinkable. It would potentially criminalise vast numbers of individuals who had committed no offence other than to breach the curfew. We would never tolerate a government who sought to introduce it.

And even if the restriction of civil rights were justified in terms of its desirable outcome, where is the evidence that such an outcome would arise. The imposition of men in their own homes might well have the unintended consequences of significantly increasing levels of domestic violence. The goal of the safer streets would be more than outweighed by the displacement of violence elsewhere. And so it might be with children. Many children may be out in the evening in order to avoid abuse or violence at home. The imposition of a blanket curfew which forced them home would place them at a greater not lesser risk of harm.

The denial of the right to freedom of association will breach Article 15 of the UN Convention on the Right of the Child. There is no evidence that the presence of children under ten on the streets is threatening public order. There is no evidence that, even if it were acceptable to justify a blanket ban on grounds of protecting children, it would achieve its goal. In any case, powers to take action to protect individual children at risk already exist. Curfews will serve to further demonise children and young people, criminalise normal and acceptable social activity, enhance conflict between younger and older people and potentially place some children at greater risk of harm. They should not be introduced.

Joe Parfery: Chair of the Hillhouse Community Council

According to Strathclyde Police and their community officers, this campaign is still ongoing in Hillhouse with serious attention being offered on a Thursday, Friday and Saturday – bodies being available. The other days of the week? Well who knows.

Our last community constable, David Walker, has been promoted and moved to Glasgow. During the interim period of replacement, 3 serious assaults took place in Hillhouse. Slow police response enabled assailant's time to quit the scene.

The children at risk factor was nullified when one of the assaults took place at 4 o'clock in the afternoon, by the library entrance, where a number of young school children with a teacher were choosing books. The assault included 4 young men with iron bars beating up another. If this incident had overflowed through the library doors, a major calamity could have resulted.

This escapade, and another involving harassment of elderly people in the Clerkwell Terrace sheltered housing complex prompted our two local councillors to call an immediate meeting of residents and community police to address these incidents. A police sergeant and four constables attended. Apologies were offered by the police for lack of cover while David Walker was away, however, in future the area will be covered day shift and night shift, holidays permitting. Being very cynical as I am, the young warlords will no doubt find out when holidays are, and act accordingly. In the meantime, the local drug dealers are pushing their wares quite openly, and in different locations.

The Spotlight Campaign is targeting the wrong age group. Young children are naturally curious and easily influenced by peer groups into doing things the others do, not fully comprehending the outcome of their actions. Older people tend to forget when they were young when they begin a statement with, 'When a wis a boy, we didnae carry oan like that'. 'Oh', says I. 'Whit aboot puting squibs through old people's letterboxes knowing they couldn't chase after you. Or tying string to opposite door knobs in a close and run away?'

Certainly some of the antics of our young people leave a lot to be desired, but at least so far they have not allowed themselves to be conned into taking up arms and going out to kill people in other parts of the world in the name of patriotism, or any other 'ism'.

Anyway, what have we done for them? What kind of support or encouragement have we offered them in their frustration of trying to get a job so that they feel less excluded from society than they do? Who really cares about them?

The *Hamilton Advertiser* carries headlines again about complaints from residents regarding South Lanarkshire Council granting an Entertainment License to the youth cafe Universal Connection at Woodside Walk in the centre of Hamilton. Where can the young people of Hamilton go? It cost about £12 to get into the dancing and only those who have the money and are old enough can gain admission.

Again, older people like myself tend to forget that we left school when the war was on. Everyone had to assist in the war effort. Work was compulsory. No one was able to be idle. After 1945 the war was over and heralded the welfare state. We the older people now enjoyed 25 years of productive prosperity. New houses, new schools, new hospitals, free health service and free education up to and beyond university. We should reflect on these things when we consider what we were given before we start to condemn our younger generation.

From Queen Victoria's time it was compulsory for children to go to school. Not for the good of the children, but just to get them off the streets. Here we are attempting to do the same to our children. *Get them off the streets!* Like ourselves, our young people's lives are severely regulated and constricted: school from nursery to primary to secondary to possibly university or college. Or worse still, the scrap heap because there are no jobs available, and we wonder why the young people react to us the way that they do.

The Spotlight Campaign is just another of these exercises to keep our children off the streets and make them more frustrated than they are already.

Tim Gill: Children's Play Council

Children's engagement with the people and places around them are crucial for their social and moral development. Play (activities chosen by children because they want to do them) is a critical and neglected developmental process for these engagements. But play is problematic in this context. Children are being increasingly excluded from public spaces and activities, apart from specific locations or while under close adult supervision. They receive powerful messages about restriction on their freedoms: messages which say that the world is a hostile, dangerous place in which children are not welcome, and their wishes – where they want to go, what they want to do – count for little.

The Children's Play Council believes that this is de facto social exclusion of a generation inevitably leads many children to feel that they have no stake in their community. Hence we have grave reservations about curfew schemes. There is a basic moral injustice behind them, which will become quickly apparent to children (who are acutely aware of issues of fairness). The injustice is, of course, that curfews punish children who have done nothing wrong, committed no crime. So the very children on the cusp of exclusion – those who are at risk of offending but who might react positively to inclusive initiatives that acknowledge their wishes – will, if curfews are implemented, receive a powerful demonstration that official adult forces are not interested in whether their actions are any different to those actions of children who have done wrong. How will these children develop a sense of being responsible for their actions if, as a matter of principle, their actions in some circumstances make no difference to how they are treated by the system?

Curfews also reinforce the view that children have no entitlement to play out unsupervised. They imply that children who are outside in their free time are likely to be intent on causing trouble, so that as a matter of public policy children should be kept off the streets. For this reason, curfews are likely to lead to a general restriction on children's mobility (not just in the areas where they are in force) and worsening relations between children (and their families) and other residents and the police. This is especially likely to happen in areas where what is needed is not greater restrictions on children's play opportunities, but rather improvements in service and facilities to give children positive options for their free time.

Apart from being unfair in principle, curfews also seem unlikely to succeed in practise. It is difficult to see how escorting children home or restricting the movements of groups of children, will in the long run contribute positively either to the circumstances of families that may be in difficulties or to the development of citizenship. The measures also conflict with article 15 (on freedom of association) and 31 (on the right to play and recreation) of the UN Convention on the Rights of the Child, ratified by the UK in 1991. Moreover, they are arguably unnecessary, given existing police and social services powers.

One powerful alternative strategy for 'redeeming' children at risk of offending is to offer them meaningful opportunities for developing their sense of community and responsibility. Positive engagement with children can reduce levels of problem behaviour by giving them a sense of worth as valued members of the community. Play offers great opportunities for developing citizenship in this way. For example, after-school clubs and holiday play schemes are proven to reduce levels of crime and vandalism. But play provides other opportunities for positive engagement that can offer children something more meaningful than diversionary or narrowly educational activities. Estate and park improvements programmes that involve children (the heaviest users of outdoor spaces) encourages them to have a stake in the results, as well as harnessing children's energies for the benefit of the community.

Roger Smith: The Children Society (written in a personal capacity)

Curfews for children have now been piloted in Scotland and passed into new law across Great Britain. Apparently, keeping our 9 year old banged up in their homes is going to improve the quality of life for the community as a whole. Will it?...when the police come knocking at the door to say that our son or daughter has been caught playing in the streets with their mates? It's not just a question of 'children should be seen and not heard', they should neither be seen nor heard, according to our policy makers.

We are now capable of fitting children into 1 of 2 categories, 'victims' or 'villains' and in either case they should not be seen out on the streets. It's not as if the new legislation has anything to offer children by way of compensation for these new restrictions. There is nothing for them to do, but that won't matter anymore, because under the new law they wouldn't be able to get there to do anything if it was available.

Why should anybody think that this sort of approach to our children should solve anything? Will the police spend their time chasing small children around when they should be pursuing real criminals? Will children be forced into their own homes to suffer violence and abuse silently? Remember that children are far more likely to be mistreated by someone who is close to them than strangers. Will the streets be dull and silent? Will the absence of children mean that real criminals are free to roam secure in the knowledge that they will not be observed?

In reality, I think it is probable their sheer impracticality rather than their immorality which will prevent significant use of child curfews. It will, indeed be the police and other agencies who decide quite simply that they have more important things to do than stop kids playing. Despite this, the curfew will still do significant damage, by conveying to our kids a view from the adult world that they and their interests are not worth very much. We have heard quite plainly over the years their soulful lament, 'there's nothing to do around here'. And, our response has been lamentably soulless; 'that's not our problem, you are'. If we take this offhand attitude to them, why should we be surprised that children are rebellious.

Perhaps children themselves should take a leaf from the women's movement and 'reclaim the streets!'

Scottish Human Rights Centre: Legal Issues – Hamilton Child Safety Initiative

The Scottish Human Rights Centre has been opposed to the Child Safety Initiative since it was first announced. In Scotland, the police do not have a general power to stop people who are going about their lawful business and suspicion of criminal activity is required before an officer will question individuals. As the Initiative's main aim, is not crime detection, what is the justification for questioning children or even detaining them, removing them to their homes or to a police station?

A number of statutes have been cited by the police in response to this.

The Children and Young Persons (Scotland) Act 1937 identifies the offence of parents neglecting a child, but does not allow the police to remove a child. The

Children (Scotland) Act 1995, replacing the relevant part of the Social Work (Scotland) Act 1968, allows the removal of a child to a place of safety to prevent 'significant harm', if sufficient grounds exist. However neither of these pieces of legislation have been used as part of the Hamilton Initiative. Even the general duty of the police to protect life and property in the Police (Scotland) Act 1967 is only relevant where the child concerned is clearly in danger.

As it would appear that police activity cannot be justified in terms of statutory provisions, it should be noted that in law there is no detention if the children go with officers voluntarily, making it difficult for a child to complain that police action was illegal.

However, as it would seem unlikely for a child in these circumstances to refuse to go with the police, it is arguable that real consent was given. This may be sustainable in one context of the European Convention on Human Rights, currently being incorporated into UK law, as judges seek to interpret the Convention in a purposive way.

Article 8 of this Convention which respects the rights to respect for family life, may also be being disregarded by police activity as parents are not being allowed to decide where their children should be and when.

The Convention's Fourth Protocol protects the rights to liberty of movement, and although not binding on the UK government, moves towards the recognition of these rights have been indicated. Clearly, the police activity in Hamilton has infringed liberty of movement. Although justification for infringing this liberty is possible in certain circumstances, there would be the same difficulties in relation to the protocol as those in relation to Article 8.

Justification for the interference with Article 8 must be necessary for the protection of health and morals, or for crime prevention, but would not be possible as this would have to be in accordance with the law, and no legal basis has been found. Even if there were such a law, it would have to be shown that action was meeting a 'pressing social need' and be proportionate in response to this.

Other international obligations protecting the family and freedom of association and movement are provided by the United Nations Convention on the Rights of the Child and the International Covenant on Civil and Political Rights.

Justification under Scottish law for the initiative cannot be found and it apparently breaches international agreements as well as new provisions under UK law.

Scared of the Kids?

Bibliography

Allen, B. (1998). 'New guidance on the use of reasonable force in schools 1998', *British Journal of Special Education*, Vol. 25, No.4.

Amis, D. (1997). *Adolescence Risk and Independence: Preliminary Findings.* (London: Families For Freedom Pamphlet).

Anderson, S. and Leitch, S. (1996). *Main Findings from the 1993 Scottish Crime Survey.* (Edinburgh: Scottish Office Central Research Unit).

Anderson, S. (1994). *Cautionary Tales: Young People, Crime and Policing in Edinburgh*, (Avebury, Aldershot).

Aries, P. (1962). *Centuries of Childhood.* (London: Pimlico).

Article 12 in Scotland (1998) *Curfew and crime – what young people think.* (Edinburgh: Save the Children).

Asquith, S. (1998). *Children, Young People and Offending in Scotland.* (Edinburgh: The Scottish Office Central Research Unit).

Atkins, C., Bee, S. and Button, F. (2007). *Taking Liberties.* (London: Revolver).

Barnardo's (1994). *The Facts of Life: The Changing Face of Childhood.* (London: Barnardo's).

Barnardo's (1995). *Playing It Safe.* (London: Barnardo's).

Goldson. B. (1998). AJJUST NOW . *The Journal of the National Association for Youth Justice*, Issue No. 43, pp. 12.

Beck, U. (1992) *Risk Society: Towards a New Modernity.* (London: Sage).

Bennett, A. and Kahn-Harris, K. (2004) *After Subcultures: Critical Studies in Contemporary Youth Culture* edited by Hampshire: Palgrave MacMillan.

Best, J. (1999) *Random Violence: How We Talk About New Crimes and New Victims.* (Berkley: University of California Press).

Blatchford, P, (1999) 'The state of play in schools', in M. Woodhead M (ed) *Making sense of social development.* (London, Routledge).

Bratton, W.J., Dennis, N., Mallon, R., Orr, J., and Pollard, C. (1997) *Zero Tolerance: Policing a Free Society.* (London: IEA Health and Welfare Unit).

British Medical Journal, 3 August 1996.

British Medical Journal, 5 June 1999.

Calcutt, A. (1998) *Arrested Development.* (London: Cassell).

Campbell, B. (1993) (Goliath. London: Methuen London).

Coalter, F. and Allison, M. (1995) *Young people in Wester Hailes.* (Edinburgh: The Wester Hailes Partnership).

Cohen, S. (1980) *Folk Devils and Moral Panics.* (London: McGibbon & Kee/Paladin).

Coleman, J. (1999) *Key Data on Adolescence.* (Brighton: Trust for the Study of Adolescence).

Cook, D. (1997) *Poverty, Crime and Punishment.* (London: Child Poverty Action Group).

Corrigan, P. (1979) *Schooling the Smash Street Kids.* (London, MacMillan).

Corsaro, W.A. and Eder, D. (1990) 'Children's Peer Cultures'. *Annual Review of Sociology* Vol. 16, pp. 197-220.

Cummings, D. (1997) *Surveillance and the City*. (London: Urban Research Group).

Cummings, D. (1999) *In Search of Sesame Street: Policing civility for the twenty first century*. (Sheffield: Sheffield Hallam University Press).

.Davis, J. (1990) *Youth and the Conditions of Britain*. (London: Atlantic Press).

Davis, M. (1990) *City of Quartz*. (London: Vintage).

Dennis, N. (1997) *Zero Tolerance: Policing a Free Society*. (London: London Institute of Economic Affairs).

Dennis, N., Erdos, G., and Robinson, D. (2003) *The Failure of Britain's Police: London and New York Compared*. (London: Civitas).

Deane, A. (2005) *The Great Abdication: Why Britain's Decline is the Fault of the Middle Class*. (Exeter: Imprint Academic).

Erwin P (1993) *Friendship and Peer Relations in Children*. John Wiley & Sons Ltd.

Farrington, D. (1994) *The Influence of Family on Delinquent Development: proceedings of a conference on Crime and the Family*. (London: Family Policy Studies Centre).

Fisher, S. and Holder, S. (1981) *Too much too young*. (London: Pan).

Fraser, P. (1999) *Community Safety Community Solutions*. (London: NACRO).

Furedi, F. (1997) *Culture of Fear: Risk taking and the morality of low expectations*. (London: Cassell).

Furedi, F. and Brown, T. (1997) *Disconnected: Ageing in an Alien World*. (Kent: Reconnecting).

Furedi, F. (2001) *Paranoid Parenting*. (London: Allen Lane).

Field, F. (2003) *Neighbours from Hell: The Politics of Behaviour*. (London: Politico's).

Furlong, A. and Cartmel, F. (1997) *Young People and Social Change: Individualization and Risk in Late Modernity*. (Buckingham: Open University Press).

Fyvel, T.R. (1961) *Insecure Offenders: Rebellious Youth in the Welfare State*. (London: Chatto and Windus).

Giddens, A. (1992) *The Transformation of Intimacy*. (Cambridge: Polity Press).

Giddens, A. (1994) *Beyond Left and Right*. (Cambridge: Polity Press).

Gilbert, F. (2006) *Yob Nation: The truth about Britain's Yob Culture*. (London: Portrait).

Glassner, B. (1999) *The Culture of Fear: Why Americans are Afraid of the Wrong Things*. (New York: Basic Books).

Greenfield, J., Jones, D,. O'Brien, M., Rustin, M. and Sloan D – *Childhood, Urban Space and Citizenship: Child Sensitive Urban Regeneration*. Economic and Social Research Council: (Background Information).

Hagell, A. and Newburn, T. (1994) *Persistent Young Offenders*. (London: PSI).

Henderson, P. (ed) (1995) *Children and Communities*. (London: Pluto Press).

Hendry, L. (1993) *Young People's Leisure and Lifestyles*. (London: Routledge).

Hill, M. and Tisdall, K. (1997) *Children and Society*. (Addison Wesley Longman Ltd).

Hillman, M., Adams, J. and Whiteleg, J. (1990) *One False Move...A Study of Children's Independent Mobility*. (London: PSI).

Holman, Bob. (1995) *Children and Crime*. (Oxford: Lion).

Home Office (1995) *Young People and Crime*. (London: HMSO).

Home Office (1997) *No More Excuses: A New Approach to Tackling Youth Crime in England and Wales.* (London: HMSO).

Home Office Research Study 140 (1995) *Young People, victimisation and the police: British Crime Survey findings on experiences and attitudes of 12 to 15 tear olds.* (London: HMSO).

Hough, M. and Mayhew, P. (1985) *Taking Account of Crime: Key findings from the 1984 British Crime Survey.* (London: HMSO).

Hughes, G. (1998) Understanding Crime Prevention. (Buckingham: Open University Press).

Jacobs, J. (1961) *The Death and Life of Great American Cities.* (New York: Vintage).

Jenkins, S. (1994) Against the Grain. (London: John Murray).

Jenks, C. (1996) *Childhood.* (London: Routledge).

Jones, H. (1965) *Crime in a Changing Society.* (London: Penguin).

Jowells, R. (ed) (1995) *British Social Attitudes: the 12th report.* (Dartmouth: Dartmouth Publishing Company Limited).

Kathleen McCoy: www.parentsplace.com

Keniston, K. (1971) *Youth and Dissent: The Rise of the New Opposition.* (New York: Harvest).

King, M. (1997) *A Better World for Children.* (London: Routledge).

Lasch, C. (1977) *Haven in a Heartless World: The Family Besieged.* (New York: Basic Books)..

Lasch, C. (1979) *Culture of Narcissism: American Life in An Age of Diminished Expectations.* (New York: Norton).

Leach, P. *Physical punishment of children in the home.* No. 166. (London: National Children's Bureau).

Lyons R (http://www.generationyouthissues.com) Vetting of Voluntary Workers.

Lyons R (http://www.generationyouthissues.com) Vetting of Voluntary Workers.

Margo, J. and Dixon, M. (2006) *Freedom's Orphans: Raising Youth in a Changing World.* (London: IPPR),

Maquire, M. and Pointing, J. (eds) (1988) *Victims of Crime: A new deal.* (Milton Keynes: Open University Press).

Maquire, M., Morgan, R. and Reiner, R. (2002) *The Oxford Handbook of Criminology Third Edition.* (Oxford: Oxford University Press).

Mason, J. (1996) *Qualitative Researching.* (London: Sage).

McGallagly J, Power K, Littlewood P and Meikle, J (1998) *Evaluation of the Hamilton Child Safety Initiative.* (Edinburgh: The Scottish Office Central Research Unit).

Mitterauer, M. (1992) *A History of Youth.* (Oxford: Blackwell Publishers).

Moorcock, K. (1998) *Swings and Roundabouts.* (Sheffield: Sheffield Hallam University).

Morse, M. (1965) *The Unattached.* (London: Penguin).

Muncie, J. (1999) *Critical Social Policy,* Vol. 19. (London: Sage).

Muncie, J. (1999) *Youth and Crime: A Critical Introduction.* (London: Sage).

Muncie, J. Coventry, G. and Walters, R. (1995) 'The politics of youth crime prevention' in L. Noaks et al *Contemporary Issues in Criminology.* (Cardiff: University of Wales Press).

Newell, P. (1989) *Children Are People Too, The Case Against Physical Punishment.* (London: EPOCH).

NSPCC Briefing Note, August 1999.

O'Malley, C and Waiton, S. (2005) *Who's Antisocial: The Politics of Antisocial Behaviour.* (London: Academy of Ideas).

Orr, J. (1997) Launch speech of the Child Safety Initiative, Hamilton, 23 October.

Pearson, G. (1983) *Hooligan – a history of retrospective fears.* (London: Macmillan).

Pitts, J. (1988) *The Politics of Juvenile Crime.* (London: Sage).

Pitts, J. (1995) 'Scare in the Community: Part 1: Youth Crime'. *Community Care* 4-10 May.

Pollock, L. (1983) *Forgotten Children: Parent-Child Relationships from 1500 to 1900.* (Cambridge: Cambridge University Press).

Roberts, H. and Sachdev, D. (1996) *Young People's Social Attitudes.* (London: Barnardo's).

Roker, D. and Coleman, J. (1995) *Teenagers in the Family.* (London: Trust for the Study for Adolescence).

Rose, D. (1995) *In the Name of the Law.* (New York: Vintage).

Rutter, M. and Smith, D. (1995) P*sychosocial Disorders in Young People.* John Wiley & Sons.

Rutter, M., Giller, H. and Hagell, A. (1998) *Antisocial Behaviour by Young People.* (Cambridge: Cambridge University Press).

Scraton, P. (Ed) (1997) *'Childhood' in 'Crisis'?* (London: UCL Press).

Scottish Executive press release: ref no. Justice – SE0598.

Scottish Office (1995) *Housing and antisocial behaviour: the way ahead.* (Edinburgh: Scottish Office).

Shimamura, H. and Snell, C. (1996) *They don't play out like they used to, do they?* (Available from author).

Sommers, C. and Satel, S. (2005) *One Nation Under Therapy: How the Helping Culture is Eroding Self-Reliance.* (New York: St. Martin's Press).

South Lanarkshire Council (1997) *Information,* 23 October 1997. Census.

South Lanarkshire Council (1997) *Information,* Child Safety Initiative, 23 October. Census.

South Lanarkshire Council (1998) *Access to Leisure and Entertainment: Findings from a Citizen's Jury.*

South Lanarkshire Council: Chief Executive's Service(May/June 1997) *Focus on Hillhouse: Scotland's First Citizens' Jury.*

Springham, K. (1998) *Time to go Home Says Who?* Glasgow: Scottish Human Rights Centre.

Squires, P. and Stephen, D. E. (2005) *Rougher Justice: Anti-social Behaviour and Young People.* (Devon: Willan).

Stirling Council (1997) *Are you getting enough...opportunity?*

Sutton, J. and Smith, P.K. (1999) *Aggressive Behaviour,* Vol. 25, No. 2, pp.97-111.

System 3 (1996) South Lanarkshire Community Survey Final Report.

System 3 (1996) South Lanarkshire Community Survey: Executive Summary.

Tilley, N. (2005) *Handbook of Crime Prevention and Community Safety.* (Devon: Willan).

Valentine, G. (1996) 'Children should be seen and not heard..' *Urban Geography*. Vol. 17, No. 3, pp. 205-220.

Valentine, G. (1997) "Oh yes I can. Oh no you can't': Children and Parents' understanding of kids' competence to negotiate public space safely'. *Antipode*, Vol. 29, No. 1, pp. 65-89.

Valentine, G. and McKendrick, J. (1997) Children's Outdoor Play: Exploring Parental Concerns About Children's Safety and the Nature of Childhood. *Geoforum*, Vol. 28, No.2, pp.219-235.

Vulliamy, G. (1999) *Meeting need and challenging crime in partnership with schools*. (London: Home Office Research).

Waiton, S. (2007) *The Politics and Antisocial Behaviour: Amoral Panics*. (London: Routledge).

Wegs, R. (1999) 'Youth delinquency and 'crime'', *Journal of Social History*, Vol. 32, No. 3, pp. 603.

Wheway, R. and Millward, A. (1997) *Child's Play: Facilitating play on housing estates*. (London: Chartered Institute of Housing).

Wilson, J. and Kelling, G. (1982) 'Broken Windows'. *Atlantic Monthly*, March pp. 29-38.

Wilson, S. (1984) 'The Myth of Motherhood as a Myth: The Historical View of European Child Rearing'. *Social History* Vol. 9, No. 2, pp. 181-198.

Wyn, J. and White, R. (1997) *Rethinking Youth*. (London: Sage).

Young, J. (1986) *Confronting Crime*. (London: Sage).

Young, J. (1994) 'Incessant Chatter: Recent Paradigms in Criminology', in M. Maguire, R. Morgan, and R. Reiner, *Oxford Handbook of Criminology*. (Oxford: Clarendon Press).

Young, M. and Wilmott, P. (1957) *Family and Kinship in East London*. (London Routledge).

Youniss, J. (1980) *Parents and Peers in Social Development: A Sullivan-Piaget Perspective*. (Chicago: University of Chicago Press).

Zimring, F. (2000) *American Youth Violence*. (New York: Oxford University Press).

Scared of the Kids?

Index

Note

All document titles, Acts of Parliament, international conventions, the names of studies and television programmes are given in italics.

A

Adolescence, Risk and Independence 120

Adolescents: Peer pressure and Your Teen 118

adolescents, intolerance of 110-12

adult-child relations, author's recommendations 166-7

adults 129-47
   complaints about young people loitering 90-1, 96, 131, 133, 156, 162
   concerns for young people's safety 134-5, 171
   feeling of vulnerability 135
   isolation from young people 129, 135-6
   lack of confidence 129, 135, 143
   lack of respect for 134
   lack of tolerance of young people 135
   lack of trust towards one another 138-41
   lack of trust when working with children 48, 49, 50
   over 60 135-6
   over 80 136-7
   perceived as strangers 137-8
   speaking to young people 131-2

Age Concern 130

Ageing in an Alien World 135

Aggressive Behaviour 95

Ahrendt, Daphne 30-1, 33

Airdrie, pilot research project 69

alcohol misuse *see* drinking by youth; street drinking

Allen, Bernard 139-40

Amis, David 120

annoying citizens, a new law 24

anti-crime campaign or child safety initiative? 57

anti-youth crime measures, truancy 42

antisocial behaviour 30, 37
   demand for new laws 130
   a growing concern 39
   petty *see* petty antisocial behaviour in public 24
   author's recommendations 167
   reduction of 37
   on the spot fines 161
   term 23, 41

Antisocial behaviour by young people 28-9

Antisocial Behaviour Disorders (ASBOs) 24-5, 83, 84

anxiety *see* crime, fear of; culture of fear

Arnett, Prof. Jeffrey Jensen 140

Audit Commission (1996) 38

authoritarian attitudes 103, 111

authoritarian policing see policing, authoritarian

B

bad manners, focus of policing 23, 30

Bailey, Dr Susan 41-2

Baird, Stuart 48

Baisden, Carol 142

Barnardo's, survey 28, 67, 73, 132

Beck, Prof. Ulrich 31-2

bedroom culture 66, 112

Beyond Left and Right 31-2

Bill, The 27

Blair, Prime Minister Tony 83

Blatchford, Peter 67, 75, 95, 116

Blunkett, David 42

BMJ, drug abuse 43, 85

Bratten, William J., New York City Police Commissioner 23

breaktime *see* schools, breaktime

British Crime Survey (BCS) 26
attitudes of 12-15 year olds 108, 115, 117
increase in reporting to police 29
Young people, victimisation and the police 117

British Medical Association, crime and security issues 44

British Medical Journal *see* BMJ

British Social Attitudes Survey 111-12

British Social Attitudes, twelfth annual report 30-1

broken window approach 23

Brook, Lindsay 31

Brown, Tracey 135-7

Brundle, Georgina 141

Brundle, Mike 141

bullying 67, 95, 115-16

Burnbank, interviewees 62

C

Cahill, S. E. 72, 84

Cambridge Study, the 41

Cameron, Sandy 55-56

Campaign for the Registration of Adults Working with Young People and Children (Cry) 49-50

Campbell, Beatrix (Bea) 26, 83

Cape, Prof. Ed 31

caring professions 37-8, 40, 43

CCTV
advice from Strathclyde Police 44
children's demands for 111
concierge system 130-1
deployment in UK 27
following death of Philip Lawrence 47
Glasgow 22
public support for 30, 83, 112
Author's recommendations 165
spread of 84, 130
Waverley Station 151

censorship 30

Centre for Action on Staff Safety 44

child abuse at home 172

Child Safety Initiative (CSI)
alternative to 161
bad parents 65, 142
impact on adults 129-44
launch of 55-6, 104
opposition by Scottish Human Rights Centre 176
paedophile court cases 73
reasons for 55-6, 57, 65-6, 77
support for 57, 134
see also Hamilton Curfew; Hillhouse

child safety orders 24, 38

child-adult relations 166-7

Childhood 95

Childhood and Public Life 72-3

ChildLine 74, 142

children
curfew on 65-82
defined 62
diaries of activities 67-8, 70
fear for 84, 132
free time 62, 77-8
general image of 42
limits to their lives 153
need to be street-wise 166
parental fears for 66

peer relationships 75-7, 153-4, 171, 173

power to reject adult authority 140

protection of 37, 38, 171

public fear of 43-6

punished by curfews 174-5

safety of 33, 37, 38, 69-70, 71-2

Scottish Office research 41

space 62, 66, 68, 77

street culture decline 84

threat to teachers 45

and trust 138-9

as victims 116, 120, 121

views on talking to strangers 74-5

violence against 139-40

walking by themselves 69

Children Act 1989 139-40

Children Acts 1907, 1933 27

Children (Scotland) Act 1995 176-7

Children, Young People and Offending in Scotland 42-3

Children and Young Persons (Scotland) Act 1937 176-7

Children's Outdoor Play: Exploring Parental Concerns About Children's Safety and the Changing Nature of Childhood 66

Children's Play Council 174-5

child's play *see* play

City Watch 22

civil behaviour v. criminal behaviour 26

Clark, Charles 42

closed circuit television *see* CCTV

Coatbridge 103-4

communities, isolation within 122

community policing 98

community safety, initiatives in Newcastle and Leeds 26

Community Safety, Community Solutions 30

community safety and crime in South Lanarkshire 57-8

community solidarity 21

complaints *see* adults, complaints by

concierge fenced-in flats 130

author's recommendations 165

consultation process 163-4

Corrigan, Paul 89

crime

falling 28-9, 48

fear of *see* fear of crime

personal experiences 114

prevention 37-50

redefined as problem for radicals 25

rising 27-9

violent 27, 28

youth 29, 42

Crime and Disorder Act (1998)

authority for curfews 61, 65, 172

causes of offending 39

child misbehaviour 38

codifying intolerant approach to young people 92

new level of policing 24

and Scottish law 25

crime reduction measures 37-8

crime waves 27, 28

Crimewatch 27

criminal behaviour v. civil behaviour 26

Criminal Justice Act 1994 27

criminalising of activities 97, 166

criminals, potential 37, 38-40, 41

cruelty to animals 39

CSI *see* Child Safety Initiative; Hamilton Curfew; Hillhouse

Cullen report 47-8

culture of fear 21, 31-3, 43-4, 97-8

Culture of Fear 32, 115

Cummings, Dolan 93

curfews
  9 pm 65
  definition 170
  on children 65-82
  consequences of 174-5
  history 15-16
  statistics for and against 105-6
  on youth 83-102

D

Davis, John 104

developing citizenship through play 175

Dewar, Donald, Scottish Home
  Secretary 62

diaries of activities 67-8, 70, 88

Dickson, Ronan 50

discipline
  adults' confidence undermined 143
  complicated by the *Children's Act
    1989* 139-41
  and parenting 136
  schools 152, 157

Ditton, Prof. James 151

Dobson, Frank 83

doli incapax 24

Dowds, Lizanne 30-1, 33

drinking by youth
  at risk from themselves 120
  demand for policing 109-10
  reason for crime 132
  reported in press 85
  see also underage drinking

drug use 39, 43, 85, 120, 132

Dunblane 46-7

Duncan, Craig 140

E

Earnock, interviewees 62

East Lothian Council *Breaking the Cycle*
  youth anti-crime plan 39

Easterhouse estate 42, 152

Education Act 1996 140

Education Institute of Scotland (EIS)
  45, 86

elderly, the
  coping with neighbours 130
  lack of respect for 134
  recommendations to help 167
  security concerns 130

enforcing good behaviour, in schools 42

entertainment industry, and crime 27

Euromale study 49, 138

European City of Culture, Glasgow 21

*European Convention on Human Rights,
  Article 8* 169, 177

*European Convention on Human Rights,
  Fourth Protocol* 177

F

Fair Play for Children, campaign 67

Fairhill 55
  interviewees 62

Falkirk High School 48

Farrington, Prof. David P. 40-1

fear of crime 30-3
  crime across society 130
  greater increase than crime 29
  in Hillhouse 132
  policing of 27, 93-4, 97
  and prevention of crime 37-50
  in Strathclyde 22

football hooligans 23

Forna, Aminatta 143

Fraser, Penny 30

Fraser, Superintendent Donald 152
free time of children *see* young people, free time
freedom of choice in play 171
freedom and responsibility, author's recommendations 167
Furedi, Prof. Frank 32-3, 120, 135-7

G

Gallie, Phil, Conservative MP for Ayr 22
generation gap 156-7
Gibb, Moira 122
Giddens, Anthony 31-2
Gill, Tom, Children's Play Council, comment on curfews 174-5
Giller, Henri 28-9
Giuliani, Rudolph W., Mayor of New York City 23
Glasgow
  1999 year of architecture 49
  European City of Culture 21
  Evening Times 138-9
  gang fighting 86
  policing in 22, 23
Glasgow Development Agency 22
Glasgow District Council 22
Goldson, Barry 24-5
Goliath 26
graffiti 93
Greater Manchester Police 92
Gruchy, Nigel de 45, 151
gun controls 50

H

Hagell, Ann 28-9, 40
Halloween 78
Hamilton

better facilities for young people 162-3
internet drop-in centre 162
Hamilton Advertiser 174
Hamilton Curfew 30, 55-64, 83
  aims 55-6, 57, 65-6, 77, 95
  amid culture of fear 21
  criticism of 121
  extension of 161
  fear of crime 93, 94
  increased awareness of risk 144
  justification for more safety campaigns 27
  multi-agency initiative 37
  and new crimes 24, 25
  part of Operation Spotlight 22
  police intervention statistics 58
  protecting adults from young people 50
  regulating public space 84
  research methods 59-62
  support from adult public 129-30, 132, 134, 161
  see also Child Safety Initiative; Hillhouse
Hamilton, John, Chief Constable of Fife 59, 161-2, 163-4
Hamilton, Thomas 46-7
Hendry, Leo 90
Hewett, David 140
High Earnock, interviewees 62
Hillhouse 55, 56-7, 58
  adults' complaints about young people 156-7
  adults' contact with young people 131-2
  attitude of adults 129-44
  children interviewed on impact of Hamilton Curfew 65
  children limited by curfew 74-7

children not in any significant
danger 71-2, 132-3
children's free time and space 67-9
fear of crime for children and
young people 132
highlighting potential dangers 152
need for better facilities 162-3
people avoiding certain areas 144
regulation of public space 84
research by Scottish Office on
adults 132, 133
research on impact of curfew on
12-15 year olds 87
research methods for this book
59-62
young people and the curfew 87-98
Hillman, Prof Mayer 66, 75, 76, 115

holiday play schemes 175

hospitals 44

Howard League, The 71

Howarth, Valerie 74

I

identity cards 30

Institute of Childcare and Social
Education 49-50

*International Covenant on Civil and
Political Rights* 177

International Crime Victimisation Survey
30

J

Jenkins, Simon 27, 28

Jenks, Chris 95

Johnson, Nick 49

K

Knight, Simon 140-1

L

Laming Guidance (1997) 140-1

Landsdown, Gerison, Director of the
Children's Rights Office 77

Lawrence, Philip 45, 46, 47

Leach, Penelope 139

Leeds, community safety initiative 26

leisure time 90

Libertarianism in Retreat 31

Liddell, Helen 45

Livingston, Ken 83

local child curfews, comment on 24

London School of Economics 66

Lyons, Rob 48

M

McAvoy, Douglas 47

McCabe, Tom 55-6, 65, 94, 95

McCoy, Kathleen 118

McGuinness, Catherine 138-9, 142

McKeganey, Neil 85, 86

McKendrick, Dr John Holland 66

McLean, Alan 152, 157

McLeish, Henry 59, 161

Major, Prime Minister John 83

Martin, Linda 93, 133

Meikle Earnock, interviewees 62

Meikle, Janice 71

Millward, Alison 66

mistrust of adults working with
children 48, 49, 50

Moorcock, Kate 67, 74, 75

MTV, Youth Anti-violence website
118

multi-agency initiatives 37-8, 42, 141,
149, 157

Muncie, John 28, 38, 39

Murray, Charles 83

N

NASUWT 45, 46, 151, 152

National Association of Schoolmasters/Union of Women Teachers *see* NASUWT

National Centre for Play 170-1

National Union of Teachers 47

neighbourhood warden schemes 37

neighbours, and the elderly 130

Nestlé Family Monitor 66-7

New Labour 21
  and crime 24, 25, 26, 58

Newburn, Prof. Tim 40

Newcastle, community safety initiative 26

Newson and Newson 66

night-club curfew 22, 29

Niven, Gordon 45

noise, complaints about 25

noisy school children, focus of policing 23

Nottie, John 85, 86

NSPCC 73-74, 75

nuisance behaviour 30, 92, 105, 108
  differentiated 166
  in Hillhouse 155
  intolerance of adults 152
  removal to new venue 162
  rise in phone calls to police 130

O

offensive weapons 29

Operation Blade 21

Operation Spotlight 22, 23, 29-30, 173, 174

Orr, John, Chief Constable
  attack on parents 65
  CSI support 161
  intolerance to "yobs" 94
  launch of CSI 55-6
  need for improving people's behaviour 25, 30
  success of CSI 59
  weapons searches 86
  young children 67-8, 71
  Zero Tolerance Policing a Free Society 22-3, 93

Ovens, Nancy, ViceChair - Play Scotland 77
  comment on curfews 170-2

P

paedophiles 38, 46, 65, 73
  court cases 65, 73
  Euromale study 49
  security measures 50

parenting orders 24

parenting and outside agencies 141-2, 143

ParentLine 142

parents
  as chaperones 119
  fears for children 65, 72
  irresponsible 65, 77, 129, 142
  responsibilities 68-9, 70-1
  separated 39-40
  skills no longer appropriate 136-7
  supervision of 113-14

Parfery, Joe, Chair of Hillhouse Community Council
  comment on curfews 173-4
  curfew's limits on children 75
  dangers faced by children 72
  insecurity among the elderly 94, 130

Payne, Sarah, murder of 73

191

Pearson, Prof. Geoffrey 28

peer protection programmes 117-18

peer relations
  bullies and abusers 95, 115
  child and adolescent development
    75-7, 153-4
  importance for young people 89-90,
    122
  pressure 94-6
  problems 154-5, 163
  reduced opportunities for young
    people 171

Pellegrini, Prof. Anthony D. 67

pessimism about present-day society
  32-3

petty antisocial behaviour
  phone calls to police 156
  potential criminal label 42
  author's recommendations 167
  vandalism and rowdiness 134

petty behaviour, elevated into acts of
  abuse 116

planning of housing estates 166

play 136-7
  access to outdoor environments 171
  importance of freedom of choice 171
  recommendations of author 167
  recommendations of Children's
    Play Council 174-5
  recommendations of Play Scotland
    170-2

Play Scotland 170-2

police harassment 27

policing
  authoritarian 161-2
  author's recommendations 166
  baby-sitting service 157
  caring, protective 98
  contradictory 108-9

demand for 164
drinking 110
"heavy handed" 96-8, 164
increase in 106-8, 122, 153
prejudiced 157
safety initiatives 166

Power, Kevin 72

Prescott, John, MP 92

press, the, youth crime stories 85

Pritchard, Colin 75

Psychological disorder in young people 103

public drinking bans 22, 23, 84

public space
  author's recommendations 165-6,
    167, 175
  without the public 157

public space regulation
  consequences 98
  demands for 83, 103
  on housing estates 84
  through CCTV and police 111
  of undesirable people 93
  of young people's behaviour 96-7

R

radical
  criminologists 21
  sociologists 21

Railtrack, leaflet on personal security
  151

recommendations to encourage
  community trust 165-7

reflexive modernity 31-2

research methods re Hamilton Curfew
  59-62

rights, conflict between adults and
  young people 94

risk awareness 114-17
  adults' perception of 119-21

following media coverage of Hamilton Curfew 144

in Hillhouse 152

risk indicators and future criminality 39-40

Risk Society 31-2

Rivara, Prof. Frederick P. 40-1

Robertson, George, MP 47, 65

Rose, David 28

Rosenbaum, Prof. Dennis 39

RSDi research company 49

runaway world 31-2

Russell, Fran 71

Rutter, Michael 28-9

S

Safe Clubbing campaigns 120

Safe Greater Easterhouse Project 42

Safe Open Spaces Initiative 73-4

safety on the roads 171

safety and young people *see* young people, safety

St Jude's Primary School, Barlanark 19

St Michael's security system 47

Save the Children
comment on curfews 169-70
research 106

schools
after-school clubs 175
breaktime 67, 75, 116
caged-in 165
crime prevention 38
dislike of 39
disruptive children 44
enforcing good behaviour 42
homework clubs 67
lunch break problems 67
recommendations for 167

safety in 45, 46-7
teaching acceptable interpersonal skills 42

Scotland's First Citizens' Jury, Hillhouse 93, 133
purpose of 164
report outlining recommendations 56-7, 58

Scottish Crime Survey 108, 114

Scottish Human Rights Centre
comment on curfews 176-7
facilities in Hillhouse 163
increase in resentment towards police 106
police interventions not crime related 91

Scottish law 25

Scottish Office
crime prevention strategies 42-3
evaluation of impact of CSI 91, 106
predicting potential criminals 41
report on children as threat to teachers 15, 16
research into adults' feelings 103, 133
research into CCTV introduced in Glasgow 151-2
research into children and crime 41

Scottish Secondary Teachers' Association 45, 140

Scouts, the 48

security fences 130

Shimamura, Hitoshi 92, 121, 154

silence, right of 30

smacking 136, 139, 142

Smith, Roger, The Children's Society, comment on curfews 175-6

Smith, Ronnie 85

smoking family 40

Snell, Chris 92, 121, 154

Social Exclusion paper Teenage Pregnancy (1999) 40

social institutions, weakened 32

Social Work (Scotland) Act 1968 177

socially excluded, empowerment of 26

society fragmentation 32-3

South Lanarkshire Council, community safety 57-8, 163-4

South Lanarkshire Youth Council 111

Spotlight Campaign *see* Strathclyde Police, Operation Spotlight

spying on your child 113-14

statistics
court 28
crime 28, 33
police 28

Stirling 108, 111

Stoker, Brian 67

stop and search powers 84
recommendation to stop 166

stranger danger, awareness in Hillhouse 73, 74-5

stranger danger campaigns 137-8, 171
author's recommendations 166-7

Strathclyde Elderly Forum 93

Strathclyde Police
Blantyre 161
children 65
falling crime 29
hospital security 44
increase in policing 29-30, 154-5
intolerant attitude 93
knife carrying statistics 86-7
Larkhall 161
Operation Blade 21
Operation Spotlight 22, 23, 29-30,

173, 174
regulating public space 58, 93
Safer Streets initiative 85-6
safety 115
searching of people 23

Strathclyde University 22

Straw, Jack J. W., MP, Home Secretary
curfew aimed at under 10 year olds 61, 65, 161
long-standing plan for curfews 58
views on policing 25

street drinking
ban 22, 29, 109-10
focus of policing 24, 56, 103-4, 155-6
Glasgow District Council ban 22, 29
unimportant in past 155
young people in favour of phoning police 109-10

street robberies 23

Sturgeon, Nicola, MSP 152

Sudjic, Deyan 49

surveillance cameras see CCTV

Surveillance in the City 93

T

teachers, assaults on 45, 46

teaching acceptable interpersonal skills 42

teenagers
chaperoned by parents 119
defined 62
fear of 84
peer pressure 56, 94-6
pregnancies 39, 83
safety concerns 105

third citizens' jury 164

Thomson, Campbell 93-4, 133

time *see* leisure time; young people, free time

Too Much Too Young 105

torch lit demonstration 22

truancy 42

Trust for the Study of Adolescence 28

U

UN *Charter, (Article 31)* 170

UN *Convention on the Rights of the Child, Article 3* 169

UN *Convention on the Rights of the Child, Article 12* 169-70

UN *Convention on the Rights of the Child, Article 15* 169, 170, 172, 175

UN *Convention on the Rights of the Child, Article 31* 175

underage drinking 23, 30, 40, 56

unemployment in South Lanarkshire 58, 164

Unison 46

urban space 65

US-style retirement villages 131

Utting, D. 39

V

Valentine, Gill 66, 69, 70-1, 72, 84, 90, 112, 116

vandalism 93, 134

vetting of staff 48, 50

victim of the crime 26

victims and villains 37, 56, 83, 98, 169

victims or villains, children categorised as 176

violence
against children 139-40
towards teachers 46

violent school pupils 45, 67

W

Walker, David 173

warden-scheme 143-4

Waverley Station 151

West, Fred 46

Wheway, Rob 66, 76

Whitehill 55

Y

Young, Prof. Jock 25-6, 33

young offenders, persistent 40

young people
adult perception of 120
adults' intolerance 135
bother from older teenagers 108
clubbing 120
control of 43
Crime and Disorder Act (1998) 24
defined 62
development problems 156, 163
dispensing with diaries of activities 88
drugs 40, 83, 85, 87, 103
equal treatment of law breakers 40
fear for 132
fear of 132, 156
free time 62, 83, 105, 113
image and self-image 103
independence or parental supervision 113-14, 121-2, 153
intolerance of other young people 165
lack of leisure facilities 164
peer relationships 116, 171
persistent young offenders 40
police interventions 89, 90, 91
protection of 37, 38, 171
regulation of their lives 37, 83, 105, 112-13
rights for 156
safety 114-17, 119, 164, 165

195

separate class of people 103, 135
space at night 62, 88-90
today and fifty years ago 104-5
as victims 116-17, 119-21
villains and victims 98, 117
see also children; teenagers
Young People New Media 66, 112-13

Young people victimisation and the police 117

Young People's Social Attitudes 28

Youniss, James 75-76

youth clubs 46-7, 135-6
demand for 162-3

youth curfews *see* curfews

youth drugs problem 83

youth provision, author's
recommendations for 167

youth training schemes 37

youth workers, demand for 162, 164

Z
zero tolerance 21-36, 88, 92, 151
Zero Tolerance Policing a Free Society 22-3,
93